The Best Worst Dog I Ever Had

Larry Ehrhorn

Paperback ISBN: 9798387979545
Title: *The Best Worst Dog I Ever Had*
Author: Larry Ehrhorn
Digital distribution | 2023
Paperback | 2023

Dedication

For my parents, Wilbert "Bud" Ehrhorn and Doris Waldo Anderson, who gave me everything but passed before having witnessed what they had created.

And my lifetime dogs: Macbeth, Macduff, Dickens, Teddy and Ernie, none who ever learned to read, but sure helped me to a fuller and happier life.

Special Acknowledgements

These people helped me a great deal!

My son Larry, chief technical adviser ("Dad, you should never be allowed to touch a computer!")

Mary Harker, second in charge of proofreading ("Is "their" spelled "ei" or "ie"?)

Becky, wife, proofreader nurse, psychologist, etc., etc., etc.

Jack, my current dog—spiritual adviser

Rainbow Bridge
Author unknown

Just this side of heaven is a place called Rainbow Bridge.

When an animal dies that has been especially close to someone here, that pet goes to Rainbow Bridge. There are meadows and hills for all of our special friends so they can run and play together. There is plenty of food, water and sunshine, and our friends are warm and comfortable.

All the animals who had been ill and old are restored to health and vigor. Those who were hurt or maimed are made whole and strong again, just as we remember them in our dreams of days and times gone by. The animals are happy and content except for one small thing; they each miss someone very special to them, who had to be left behind.

They all run and play together, but the day comes when one suddenly stops and looks into the distance. His bright eyes are intent. His eager body quivers. Suddenly he begins to run from the group, flying over the green grass, his legs carrying him faster and faster.

You have been spotted, and when you and your special friend finally meet, you cling together in joyous reunion, never to be parted again. The happy kisses rain upon your face; your hands again caress the beloved head, and you look once more into the trusting eyes of your pet, so long gone from your life, but never absent from your heart.

Then you cross Rainbow Bridge together.

Twelve Axioms All Dogs Inherit at Birth

When dogs are born, they inherit twelve imbedded guiding principles. Each dog may use them all or just periodically run across the need to use them. They explain how dogs can guide themselves through life without human contact, needed or not. These help to explain the unexplainable acts of some dogs.

1. All dogs are smart, even the dumb ones.
2. Walking on four legs requires extreme skill; no human can do it.
3. To show sincere pleasure, wag your tail; purring is for cats.
4. You can chase something up a tree, but never try to pursue it or you'll look foolish.
5. No matter what you're told, there is no such thing as Kibble Supreme, so deal with it; kibble is kibble.
6. What you can't get with your paws, you can usually get with your soulful eyes.
7. When in doubt, always rely on your sense of smell.
8. Never make a person choose between you and a cat, unless it's a man. A woman will usually choose the cat.
9. It's okay to be frightened by loud noises, just like people are.
10. All dogs can swim; nobody told them that they couldn't.
11. Dogs get smarter faster than people because they live in dog years.
12. Rainbow Bridge is a real place; just don't hurry to get there.

Christmas 1950   *ZsaZsa*

Chapter 1
Every Good Life Begins with a Dog

"Those are the moments that I think are precious to a dog—when, with his adoring soul coming through his eyes, he feels that you are really thinking of him." James Galsworthy, novelist

"God spelled backward is dog." I first heard that cliché when I was six-years-old and thought it was sacrilegious and an express ticket to hell, and I wasn't even religious. As I grew older and more mature, I pretty much erased the heresy from my mind. A deeper idea began to slowly permeate my mind and claimed ownership of a small part of myself. By the time I turned thirty, I felt that I had a fuller understanding of goodness, because every dog I had owned or even met showed me something enlightening, like a tutor trying to convert an average high school freshman into a genius. It seemed that a dog would elevate my being closer to becoming a more wholesome person. I began to think that if I could mold myself into a human with all the qualities of a dog, I would lead a happy, productive life. French leader Charles de Gaulle wrote, "The more I get to know men, the more I find myself loving dogs."

I do not remember my first dogs. In 1950 my parents, brother and I lived in a small apartment above a chop suey take-out in Oak Park, Illinois, a western suburb abutting Chicago. How we all existed in that third floor walk-up, which was always fragrant, I will never comprehend, except for the fact that I was only three, had two parents a brother, and two dogs. What did I know or care?

To be honest, I cannot find a faint memory of either Ginger, German shepherd or police dog as they were commonly called, or Suzie, the beagle. Most people cannot recall their first memory. Try it. When I got older, like ten, I found the only picture of the whole family, including my dogs. It was a black and white photo, taken around Christmas. In this picture Ginger sat on the floor in front of a couch that was holding the rest of us. Suzie was on the end partially sitting on Mom's lap. I was next to Mom and had my face buried and hidden like any obnoxious three-year-old, next to Dad.

Amazingly, as much as I love dogs today, I have not the vaguest recollection of those two. A couple of years later, we moved to a small house in Elmhurst, a suburb about twenty miles west of Chicago. I have no idea what happened to Ginger and Suzie, but they did not go with us to our new home. The good side to my lack of recall is that I did not cry or feel heartbroken in their absence, like I did with all my other dogs. My first two dogs had just disappeared.

As I grew older and had my own dogs, I often looked at that old Christmas picture that did not set off memories but made me ponder their disappearance even more. The fact is that I did not miss them. Why? Looking at that lone photo, I wanted to know if they ever got walked. There was a park across the street, but I do not remember going there to play with them. At two or three, I was not allowed to take two dogs alone across the busy thoroughfare to play with them. What did they eat? Where was their water bowl? Did they have toys? I thought it odd that I had never asked my parents about those details, but, as so often happens, questions were postponed until it was too late and the answers died with them.

The next twenty years passed faster than dog years. When I turned eight our first family dog briefly came home courtesy of my older brother Duke (real name). When my parents came home, they were both stunned and bewildered at the presence of a black and white mutt in our tiny living room.

Nonchalantly, Duke explained, "That's Pepper. A cab driver gave him to me. Asked me if I'd like a dog, so I said, 'Sure.'"

Mom was still standing, thinking on her feet. My dad stood silent, either stunned or willing to let the wife field this one.

Ma spoke first, "What kind of cab driver rides around all day with a dog and then decides to give him away at a junior high school?"

That one stumped Duke, "I don't know. He's there every day to pick-up some rich kids." Good answer.

Better and quicker response. "Well, if he's there every day, then I will go to work early and return his dog. We can't keep him. I like dogs and hope to have one someday, but not today. There's no fence in the back yard and we're gone all day. We need a bigger house. Two bedrooms with one shared closet does not leave room for a dog. He can stay the night, but tomorrow he goes back to riding a cab. Besides, maybe Pepper was training to be a substitute driver." Mom tried to leave on a high note, but her humor fell short, especially with the controversial dog sitting right there looking happy to be in a house. Dad never said a word. Not sure that he didn't want a dog. Just not this one.

Duke and I didn't feel like we had done anything wrong or were being scolded, but I felt sorry that Pepper was being expelled. He was friendly and seemed to like me. It was probably the first time that I had felt a bond between me and a dog. Nothing major, just a connection.

The link grew stronger that night when he instinctively jumped into bed with me. I ruffled his head and rubbed his belly, which reflexively caused his leg to twitch like he was pedaling a bike. The more he licked my face, the more tears I leaked between my sniffling and giggling. Maybe he just liked the salt.

"Good night, Pepper. Wish you could stay," and I surprisingly cried openly. Duke may have brought him home, but Pepper seemed to want to be my dog. So did I.

Eventually I fell into a deep sleep, and when I was awoken for school, Pepper was already gone. I asked Duke where Pepper was, hoping that he was just outside on a walk with Mom.

He answered dejectedly, "Mom left early with him to see if she could find the cab driver. He's gone, Lar, but he had fun his short time here. Maybe someday."

One day and one night and I wished for a dog to be permanently mine. I never saw Pepper again, nor did I ever forget him.

That same year we continued our westward migration to Wheaton, thirty miles west of Chicago. It was real suburbia – huge yards, white picket fences, and plenty of dogs being walked on leashes. After Pepper's exile, I hadn't forgotten about getting a fulltime pet dog, and I couldn't help but smile whenever I saw one. Hopefully, our new larger house in suburbia would bring a change.

One Saturday my mother told me to get in the car. Not Dad, not Duke, just me. We drove a few miles to Lombard, and got out at a small yellow brick house. Ma knocked on the door and an older man answered.

"Doris?" he asked. "I'm Chuck Rubner. Please come in."

Mom went in and I silently followed. There was an unusual smell in the house, but I couldn't recognize it. Surely not fresh cookies in the oven.

"They're in here" and he led us to the kitchen. Suddenly there was the piercing sound of yipping attacking us from his kitchen. When we entered the room, the first thing I saw, but certainly not expecting, was a mother dog lying on her side in an oversized dog bed. Surrounding her and slipping on the linoleum floor while climbing over each other, were four yelping basset hound puppies. And I thought Tuesday Weld was cute.

I cautiously approached them and kneeled but my presence was secondary. Their mother emitted a low growl.

"Are they ready?" asked Ma.

The owner replied, "They're ready. We usually wait eight weeks, but the vet said that six was okay if they felt comfortable. Some breeders believe that if you take the pups away from their mother too soon that they tend to be less trusting and may grow-up with temperament issues. But we've already sold two yesterday and things seems to be working just fine on this end. Did you want a male or female?"

Was I hearing this? Were we going to take one of these fur balls home? They began licking my hands and climbing my shoes. "I think a male. What do you think, Lar?"

"I want them all," which earned a chuckle from the owner. I wondered if he would trade them all for my brother Duke, a fanciful wish.

"Pick one," Ma commanded.

They were all on me, and the decision was made because one had a brown ring around his eye, and he could actually step on his ears.

"This one," I said as I picked him up and a stream of urine poured forth. Was he overjoyed or protesting?

"They all need some housebreaking," Mr. Rubner joked.

As I was laughing, I noticed that the mother dog glared, part of her head on the edge of her bed, resigned to another unpleasant fate that she could not stop. Awful for the mother to see her litter disappear; hopefully good for the pups in a new home but, of course, she had no clue about what would happen to any of her children.

"We'll take good care of him, I promise," I whispered to the mother. She blinked her eyes as though she understood and hoped it was true. Many years later during a typical high school sleep-inducing English class, I snapped awake when Mrs. Haag read some Shakespeare quote, "The eyes are the windows to the soul." Years later that quote triggered my memory back to Dexter's mother's soulful eyes, and made me wonder what kind of life that was for a female dog – to give birth to five "kids," and after six weeks of bonding and nursing and nurturing, to have total strangers come into the room, and, one by one, take away all of her children, never to be seen again. Twice I had patted her on the head and repeated, "I promise." She had replied with another sigh. Her eyes conveyed the loss that I would feel throughout the years after losing four of my own dogs.

I picked up the pup while Ma and Mr. Rubner completed some business matter before we left. Dad and Duke eagerly greeted our new nameless family member.

"What's his name?" asked Dad, who had already known about the recent surprise addition to the family.

"Whatever we want," answered Mom coyly.

"Do you still want to name him after a saxophonist?" he replied, surprised but not angry.

"Yes, but I also happen to like the name, and I have heard of other dogs named Dexter."

"Dexter?" Duke and I reacted simultaneously.

She looked at us like the decision had been made before we had even gotten the dog.

"Yes, Dexter. I like the sound of it. In fact, I even picked out his first name."

"First name? I thought you said it was Dexter," I replied puzzled.

Now the truth came out. "Yes, Dexter. Dexter Gordon, who played saxophone with Louis Armstrong, is going to be a show dog but the Kennel Club requires two names for registration purposes."

Duke and I never expected a music history lesson, although Mom told us countless times that she had played her violin at a birthday party for Carl Sandburg's daughter. Again, another neglected question until it was too late. I had no idea who Sandberg was until high school when we read a poem titled, "Chicago." The poem encompassed everything I had experienced during our occasional visits to the city.

Irritated, "I don't get it. Is he our dog or not? Can't I play with him and stuff?"

She could tell that I was disappointed and confused.

"Of course he's our dog. But I've always wanted a show dog, sort of a hobby. It'll be fun. Dexter and I have to attend classes, and there will be special dog shows for basset hounds held in fancy downtown hotels. We can all go. It'll be a year before he's ready, so don't worry and enjoy Dexter."

"What is his first name?" Dad asked, a point that Duke and I had forgotten.

She smiled and declared with a straight face, "Miserable."

The three of us stared at her as though she had proudly announced, "Hitler."

"Explain, Doris," said our rarely perplexed father.

She had had this planned for a long time, I could tell.

"Because he's a basset hound. His eyes and droopy ears make him look so sad and miserable. It's more fitting than 'Happy,' don't you think?"

Thus, Miserable Dexter, basset hound show dog, became our first family pet.

"Can he sleep in my room?" I pleaded. Fond remembrances of my only night with Pepper built hope for even more bonding with full-time Dexter.

After what seemed forever, Ma hesitantly agreed. "Okay, we'll put his new dog bed in your room, but he cannot sleep on your bed.

Puppies need to be trained right from the start or they may develop bad lifetime habits. Understand?"

That answer puzzled me. What bad habits would I teach him? Duke was the one who smoked, though my parents didn't know it yet, unless they played along with their "cool" teenaged son. I smiled at the picture of Dexter lounging in the back yard hidden behind our apple tree, sharing a cigarette with Duke.

What eight-year-old boy is not willing to have his dog sleep in his room? Of course, Dexter was with me in my bed from the first night. Sometimes we'd get caught, but Ma only chased him down, so apparently doggie discipline was not her strength. We paid dearly for that selfish weakness.

Dexter and I grew closer. He followed me everywhere. I often played fetch with him, but his stubby basset legs were not created for running too fast without causing exhaustion. My dad said that Dexter looked like a canine version of Charlie Chaplin, a reference I did not understand for many years.

Every Tuesday and Thursday nights, Mom loaded Dexter into the Nash and left for a couple hours. When I asked where they went, she smiled and said, "School."

"Can I go with?" I asked without much thought. What kid would want to go to school at night, even with his dog?

"Sorry, Lar, abut I'm afraid you might be a distraction. He'd probably see you and want to play, and he needs to learn who's in charge if I'm going to enter him in a show soon."

I'd forgotten that Ma got Dexter to be a show dog, a picture my imagination could not create. Almost a year had passed before Mom and Dexter finally came home with a framed graduation certificate. I was never sure who that diploma belonged to – Mom or Dexter? Maybe they shared it.

Almost a year after their graduation, my mother proudly announced that we were all attending their first professional dog show on a Sunday next month. It was being held at the Bismarck, a fancy hotel in the Loop. We all spruced-up and drove downtown with Dexter panting and hanging his head out the rear window. His ears were big enough that I thought the car might fly, but there is a major difference between fantasy and science.

Once Dad found a parking space, Mom attached a special collar and leash like they had always taken to school, and we all walked to the hotel. It was so strange watching my dog stroll down the wide city sidewalks, stopping to sniff doorways and fire hydrants. His snout vibrated like a short jack hammer at all the unusual smells that permeated the lot of us. It was like Chicago was covered by a dome that captured unique city scents and sounds – buses, taxis, police horses, the el trains with their squealing brakes, buildings and people and city smells of industry and humanity. Dexter started to lead us into the United Artist Theatre box office and lobby, but Ma had control of the lead. Years later I grew to appreciate Sandburg's poem about Chicago because I had experienced it.

It was a perfect Sunday afternoon, and I would have been willing to walk all day in that beautiful place with all of my family. Then we arrived at the entrance to the hotel. The lobby was busy and cavernous, really quite exciting and luxurious. All the golden molding and plush red carpet took me to a new "wow" level. Our amazing journey continued when the polished elevator doors opened, and Ma took the lead without hesitation. Dexter looked confused and frightened when the doors closed. He sat there and stared at us as if wondering if we were going to save him from some horrible fate. He looked miserable.

We got off at the third floor, where the ballroom was located. Dexter made a beeline to a silver cylindrical upright ashtray and immediately lifted his leg and relieved his tension. Ma was shocked and couldn't stop him in time.

'That's all right, Ma'am. That's why I'm here," said a high-school-aged kid in a brown uniform with the words "Bismarck Hotel" stitched on his pocket. He quickly knelt by the ashtray, sprayed the victimized carpet, and lightly blotted the area with a special green sponge with the hotel's name on it. Don't know what he would have done if Dexter had really unloaded. Had to wonder where that kid would be in ten years – manager of dog waste or politician.

Mom led Dexter to a long check-in table and received a number, which she pinned to her dress, and a program. We all entered the massive ballroom, which was also elegant with a huge chandelier and a stage at one end. Dad, Duke and I took spectator seats along the wall. Dad checked the program, then passed it to Duke and me. On page 36 he pointed to the entry: "Miserable Dexter," followed by a bunch of cryptic breeder names and lineage and owner "Doris

Ehrhorn." I guess I didn't come into play anywhere, even if I was Dexter's favorite.

The actual show was slow and boring. I had had more fun walking from the car to the hotel. Finally, Mom and Dexter took center floor with two other owners and their dogs. The dogs and owners pranced rather awkwardly in a circle, and the judge opened each dog's mouth and held its tail straight back. Checking for cavities, I guess. Apparently Dexter chose not to cooperate with the silly behavior and snapped sharply at the judge's hand. Maybe Dexter was so miserable that he didn't pay close attention during his classes. Finally the judge took three ribbons and a small gold trophy from the awards table. He gave one owner a trophy and a blue ribbon, and gave the other two participants' ribbons no trophies. Ma took her white ribbon, led Dexter off the floor and waited for us in the hall. Was that it? A year of training for that?

"Did you see that?" Mom barked at Dad.

"Yes, I saw. Everybody saw. Did he draw blood from the judge?" Dad asked, but I think I could detect a smirk and a stifled laugh.

I saw the ribbon Ma was holding. "Did Dexter win something?"

She gave me the ribbon marked "Third Place."

"Did he finish third? Out of all these dogs, that's pretty good, right?" My foolish, naive comment was meant sincerely, but I quickly blushed as I realized the truth.

She couldn't help but smile. "There were only three dogs in our grouping," she replied but her anger had gone elsewhere.

"But it was his first try, so that's pretty good." Ma patted me on the head and led us all to the lobby. Show over.

The trip home was light-hearted, even though everyone except me thought that we had lost. I rolled down the back window again and Dexter relived his trip into the city. I was glad that the show was over and that I still felt the same joy that I had always shared with my dog. I was afraid that he might be transformed into a prancing, groomed show dog, and not the dog that slept in my bed and played fetch with me.

We even stopped by an A&W root beer stand on the way home, where I walked Dexter in the parking lot and he had the opportunity to water their bushes. When we returned to the car, four floats and a small dish of ice cream awaited us. People with two hands each got a float, and I held the dish for Dexter, who eventually licked the bowl clean, his black nose and snout covered. It was the best day ever in my still young life. That day did have a permanent influence when I got older. Someday I hoped to recreate that day with my own show dog.

There were only two other dog shows in the career of Miserable Dexter. His performances were consistent. Dexter always took third place, but in his final show, he took third out of five dogs, so we all agreed to consider that show as a first place win, because he had beaten two other dogs. Logic of a show dog owner.

When Dexter was four and I was twelve, our relationships in the family came crashing down. I had been sick with something that kept me out of school and bedridden for three days. Of course, Mom frequently checked my temperature and brought me nourishment. One afternoon something disastrous happened, but I did not actually see the incident. I awoke to the screams of my mother, with Dexter growling and snapping his jaws. By the time I was fully conscious, I could see Ma's arm bleeding and her rushing from my room. She was quick, but not as fast as Dexter in pursuit. I rolled out of bed and followed them.

Mom kept yelling," No, Dexter, no! Bad dog!" as she still held her bleeding arm and stepped up on the couch, while Dexter continued his barking and snarling. It was scary to watch, but I didn't hesitate to grab Dexter from behind and pull him away.

Once it appeared that I had some control over my/our dog, Mom stepped down from the sofa and went into the bathroom, trying to hold back her tears. I was the only other one home and did not know what to do, so I held Dexter tightly, not in a threatening way, and awaited my mother's return.

She came out of the bathroom with a cold wet hand towel wrapped firmly on her wounds. Her eyes were still watery, but she seemed to have lost some of her rage. She took a step closer to us and Dexter growled again, baring his teeth.

"I'm sorry, Lar, but Dexter has to go. He won't let me near you anymore, even when you're sick or sleeping. He's become over-protective and he can't be trusted."

I grabbed him tighter, hoping that she could see that I had complete control over him, but it did no good.

"Carol Sutcliffe at work mentioned that she was thinking of getting a dog, and she doesn't have any kids at home anymore. He would go to a very nice home with someone who could use his company, and be taken good care of."

I was surprised that she would so easily decide to get rid of him; after all, she was the one who wanted a show dog and had gone to classes and shows with him. Certainly those memories must have meant something.

My tears flowed freely, unsure if they were for my mother or my dog. Ma would always be there for me. I began to accept the idea that I may have to picture the rest of my life without Miserable Dexter.

"If he still lives in town, will I at least be able to see him?"

Ma did not hesitate, "No, I don't think that would be in their best interest. He's too attached to you and too protective. I should have kept Dexter in a separate dog bed in the utility room. It's just too late now. He won't change. And there's something you don't know, Larry, that might help you understand."

She looked like she was deliberating her own statement. "What?" I asked impatiently.

"Your dad and I were both going to tell you in a few weeks, but it seems more appropriate now." Even longer pause. "I'm pregnant and we're going to have a baby in September. You can see what Dexter did to my arm, and I was an adult who was able to get away from his snarling teeth. Just imagine what he might do to a helpless infant. Like I said, he's past the point of being trusted. I'm not saying that he would ever hurt a child, but it's just not worth a gamble."

That was not the answer I had expected. She was going to trade my dog for a baby sister or brother. Inside I smiled because I thought how similar it was when I was hoping that Mr. Rubner would be willing to trade his litter of basset hounds for brother Duke. For the next two hours I sat on the couch with my dog, petting and scratching his neck, while we waited for Dad to get home. Poor dog had no clue that he had done anything wrong, and he certainly would have no idea of why he had to leave.

Finally Dad walked through the door and he could tell instantly that something was wrong. I could not stop the waterworks and hoped that Dad could rescue us. Without a word he went straight to the kitchen, where Mom was cooking something that sizzled. The sound made it difficult to overhear their conversation, but I could tell that he was surprised and worried when his voice got louder, "Are you all right? Do you need a doctor?"

The only reply I detected was that Mom had started to cry harder. Soon Dad returned and looked at us with little sympathy. Dexter wagged his tail once, perhaps trying to generate support. No such luck. He had crossed a line.

"Sorry, Lar, but Dexter can't live here anymore. That's final, so please get used to it. Your mother explained why, and I hope you will grow-up to always look out for your younger brother or sister. Dexter will be gone as soon as we can find a good home for him. We don't mean to sound cruel, but who knows when another disaster may strike? Sorry."

So ended the presence of Miserable Dexter, basset hound supreme, dog show ribbon winner, my over-protective bodyguard and best friend.

Life was painful for a few days, when, like Pepper, they took away Dexter while I was at school so that I didn't have to watch him leave. I had cried and pouted for three days, hoping that my parents would find a change of heart, but I didn't expect them to. During those remaining days Dexter still slept in my bed, having no inkling about his uncertain future. Mom never came near me again in Dexter's presence. Yet, when I wasn't present, she would still pet him and give him treats like nothing had ever happened.

On Friday I came home from school in a despondent mood despite a two-day weekend without school. I had prayed for Dexter's immediate transformation and my mother's forgiveness, wishing that time could travel back a week and all was as it should be. When I walked through the door, I did not receive my usual greeting. No sound of scampering toenails across the linoleum kitchen floor. No excited panting, flying ears, or boundless enthusiasm attacking me at full force. I stood frozen because I knew.

"Sorry, Lar, but Dexter went with Mrs. Sutcliffe this afternoon. She'll keep me posted about him. Be sad, but don't worry. He'll be fine."

I knew that it had been inevitable but never gave up hope. If only I hadn't been sleeping when Ma had come in to check on me. If only I hadn't been sick. I really didn't blame myself so much, but fate seemed to play a major role. I did promise Dexter's mother that I would take good care of him. Hopefully, Mrs. Sutcliffe would be a positive extension of my vow.

Sniffling, I managed to say, "You could have told me, so I could have said 'good-bye.'"

"As hard as this is to believe, this way is easier. I hope you don't mind, but Dexter asked me if he could take that smelly pair of socks that you tied in a knot to play fetch and tug with him. I sent them with him and he thanked me."

I looked at Ma as though I actually believed for a moment that Dexter could talk.

"Sure. Then he'll have something to remember me by."

She smiled, "He didn't need your smelly socks to remember you. He'll never forget you, just like you'll never forget him." True words I never forgot either.

It was years later after I had had my own son that I began to understand the bonding of any parent to care for and shelter a child, not unlike Dexter's own mother, and that my mother emulated. I may have caught a glimpse of Dexter one more time in my life. At age twelve I was too young to get my driver's license, but I could ride a bike forever. Months after Dexter was gone, I found Mrs. Sutcliffe's address in the phone book. I decided to venture the two miles across town, hoping to catch a glimpse of him, even though I had promised myself and my mother that I would not search for him.

I found the house easily. Mrs. Sutcliffe had a white-picket, fenced back yard. A few times I thought I could see a moving body walking around inside the fence line. I never dared to get too close to look, fearful that Dexter might see or smell me and start barking, which would have made me feel glad, but not worth the risk.

One day I pedaled to her house and she was just coming out the front door, leading a dog on a leash. We had never met, so there was no risk of being recognized by her. But was that my dog? To be sure I rode around the block and came back looking straight at them. It was Dexter – same ears, sad eyes, and show dog jaunt. He may have been a little heavier, but I decided that it was him. I wanted him to look at me to see if he still recognized his boy. But we never made direct eye contact. He looked healthy and content, so I felt empty but satisfied that I had at least seen him and that I had kept my promise to Dexter's mother. It was the last time I ever saw my best canine friend.

During my childhood I can only recall brief relations with dogs – one-night Pepper, four-year Dexter, and my last mutt. When I was a fourteen-year-old junior high school student, Ma asked me to go with her to see Aunt Amy in Chicago. I really had no desire; it was a beautiful, sunny day, and visiting my spinster aunt Amy was as much fun as having a root canal without anesthetic. But Ma really seemed to want my company, citing driving home alone in the dark. Dark? Did that mean the whole day? Dad, Duke, or my new sister Lynn were not invited, which I thought odd. Something was happening, and I had no other plans, so I succumbed to my mother's wishes.

My aunt lived on Augusta Boulevard in a brownish and red brick four-flat apartment. She ran a dry cleaner pick-up service out of her ground floor flat. Every year my uncle Raymond would haul down freshly cut Christmas trees to sell from an empty lot next to Amy's building. He was also the one who took Ginger and Suzie back to Michigan to lead full lives of running free on his own land. At least that's what I was told years later when I finally asked about that old Christmas photo of us. I never asked for details, but I liked the idea that they were happy then.

We entered the front Dutch door, and I could hear some high-pitched yelping. Passing through the living room and into the kitchen, I looked down and saw a boxful of puppies. There were five, big enough to climb over each other and chew each other's ears. No sign of their mother. I kneeled and started to pet one. The other humans filtered in behind me, enjoying the show.

Ma began the explanation, "Uncle Ray is visiting from Bagley, and a farm friend offered him this litter of puppies to take with him to sell and give to good homes. Ray remembered how attached you got to dogs, and thought that we might want one. Your dad said it was okay, and Lynn has just started walking, so I think they might grow-up to be good friends. And now we have a fenced-in yard. I didn't want any argument over which one to choose, so I thought I'd let you pick. I think you've shown the closest attachment to all or any dogs. Believe it or not, I still feel guilty about having to get rid of Dexter. I know how connected you two were."

I was stunned, unsure of what to say or do.

Gruff, old Uncle Ray stepped in. "They're pretty much all the same, Lar. What we refer to as a Heinz 57 mix. Without permission, some local farm dogs decided to have a family. I'd say they're all pure mutt. No show dogs there."

I looked at Ma to let her know that I had caught the "show dog" reference. She nodded to assure me that she had no desire for any more last place ribbons, and that this dog was pretty much mine.

One by one we picked them out of the box and put them on the floor. They were mostly black or blonde with white or a combination of all three. All cute, no matter what the pedigree or lack of. Two puppies decided to water Aunt Amy's linoleum. Others tried to run and slid, so they did it again. It was like exercise hour in the prison yard. One licked my hand, so, of course, I immediately chose it, which added more puppy kisses to my face. What kind of a person can say, "No," to puppies? I raised it above my head and checked her coat – all blonde with white patches and little bent ears.

"What about this one, Ma? He seems nice."

"She smiled and replied, "He's a she and I think she's just fine. What are we going to name her?"

Somehow my mouth opened and I replied as though a demon was speaking through me. Where else could such a name come from?

"What about Zsa Zsa?"

Bewildered mother, "Zsa Zsa? Where did that come from?"

Bewildered son, "I don't know. She looks like a Zsa Zsa. All blonde. You know, like Zsa Zsa Gabor?"

"I know who Zsa Zsa Gabor is. But for a dog?"

Uncle Ray was enjoying the conversation. "Yeah, Doris, what's wrong with that name for a dog?"

"Yeah, why not?" asked Aunt Amy, equally amused.

Seeing no easy way out of the situation, Ma sighed, took the high road and played along. "Zsa Zsa it is, then. I picked Miserable Dexter, so who am I to judge? Besides with some much mixed lineage, maybe she is Hungarian, too." A reference I did not understand.

After some Swedish coffee cake and coffee, we were ready to leave, with me holding Zsa Zsa. I sensed that her litter mates knew that they would never see one another again. The puppy kisses had stopped, and she kept looking back at her brothers and sisters, like Dexter had done. Seeing her being carried in my arms, they couldn't know, but they seemed to feel that this was a final farewell, and barked. Zsa Zsa barked back, and I felt guilty and sad, but hopeful that we'd become best friends and that she would have a wonderful life.

When we got back to Wheaton, Dad and Duke were surprised and couldn't wait to hold her. Lynn was resting on the couch, and Zsa Zsa jumped up and gave Lynn a few doggy greetings, which caused giggles to no end. They would be just fine.

We put her in our fenced-in yard, and she ran like a greyhound (the bus, not the dog), while we semi-chased her. Two days later, she was comfortably settled in her new home – dog bed, water and food, squeak toys, treats, and a sense of safety.

Zsa Zsa usually slept with me, but as Lynn and Zsa Zsa grew older together, Zsa Zsa migrated to Lynn. Sometimes Zsa showed her independence and was able to climb up some short folding steps that we kept by the washer and dryer. She slept on top of the appliances. Ma had spread a large towel on top for a sheet, and she really loved it in the cold winter and the warm dryer was running. During the hot summers sometimes, Zsa Zsa would drop into the utility sink next to the washer and enjoy the cool retreat. Fond memories of watching her asleep, curled-up in that tub. Luckily, the water never gushed on her while she was sleeping.

I do not remember much else about Zsa Zsa before I left for college. We shared three years of car rides, long walks, playing in the snow, watching movies and eating popcorn with the family. I only saw her during the summer and school breaks. She pretty much became Lynn's dog.

Good old Zsa Zsa – no temporary drifter, no show dog, no trouble, just twenty pounds of loving, family dog, the way a dog's life and family should be.

One cold night in DeKalb, the phone in my dorm room rang. It was my mother.

She had been crying." We had to put Zsa Zsa to sleep today, Lar. You knew that her systems were failing, kidneys especially. She hadn't been comfortable for a long time. No more pain. She was a good old dog. Just thought I should let you know. Sorry, Lar."

My brain went numb and I couldn't speak. I hung up and cried. My roommate was out, so I grateful to be alone for a while.

For the rest of my pre-adult years, the canine-inflicted sorrows began to dissipate, though never into oblivion. I will always remember and credit Pepper, Dexter, and Zsa Zsa, and, perhaps in my deep subconscious, Ginger and Suzie, for laying the foundations of my adult relations to other dogs who had shared their lives and connected with me.

I have had five dogs in my adult years. I really never knew complete backstories of them. So I decided to let them tell you where they came from and what they were thinking, stories which turned out to be quite contradictory from what I had imagined. I started with a mutt from a pet shop window, then progressed to a border collie, to a show dog, to a service dog, to the best worst dog I ever had, a rescued silky terrier, that miraculously had survived Hurricane Katrina.

I did have a hand in helping them (their penmanship is marginally better than mine), but it wasn't too difficult. Not only was I able to talk to them, as do most dog owners, but my special skill is that I can carry both sides of a conversation. Italicized words represent the dog's voice. My view is NOT italicized. Thoughts supplied by the dog, some vocabulary supplied by the author. If you don't believe me, just ask my wife. Roger Karas, writer, one-time president of the ASPCA, made this observation, "Dogs are not your whole life, but they make our lives whole." Well said.

How much is that doggy
in the window? $10.00

Turns out to be my best
"ten-dollar mistake."

Chapter 2
Macbeth–My First Worst Dog

"The first dog is the dog that gives you so much that the first dog is
often the reason for the second dog." Unknown

*I entered the world blind, deaf, toothless and incontinent. Fifteen
years later, I left it exactly the same. I think there were six of us
at first. Although we were born equally handicapped, we
instinctively felt our need for the others to keep warm and for our
mother to feed us. My brothers and sisters and I would instinctively
try to climb on and over the others in an attempt to latch onto our
mother.*

*My first sensation of affection occurred when mother began to lick
our tiny six-ounce bodies. After a few days when she bathed us with
her tongue, I strongly began to feel that the consumed mother's milk
was beginning to leak out of my body. Despite all of this eating and
purging, I doubled my weight in the first week, but I was still rather
light at one pound. Of course, sleeping much of the time did not
expend much energy. In fact, I bet that if I hadn't had so much
activity following my nose to mother's scent without the challenge of
crossing over my litter mates, my weight might have tripled*

A couple weeks after waking-up into the world, I began to wake-up to an even bigger world. My eyes and ears became functional and I sensed a whole new experience awaiting me. I could faintly see my family and wondered what I looked like to them. Mother was safe and beautiful, and I hoped I would grow-up to look like her. Selfishly, I didn't really want to look like the other pups, even though we were all the same breed – black and white mutts, often confused with border collies, but not nearly as dignified or talented.

At about the same time, two weeks after birth, another intruder entered our world. A yipping, high-pitched sound arose from someone in the litter, I think. Suddenly mother made a much louder and rapid sound that emerged from her mouth. It was scary but reassuring. All she did was open her mouth and the commanding but protective noise erupted. I opened my mouth, also, but nothing came forth. It took days of watching a sister pup recreate the first noise (Crying). Was it possible that only girl dogs could have noise come out of their mouths?

Then a brother pup yelped, much to everyone's surprise. Soon everyone but me was able to make sounds – some sharp, piercing noises, others were less forceful; still others made a low repetitive tone, like they were suffering from hunger. I noticed that several of them inhaled air before exhaling with the noise that showed awareness and that would grow into something more offensive. So, about four weeks after entering the world, I instinctively tightened my throat and exhaled.

It felt like a lump had come up my throat and shot through my mouth. The sound was like a force, and I quickly learned from watching my mother that if I opened and closed my mouth and tightened my throat, I could make a distinctive, authoritative sound. I later learned that it was called a "bark" and I was the first in my litter to do it at will and extensively. Much later I learned that barking was often inappropriate behavior, but at the moment I was the only one of my five brothers and sisters who could do it on a constant basis. I may have started slow and been the last one to make any sound, but I was the first to authoritatively bark. "Leader of the Pack" some persons called me.

Besides my dog family, there were big people who seemed to have roles in our upbringing. They mostly seemed to fill mother's bowl with smelly chunks and sometimes a soft paste-like meat that I eventually tasted and I soon got my own bowl, while fighting off my litter mates. I quickly learned that a loud bell ringing in the kitchen was followed by a serving of the tasty stuff and I was always the first to the kitchen to await the refilled bowl. After we had all eaten, some of the people would take all of us into the wonderful yard, where we could begin to run freely, not fast enough to go to anywhere, not that we'd know where to go anyway. Still, by five weeks, we all seemed to feel sharp little ridges begin to push up through our gums, and we all soon learned to snap our jaws closed in order to get something to chew or to bite.

I found that biting was best for playing with my brothers and sisters. They tried to bite back, but I was usually too quick and nipped their ears, which brought forth yips that sounded sad and hurtful. I soon learned that bites had to be used in a proper manner, such as eating the hard chunks of food that were always present.

One time, Lisa, the little girl in the human family, wanted to play, so I bit her arm. Surprisingly, she started to cry, a previously unknown reaction. Samuel, the biggest man and apparent head of the house, immediately picked me up, sharply slapped me on my hindquarters, and taught me my first human word, "No!"

My back end stung and I immediately began to yip and crawl away to avoid another painful slap. I seemed to relieve some of my pain by continuing to yip, which I realized was like Lisa's crying. Lesson learned –biting hurts and slapping hurts. Meanwhile, the adults hovered over Lisa, trying to console her. A tiny drop of blood was quickly wiped away and a band aid covered the spot. I guess because I had no blood that I did not earn a band aid, but I would have liked one like she got. I was still hurting, whether it was from the slap I had received or the guilt from causing Lisa to cry so loudly and endlessly. She was my friend.

Suddenly I felt a hand pick me up like I weighed nothing. It was Samuel and I feared what was about to happen. My puppy head was looking around to search for a route to escape anticipated additional pain. Soon we were sitting in a chair and he was holding me at eye level.

"Pup, you can't go biting people, especially fragile little girls like Lisa. It really hurts them and may cause them to be afraid of all dogs their whole lives. Do you understand me?" I was still at eye level and did not have a clue of how to react. I waited, as if I had a choice.

"Lisa, come here," still speaking without emotion. The girl had stopped crying and reluctantly came over to Samuel, who had lowered me to arm level. I looked at her in fear.

"Lisa, this little guy did not mean to hurt you. He only just got his teeth; he was only playing like he does with the other puppies. But I think I taught him not to bite little girls any more. Okay? Now I want you to pet his little head gently and say nice things to him, Okay?" My fear had gone with Samuel's gentle voice and Lisa's petting and her calling me "good girl."

"Good boy," corrected Samuel.

"Good boy," Lisa confirmed. For some unknown reason I licked her hand like she was a sibling.

I felt better when Samuel gently placed me on the floor and I returned to my dog family, who had watched in awe. I had learned one lesson – never play with Lisa again!

When I was about five weeks old, I learned another dog skill – a good dog's bathroom is the outdoors, not the inside floors. The first few weeks my system would just eliminate my body waste whenever it wanted. As I grew and became more aware of my senses, I felt that it would be better if I went somewhere other than my bedding so that it would not smell. Again, I was the first to learn this, as my litter mates would often wobble to the kitchen, the room where our food always awaited us, and let loose on the smooth floor.

We all had gradually stopped drinking mother's milk and had started to eat tiny, hard chunks soaked in water and some of that soft food that stuck to the roofs of our mouths and did not taste great but the change was good. With our new food intake came the production of more waste and a need to go outside more often. If there was a big person watching, he/she would yell the magical "No!" and take the almost guilty party outside, no matter how many times a day. At night they would put down squares of paper and their scent was almost like our own body waste. Those who could not wait (I almost always could. Good dog!) were not scolded if they messed on the pads. The people were often inconsistent with this training, because we would often hear a loud stomp of a foot on the floor and a "Bad dog!" accompanied by a sharp hindquarter slap and being gruffly taken out to the yard, followed by a loud, scary slam of the back screen door, sometimes so hard that the door would swing open again.

This reaction frightened us something awful, especially the guilty party because no one was sure who or what had caused such an outburst. Then a few moments later the storm passed and we went back to playing. If we got lucky, someone might bounce or roll a ball and play with us. It let us know that everything was all right in the world again, until next time.

Next time happened the one day when we were all in the back yard. Johan was almost as big as Samuel, but apparently much younger. I could tell by the way that Samuel ordered Johan to finish chores in a firm but playful manner. Today's chores apparently involved fixing something important called a generator sitting on the lawn. He put a large pan under the front, and loosened something, which caused a dark, sweet-smelling liquid to pour into the pan. We all watched this unusual activity intensely.

After a while Johan pulled out the smelly pan and put it near on the grass. Unable to resist playing with Johan, all of us pups immediately attacked his overalls and started to bite at his clothing. He laughed and yelled at us to "Go away now!" swatting his hand blindly but not trying to hurt any of us.

Soon he gave in decided that it was time to play with the pups and chased us as we scattered about the yard. The only pup he caught was his favorite; he even called it "Lucy," the only one of us to have a name. We did not know how old you had to be to get your own name, but we figured our time would come.

"Lucy, Lucy, what am I going to do with a four- pound lady rebel?" He held her high at the end of his fully extended arms. Lucy looked around with her little pink tongue hanging out. She actually seemed to be enjoying herself. Gently, he placed her on the grass and went to retrieve his pan, now filled with the dark fluid.

"Now, you monsters stay here while I empty this oil pan under those trees. I'll be right back."

Off went Johan followed by four pups. Only Lucy and I stayed behind as ordered; I don't know why. I watched Lucy and jumped on her back, but she quickly seemed to lose interest in playing. I did notice Lucy walking funny when she staggered to a second pan left by Johan; it was filled with some sweet-smelling green fluid. Lucy sniffed, approved, and then began to lick some like she did from our water bowl. I, too, trotted to the sweet smell of the pan's contents. Lucy, determined not to share, pushed me away, but I was quick and got around to the bowl's other side. In my eager clumsiness I stepped on the bowl's edge and spilled its contents. Most of it ran onto the grass, but Lucy stuck with it and took a few more laps. It tasted different but not something I would want much of.

"Lucy, No! Get away from there!" Johan screamed and ran full force at us as though trying to scare us. He succeeded and we scattered as far as possible as four-pound pups can run. We knew nothing of why Johann reacted that way, except for the word "No!"

In one swift pick-up, Lucy was in Johan's hand, being carried towards the house as he yelled, "Mom, Dad, I think Lucy drank some anti-freeze!"

Samuel ran though the doorway and quickly checked the area. The other pups obediently ran to the house. "Johan, put all the pups in the house. Tell Ma to give Lucy water. I'll get Duke and see if he got any."

I guess I did have a name, after all. Samuel swept me up with his big hand and forced his fingers between my little teeth, forcing open my jaws. He searched the inside of my mouth, shaking his head as he looked.

"I see a little spot of green on the back of your tongue, Duke. Did you drink any?" I assumed that Samuel knew I didn't understand anything he said, but he seemed worried. I knew "drink" but I wasn't sure how to respond. I barely tasted anything. Years later when I understood people's speech better, I realized that if I had been able to speak, I would have yelled, "Of course I drank some. Who wouldn't? Now help me out, please."

"Come on, boy, you need some water." We went in the house and he poured me another bowl of water and set it on the floor across from Lucy, who was being held there by Mother Amy. Lucy was still drinking water but at a slow rate.

Samuel shoved my snout into the bowl forcing me to start scooping water into my mouth with my tongue. I could still faintly taste that sweet green liquid, but it was fading.

Soon we were all outside again, and Lucy and I were getting special attention. I started to get a little dizzy and fell on my side. I could see Lucy coughing and throwing-up green and yellow stuff. Soon I did the same, but not nearly as much as Lucy. She was trying to walk but kept falling. Then her whole body began to shake out-of-

control. I was seeing better but was too worried about Lucy to feel sick.

Samuel barked, "It's probably too late to take Lucy to Doc Harker's. It's a good two miles. Maybe someone will pass us and give us a ride. Hope for the best. Watch Duke. Give him water, see if he'll eat anything, and try to keep him active. I should be back soon."

"Can the doc fix her?" cried little Lisa.

"I sure hope so, little one. Take care of Duke now."

With that he was out the door with Lucy's head resting on his arm. She looked back at each of us, especially me. Then they disappeared into the dark. Samuel ran down the driveway, and I wondered if it would be the last time that I would see my sister.

A couple hours later, I started to feel better, but did not want to eat anything, even though they made some special meat for me. It was night black when Samuel returned. We all looked for Lucy, but he returned empty-handed, his head hung low; he looked like he had been crying.

"Where's Lucy?" asked Lisa immediately.

"I'm sorry, kids; the doc couldn't help Lucy. She's at Rainbow Bridge now, waiting for all of us."

All the people kids and Mother Amy began to cry. Although we pups had never formally heard of Rainbow Bridge, we all seemed to become more aware of it as the years passed. It was a place where all dogs go after they die, where they play with other dogs and never experience any more pain. They stay there until one day when they hear their masters' voices, their ears perk-up and the reunion is heavenly.

Samuel explained to Mother Amy. "Doc Harker said that she drank too much anti-freeze. Three tablespoons can kill a 22-pound dog in less than twelve hours. Poor, little four-pound Lucy never had a chance. Apparently, it tastes sweet and attracts dogs, causing them to over-indulge. No sure treatment. There was a remote cure which would have cost $3,000, but it would have taken a few days to get it here and there was no guaranty that it would even have an effect on Lucy after so much time. And we really didn't have that much money to gamble on a pup; God love her. I'm sorry. Duke looks a little better, but still sluggish. Did he eat?"

Mother Amy shook her head no.

"That's too bad. Let's keep an eye on him. He probably just got a little taste. Hope and pray, Ma."

I slept with Johan on his big bed. Any time I cried, he picked me up and talked to me in soothing tones. Eventually I fell asleep.

When I woke the next morning, I felt close to being normal. Johan carried me outside, where my litter mates were waiting. They cuddled me, sniffed, and looked around the yard. Still, there was something important missing; we realized that Lucy was gone, probably forever. No one felt like playing much. We didn't know why we felt so sad, but as I got older, I realized that a life had passed. It was our first meeting with Death, but far from being our last.

As sad as the loss of Lucy was, what happened later was totally unexpected. We pups weren't sure if we were being punished for what had happened to Lucy or something else. The family had us all in the yard and were picking us up, petting us, playing, and then talking with each other. The adults all agreed that we were big enough, but for what purpose no pup could guess.

"Okay, kids, which one?" asked Samuel. "Remember, if we keep a girl, she'll be able to give us more pups."

'What does that mean?' I thought.

Soon Lisa spoke-up. "I like Duke, even though he bit me."

Johan quickly added, "Dad's right, Lisa. We really should keep a girl. I like Ruby."

Again, the adults conversed and soon Lisa began to cry softly. No pups knew what was happening and if we were going anywhere else, but for the rest of the day we all played in the yard, with Lisa paying extra attention to me. I was already exhausted and slept for a long time.

When I awoke, Johan was taking me outside to do my bathroom business. As soon as I was done, he scooped me up and placed me in a cage with the rest of the litter, except for Ruby. I feared that Ruby, for whatever reason, suffered the same fate as Lucy. Then we all saw her being cuddled in Lisa's arms.

The word "never" was not part of our perception at the time, so realizing that we would never see our birthplace or the adults who had nurtured us to this point were not major factors in our emotions. Just curiosity.

An "English" friend named Mike picked us all up in a pick-up truck at our home. We rode for a long time in a large cage. The fresh air felt good through our fur, but the unknown really took away any joy. Although the truck's cab blocked most of our view, we could catch glimpses of the sights we passed. We drove into a busy place, later known to us as a "city," with countless vehicles that were all foreign to us – buses, trucks, honking cars, and an endless rush of noises we had never experienced at our old home. It was exciting but terrifying. What next?

We drove past a large, white building with a brightly lit dome. Later we would learn that we were in a city called Madison. We turned away from the dome and Mike stopped the truck in front of a large window with displays of food and water bowls like we had at home, surrounded by pictures of dogs. We had no idea that places like this existed. And what were they?

Soon we felt Samuel and Johan lift our cage off the truck. They propped open the door of the building and carried us inside, finally setting the cage on the floor. We looked up, scared of what would happen next.

The side door of the cage opened, and Johan's big hand reached through and grabbed one of my brothers.

"We call this one Sparky," he said as he showed Sparky to another man.

"Just put him in the window, Johan. He'll be just fine."

Soon Samuel picked up another brother. "We call this one Sammie, kind of after me," and Samuel gently put his namesake next to Sparky.

Then Samuel lifted out our only remaining sister. "This one we called Amy, after my wife."

Finally, it was my turn. Johan lifted me high to the level of the other man's face, as I struggled to get back to the ground, my little legs pumping the air but going nowhere.

"And this one," said Johan proudly, "we call Duke, because he was pretty feisty and active. Might make a good sheep dog."

Looking down from my exalted view, I could see my brothers and sister, all with names now, walking around an open-topped cage, with shredded newspaper for a floor. I was set alongside them and got used to the odd floor cushion. Of course, I immediately had to pee, as did my family.

The strange man chuckled and said, "That's what the newspapers are for Samuel. Don't worry; we change them three times a day.

Always plenty of water. Common food bowl; they get plenty of nutritional food and nighttime treats. And they all go to good homes; we do background checks if we feel it's needed, but many buyers we already know. Let's go in the back and take care of the paperwork. I already have your check made out."

With that said, all the humans vanished. I became even more startled when I looked out of the cage and saw a group of people staring at us through the big window. They all seemed to be smiling, while some knocked on the window and pointed at us. We all froze, as much as puppies can.

A few minutes later, Samuel and Johan returned and looked down at us. Samuel spoke with his authoritative voice, but I thought his eyes might be damp.

"Okay, pups, you be good dogs now. We'll think of you from time to time on the farm, but I doubt we'll ever see you again. Behave now, especially you, Duke." He turned sharply and left us there, never explaining what we had done wrong. Johan dropped a quick, "Bye," and followed. Soon the crowd at the window had vanished, and a light went on above our pen.

Then a voice from above said, "Good night, dogs. We leave the light on all night for your comfort and to show you off to the after-bar-hours crowd, who like to window shop, especially for puppies. Here's a few rawhide chews to keep you busy and your puppy teeth happy. See you tomorrow."

We ignored the chews he gave us, having never seen one before, and all turned towards the window where we could see the truck ready to pull away. Johan looked and gave us a little wave as he smiled. Samuel was right – we never saw either of them again.

As the non-appointed leader, I pawed some loose paper into a small mound, settled down and nestled into the shredded paper, which I found adequately comfortable. Soon my brothers and sister decided to cuddle with each other on the same paper I had gathered; we were all touching each other. I heard one short whimper, felt someone snuggling even closer and sleep came easier than expected. We'd all had a busy day and were exhausted, not sure what tomorrow would bring.

Bath Day

Macbeth Opens Gifts

Chapter 3
Duke Finds a Home

"Dogs laugh, but they laugh with their tails."
Max Eastman(1983—1969), American Writer

1970's –The "Me" Decade, Continued social conflicts for Blacks (African-Americans soon came to be), Indians (Native Americans), women (still women), the decade that ended the slow demise of the Vietnam Conflict, and the start of the Green Revolution. Most importantly, 1970 was my college graduation, which meant that I had to leave college, try to find my way as a teacher and start a grown-up life. Teachers in 1970's were frequently referred to as "a dime a dozen." After several unsuccessful job interviews, and the constant inquisition by my parents about my success/failure in obtaining such a "prestigious" job, I had my back to the proverbial wall. So, against my twenty-two years of brainwashing and normal socialization, I was forced to leave the friendly confines of Chicago and suburbia and accept a job in the land of the frozen tundra (whatever that was) -- Wisconsin. All my life I had been raised to believe that Wisconsin was the lowest ring of hell. Even worse than Wisconsin I will never forget that once I drove eight hundred miles round-trip for a job interview in Iowa, where the first site that greeted me as I crossed the small-town limits was a faded wooden sign warning me "Howdy Stranger, Welcome to Granger," which was followed by a real pig, running in front of my car. 'Perhaps the mayor,' I thought. I floored the brakes, barely missing the walking bacon. Wild hog or escapee, I never learned or cared. That job interview consisted mostly of small talk about locals who I never met, and being forced to sit in several chairs, assured that I could choose any chair guaranteed to help my teaching. I wasn't sure what the district budget was, but they sure had chairs! Worst part of my Iowa experience was that I did not even get the job. Chair teaser! Anyway, suddenly Wisconsin started to feel like a trip to Disneyland.

There were only two weeks before public schools started, and the openings were diminishing quickly. So, I pondered what the neighbor to the north could offer a young, urbane man such as myself – the Packers, cows, less tolerable weather (though I was pleasantly surprised when we all got our first "snow day"), something called "euchre", the Brewers (what kind of state would name its only professional sports teams after a person who makes beer and/or packs meat? Was I prepared for such a breathtaking leap? Would I lose all my friends? Would I still have a noble goal in life? But, wait! There was a possible upside to this. As the old adage says, "When God closes one door, He opens another." Or something like that. Maybe I could get a dog. Any state that likes cows, must like dogs too, right?

Begrudgingly, I turned traitor to my native homeland, filled a U-Haul truck with furniture (mostly old stuff that neighbors, family and friends wanted to discard) and headed towards a town of 800 people called "Pitsville" (spelled correctly) in southern Wisconsin. It was about a three-hour drive from my parents' comfortable suburban home in Wheaton to my newly discovered bottom-half rental of an old white frame house in Pitsville, only three blocks from the school. All the way there I kept up a rather active, explanation to my imaginary dog Rover (I could always change his name), about why I was moving him and that it could have been worse–Iowa.

Moving from a megalopolis of 10,000,000 people to a town of 800 was similar to having a tooth extracted through your anus. The high school principal found the bottom half of an old house on one of the five streets in Pitsville. For $75 a month, I could live below my elderly landlord, who had put a shower for me in the basement, both ideas which seemed somewhat creepy. And it came with free on-the-street parking, which seemed to indicate that I could park anywhere. As I only saw one other car on the street in the three years that I had survived there, I did not have to worry about breaking any municipal traffic laws. Best of all, the landlord said that I could have a dog as long as I "picked-up" after it. Of course, he wanted to see the dog, but since I didn't have it yet, I couldn't very well show it to him. Thank God I soon learned that he was somewhat senile, because I had to use that excuse many times in the future. "Sure, I told you I had a dog. Remember?" The place had a large back yard – just perfect for an energetic pup, I thought, but there was no fence. I would have to train him about his boundaries or chain him to a stake.

I was never sure which came first – the name Pitsville or the town itself? Didn't really matter, because it was a long cry from Chicago. There were two locally owned grocery stores, one small eight-table restaurant (Midway Café), which also served as the central command for all town gossips, and four bars.

Cap's Tap, Dobby's Village Inn, Gene's), all usually busy, which indicated the need for escape. Interestingly, on the first day of school, all teachers were told not to be seen in any of the local drinking establishments in order to avoid possible conflict or scandal. I didn't even ask about brothels. However, it was acceptable to drink at home in private. I wasn't sure if that eliminated parties or not. Again, I began to ponder, "Is this the kind of place I want to raise a dog?"

With only one week to Day 1 of the new school year, I had to get serious about settling in and getting a dog. Probably the highlight of my new life was meeting the girl with whom I could share this misery for a while. Becky was also a first-year teacher who had moved to Pitsville from Iowa, the social climber. She taught home economics. Oh boy! A woman who is willing to live in Pitsville and can cook! Jackpot! She was attractive with shiny waist- length auburn hair that she cut short two weeks into the year. She did it for a cause – Locks of Love, a donation of her locks for cancer patients, but I think she did it to also make some real brownie points with the locals. Waist length hair to a Peter Pan cut?

The bottom line is that because we were the only two new hires, we instantly gravitated to each other and began to discreetly "hangout," which in a rural town of 800 people is like the pope sneaking-in chicks at the Vatican. Nothing else to do in Pitsville. On our third day of living there, Becky and I decided that we both needed some home and school supplies, so we decided to get "out of the Pits." Madison was our closest city of size, so I picked her up at ten from her above-the-bank apartment, which reminded me of Stephen King's hotel from <u>The Shining</u>.

The drive up Route 78 was twisty and hilly, but absolutely gorgeous, with rolling mounds and countless pastoral working farms. Around one curve a dog raced alongside our car, barking and trying to bite our rear tire the whole way. "I gotta get one of those," I said, mostly reacting to the border collie's energy.

She looked at me, puzzled, "The dog or farm?"

"The dog, of course," I replied thinking 'Is there a choice?' "I'm a full-time teacher now. How could I find time to run a farm?"

Without pause Becky responded with a truthful but stinging retort, "Exactly! When are you going to find time for a dog?"

My mind immediately envisioned my new apartment – living room, bedroom, basement shower, and decent yard without a fence. "I think he'll be fine. I'm only three blocks from school, so I could rush home at lunch to let him out. We'd have all weekend. I could stake him in the yard for a while. I really want this." Suddenly I realized that she was probably planning her future so that I would be forced to choose a new girlfriend or a new dog. Iowa vixen!

Becky could sense that I really wanted a dog after such a short time. "Okay, we'll keep an eye out." When she said "we," I really started to like this girl. Could I have both in Pitsville?

We stopped on the edge of the city at a Treasure Island department store. ("Our trash could be your treasure") I thought it the perfect motto. As a college town, there were plenty of back-to-school sales and by the end of the day we had loaded the trunk with mops, buckets, even kitchen curtains. We were both low in the inventory of "Things needed to start a new life." Besides a whole mess of junk, I decided to be prepared and bought a spiral dog stake with a twenty-foot chain for the back yard. An old boy scout motto came to mind. Becky saw an opportunity to show-off her perspective (probably some Iowa philosophy about counting chickens), but said nothing. We had almost reached the car, when out of the blue I felt a need to reward this girl in some way. "How about if I buy you lunch in Wisconsin's state capital?"

She smiled, "Sure, how do we get to the city center?"

"City center? Who talks like that? You from Iowa or something?" I kidded.

She smiled and attempted to even the score. "Okay, Mr. Chicago big city, take me to the Promised Land. My Ma warned me not to get mixed-up with some big-city galoot."

"Galoot? Is that an Iowa word? When we leave the sanctity of this car, you'd better hold my hand or you'll get gobbled-up by the big fish." I was a fast mover in those early days.

She took my hand and we walked to my 1967 Malibu, a parting gift from my parents, so that I would not forget to come home. Unfortunately, I had no idea how to get to Madison's city center. I asked some galoot in the parking lot, who pondered like he was deciding whether to help me, an apparent Illinois rube, or not. He looked at Becky, who smiled warmly, and he decided to set us straight. Good thing that he didn't know he was talking to two out-of-staters. We pulled out of the parking lot and started to drive down Nakoma Road, a straight, beautiful street with very ritzy homes. Becky kept pointing at various palaces, but she must have forgotten that I had never been to Madison, so I kept my eyes locked straight ahead. We finally came to a busy cross street and decided to follow the flow of traffic, angling right, and we were both overwhelmed by the sudden and prestigious sight of the majestic capital building. I found an open spot on the street, so we parked and began our exploration.

State Street was the major passage between the capitol and the University of Wisconsin campus, full of eclectic shops, every one selling clothing, mugs, key chains, etc. with the beloved Bucky Badger mascot embossed on everything. I didn't think I would be able to cross that major a line from my Illinois roots. I wondered how Iowa Becky would feel. Go Big Ten!

As we sauntered up State Street, heading towards the capitol, Becky suddenly grabbed my arm and pointed with her other hand. "Look! That must be a pet shop."

A wooden shingle hung over the sidewalk. "Fur, Fin and Feather" it announced.

Quick witted, I responded. "Sounds like a pet shop, but I don't have a pet yet, remember?" I honestly think that I was afraid to face the reality of being responsible for another living creature so soon after beginning my new life. However, I felt a little guilty because Becky meant well. "Let's go look, anyway. Maybe we could buy a water bowl or something. Never hurts to be ready." That was the second time that day that I recalled the boy scout motto, and I was never a boy scout. Neither was Becky.

We walked the half block and looked in the big picture window. Inside were three black and white fur balls, standing on their back legs, yelping at anyone walking by or coming into the store.

"Larry, we have to go in," she commanded; still leading me by the nose, or elbow, we entered. The three pups quickly changed sides of the window cage and came over to us with hope in their soft, irresistible brown eyes. Above the cage on the sidewall was a sign that warned, "Keep fingers out of window." Of course, I immediately stuck my hand over the edge and into the gathering of three puppies. "Snap!" came the jaws of the biggest fur ball, the one that was closest to being named Jaws, I assumed.

"Hey, sir, didn't you see the sign?" came a strong, but not unfriendly voice, as he pointed at the warning.

"Sorry, no," I lied. "Can I hold one?"

"Sure, which one?" so I pointed to the snapper. As the man reached in, the other remaining members of the litter looked sadly up at my choice, as his little legs cycled in the captive hand. They had seen this before.

The puppy was transferred to my arms and he immediately climbed my jacket and covered me with sandpaper licks.

"Can I hold him?" pleaded Becky. Of course, I had to give it to her but that was okay. No time to be selfish.

"I'm Bill, the owner here. This is a litter from a good Amish family that brings down a group every year or so. These came in four days ago, but two have already been bought. That one you picked seems to be the leader of the pack. I think Johan said his name was Duke, but, of course, you can call him anything you want."

I thought I saw the pup jerk his head at the sound of "Duke," like he was used to responding to the name. "What breed of dogs are they?" I asked as Becky started to bond under an onslaught of puppy kisses, which made her giggle.

"Just mutts," Bill replied. You won't get any purebreds here, especially on campus. Probably some collie-mix. Johan said they liked to run. That's why they're only ten dollars each."

"Sounds like our budget," coaxed Becky. Suddenly it was "our" budget, not mine. I took the dog back and held him at face level. He really liked me; I could tell; No need to ask Becky. It was my decision, but I felt like I should make her feel that I respected her opinion. Who knows how long our future together was going to last? At least a month?

"I think you should take the whole family as long as you're buying their leader. You don't want to split-up a family, do you?" she half-kiddingly suggested.

"I think we'll just take this one, Bill," I said firmly, starting to think that these were probably brothers and sisters, like when we chose Dexter and Zsa-Zsa back in childhood days.

"Should I gift wrap it for you?" he joked. I was still a bit unsure, but Bill laughed anyway. Fifteen minutes later I could see my new dog straining back to see his litter mates as though he was apologizing for something. They returned his glare and gave a few soft barks and cries as we left the shop. What could a ten-pound puppy do to stop what was happening to his family?

The three of us left the Fur, Fin, and Feather with a large bag of "necessities"—toys, bowls, treats, etc. I had to laugh at the total bill of $35.00. It was twenty-five dollars for incidentals and ten dollars for the dog. I always referred to my first dog as my "ten-dollar mistake." I could have easily bought all three dogs. I gracefully handed off the dog to Becky, while I toted the dog ware. We must have been stopped ten times with such harmless comments as, "Oh, can I see your puppy?" or "What kind is he?" I was flattered but he was my dog now, even if Becky was holding him.

Of course, I got to drive home while I watched my dog fall asleep on Becky's lap. What was going on here? Was I jealous over a dog? After a 45-minute drive, I pulled-up in front of the house and Becky reluctantly surrendered the pup, which I promptly carried to the large back yard and gently placed him on the lawn. Of course, the excited puppy acted like he had seen heaven or a remembrance of someplace similar. He immediately peed while his little head acted like a periscope and he scanned the entire area. Once the dog took off, running circles in the yard, Becky and me in mock pursuit, he acted like he had seen the yard before and had experienced freedom, not imprisonment in some window cage. Finally, I scooped him up and we entered through the back door. Exploring, he raced from the kitchen to the bedroom, to the living room, frequently slipping on the non-carpeted floors.

"What are you going to name him? You're not going to let him keep Duke as a name, are you?"

"What's wrong with Duke? That's my brother's name, but it looks like Demon might be more appropriate."

"Larry, you're an English teacher. You can't just settle on a cliché like Duke. Use your creativity," she taunted.

I could see Becky's game – shame me into trying to be clever, perhaps more sophisticated, then stomp on my ego with an inappropriate answer. "I suppose I could name him after a literary reference, like Shakespeare or Wilde," I tried.

"You'd look goofy yelling 'Shakespeare' in the neighborhood. And Oscar Wilde was gay. You wouldn't want the fine people of Pitsville thinking you had a gay dog, would you?"

This girl was good. She took control without even knowing it. I kind of really liked her, but she'd better not come between me and my dog.

"We don't have to decide now. Let it fester a few days. What's the rush?"

So we agreed to slow down with choosing a name, while we unloaded all of the dog's paraphernalia. It was ridiculously fun; purple plastic bowl next to his matching food station with kibble on one side and canned food on the other. Then the best dog toys! I threw a tennis ball, but the dog just watched it bounce and went to the water and food bowls, which he immediately used and liked. I was hoping that he'd belch. I'd save the squeak toy until later.

The next day I realized that with his energy, the dog wanted to run, but I couldn't compete all day. Fortunately, old man Johnson, the landlord and upstairs resident, took a liking to the dog (still no name) and allowed me to extend a 20-yard clothesline to the back of the yard. I put the choker chain on the dog, placed him on the grass, and off he raced! Unfortunately, the dog started to run sideways and soon was brought up short at the end of his chain. Smart dog, he soon learned that he could run farther if he ran north to south. A few sniffs followed by some trial-and-error explorations and, he quickly learned the yard's generous boundaries, but I had the feeling that he was used to even more space. He should be glad that some frat boy didn't take him to his yard less house on fraternity row. I don't think the dog had any clue about pet crates, other than his brief trip to the dog store. Bill at the Fur, Fin, and Feather, said that the puppies had come from an Amish family, where he probably could run endlessly. But what could I do?

Because he was still small and easy to catch, I took the choker chain off his neck and let him run free. I tossed the ball, and he chased it, then played keep-away. New squeak toys really sealed the deal, and dog seemed to accept his new home, at the expense of an exhausted but happy owner.

Becky came for dinner that night, a gourmet meal of spaghetti, the safest meal for a guy to make for his "date." Any guy who can't successfully cook a spaghetti dinner should be required to earn a mandatory license to date. After dinner we both started to look at our lesson plans, school to begin in another five days. The dog slept in his new bed at the end of the couch.

"So, have you picked a name for the dog yet?" Becky challenged.

I looked at the book in my lap. "You don't like Shakespeare, huh?" was the question.

"Too pretentious, even for an English nerd."

I knew that would not generate an alternative suggestion. Besides, who's a nerd? So I pretended to check the book I was reading for my lesson again. Answer!

"What about Macbeth?" I probed.

"Macbeth? Don't you think that is a bit harsh, condemning a dog to be called Macbeth? 'All hail, Macbeth, etc."

"First you're afraid that people might think my dog was gay, then pretentious, then that he would be condemned by having the same name as a brutal Shakespearean character. Besides, he was a king, good and evil, like the dog is black and white. . .'

"All right! You're just making this stuff up, but I give you credit for creativity with absolutely no pre-thought."

"Macbeth!" I shouted but poor puppy was dead to the world during such a major point of his life. "I like the sound of it, I think." Ran out of sarcasm.

"Okay," surrendered Becky, "Macbeth it is, but it may take a while to get used to it. I think you had me at the good and evil, black and white part."

She gave me a quick kiss and decided to pick-up the sleeping dog. She lifted him to her nose for a puppy kiss, but Macbeth had other interests, as he peed on her Iowa Buckeye shirt. Smart dog or political?

"Oh gross!" and she quickly made a beeline for the back door. He went outside again but really had no interest in running anymore, so we all went back inside and kind of began our lives as a fully named family.

Six months later, except for the nasty Wisconsin winter, life was good. Becky and I grew closer, and she spent the night at my place about twice a week. She couldn't move in with me, because in 1970, teachers fraternizing with other teachers pretty much stopped at after-school mandatory staff meetings or chaperoning and was highly discouraged, especially in Pitsville.

One time old man Johnson, an early riser at 5:30 a.m., caught Becky leaving my place to rush home to change her clothes for school. Becky gave him an innocent, "Oh hi, Mr. Johnson," waved and started to canter the four blocks to her apartment above the bank. Old Mr. Johnson responded only with a stern frown, which Becky translated as "You're going to hell, young lady!" I think she may have over-reacted with her interpretation, but we grew more cautious. His curt, "The rent," was all he acknowledged when I personally delivered each month's rent check. There was a change in the winds, and I don't mean just winter.

Unlike Mr. Johnson, Macbeth grew to accept Becky's presence, except when it came to our intimate moments. On his first night away from his canine family, I had made the innocent mistake of allowing Macbeth to sleep at the edge of the double bed with me. A month later I had moved his very plush, plaid, dog bed from the living room and put it on the bedroom floor next to me. He lay there, making no effort to sleep but merely looking at me with those soulful brown, still puppy eyes, and he would let out an occasional growl. Not a bark but a puppy cry that would have made Mother Teresa weep.

"Go to sleep, Macbeth," I scolded mildly.

I turned on my other side, but I could still feel those piercing eyes burning a hole in my back during a sorrowful puppy concert. Couldn't help but wonder if he was missing his littermates. He wanted them and I was a poor substitute. 'Show some empathy,' I thought. Slowly I rolled back, and I swear that dog had not moved one iota. Hesitantly, I reached down and picked-up the fur ball. He stood on my chest and proceeded to paste my face with dog saliva. I guess that I did count as a substitute for his brothers and sisters.

I lofted him above my head and told him, not too harshly but affirmatively, "Macbeth, you are the worst dog I ever had. I know you're the first dog I've ever had, but you're still the worst." He drooled on me as if to answer, "If I'm your first, then I must also be the best dog you've ever had."

I lowered him to the other half of the bed, where he proceeded to comfortably settle. He did seem to have this annoying need to be touching me. Every time I moved away, I could feel his little legs extending until his back made contact with mine. Little brat would have pushed me off the bed if I had let him. I'll never understand where a fifteen-pound mutt got so much strength and perseverance. I assumed that he had been the alpha male of his litter on the Amish farm.

The next few months created a reasonably comfortable routine. I never had to lock-up Macbeth in a portable kennel or anything. He just looked out the front window while reclining on the top of the Salvation Army couch. Good balance. I'm sure he barked plenty at anyone passing, but I never heard any complaints, not even from old man Johnson.

Most days when I made the three-block walk home for lunch, I saw his head go into search mode, his ears like a couple antennae. We'd spend most of the lunch period in the back yard, where he made full use of his time. He didn't argue when I took him off his running cable and left him alone in the house again for a few more hours. I really learned the importance of a rawhide chew for a dog. I didn't see any signs of protest. After school, I'd let him run loose more often, but then he fulfilled the curse of all puppies. He started to grow-up into that awkward, destructive, in-between stage, like a human teenager, but he was still a good dog.

One of the more interesting happenings occurred around Thanksgiving. We had about an inch of snowfall, the first of the year. I took Macbeth out, still able to carry him in both hands, and gently placed him on the snow. I don't think he had ever experienced snow. He started to high-paw, like every step was painful or he had plans to be a neo-Nazi faux border collie. After ten minutes of this circus show, he stood on all fours, no harm done.

Soon he was sniffing the powder and brought up a snout full of snow. He looked at me, like checking to see if I was okay. I laughed at his missing nose, and he sneezed and shook away the foreign substance. But then he returned to his exploration with the same results.

After a few rounds of "what-is-this?" he realized that he was not attached to his collar and started to run back and forth across the back yard. Naturally, I chased him. Soon he started to growl and fell sideways as he tried to make a 90-degree turn. He slid but was up in seconds and continued his romp.

"Looks like Snow dog isn't going to quit," Becky said, an amused reaction one day after school. A few more throws and we all went inside, where we wrapped Macbeth the snow dog in a large quilt and put him on the couch. We made some hot chocolate in the kitchen, and by the time we got back, Macbeth was sound asleep. I could imagine his brain repeating, "Best day ever!"

"Looks like we picked a good dog there, Lar," she said as she nuzzled my arm.

"Looks like it," and we kissed to unofficially seal our agreement. Months later, Becky and I took Macbeth to the nearby farm of a student and let the dog loose in a large corn field. We threw a bright orange tennis ball and he chased it a million times, always returning like a huskie leaping over snowdrifts. I don't know if he didn't realize that there was no longer any snow or if he was pretending.

A few months later, we had our first major disagreement about Macbeth.

Macbeth's only challenge to his occupying the bed with me was Becky, the alpha female. After a couple months, Becky and I became "intimate" at my place. The first times were at her apartment, usually on Saturday nights above an entire bank building, cool but scary. And so it continued during liaisons #2, #3, #4. Good and safe.

On our six-month date anniversary (easy to remember because we just checked the school calendar), I decided to be the suave, good-looking, caring boyfriend, and made her supper at my place. Of course, I would make spaghetti, only this time I put candles on the table, like in" Lady and the Tramp." How could she resist such temptation? She did comment, "Nice candles," but that was all.

After our gourmet dinner (I had thought about tacos, but the hot sauce would ruin the breath of a hippopotamus), we moved to the living room sofa and pretended to watch a Badger basketball game against Iowa. With at least a rooting interest in Iowa, we watched the entire game. Coach Tom Davis's team won, which satisfied us both, since neither of us had abandoned our home state schools. Macbeth sat next to us on the couch, but dozed-off during halftime.

Soon the making-out session started, but Macbeth still slept. Becky gave me the hush sign as we sat up and proceeded to the bedroom. We quickly dropped our clothes and got into the bed, where we continued our make-out session with interest, when we were interrupted by a jouncing at the foot of the bed.

"What was that?" blurted Becky, like a teenager who almost got caught in the back seat of her parents' Oldsmobile.

I knew. In six months, Macbeth had grown-up enough to jump up on the bed without help. He no longer needed to play the role of abandoned orphan that needed my assistance by lifting him. He was about 25 pounds, but he just took what he wanted – his half of the bed.

"Well, he can't very well stay here, can he?" Becky asked or told me; I was never sure which.

Had to try. "It's the only bed he knows. You know, he was torn from his family and taken to a new world. He has nothing else."

"Jesus Christ, break out the violins! We are not the United Nations' Orphan Dog Relief Center! He has a perfectly good dog bed right next to us. That's where the dog sleeps."

She was really getting perturbed, but she may have been right.

"But, Beck . . ." I began.

"Larry, you now have a decision to make. Tonight you are going to spend the night with a hot, Iowa chick in your bed, or with an Amish farm dog. You have ten seconds to decide."

And she meant it. "You have such a way of phrasing things. Hitler could have used you in place of Goebbels during World War II. Might have had a completely different outcome."

She responded with a smile, while intensifying her glare. "Four, five, six…"

"Okay, okay, just give me a second."

My foot shoved the canine lump at the end of the bed. "Macbeth, you have to get down now. Go on, get down!"

Miraculously, the damn dog was still half-asleep.

"Go on, move it, buddy, and get down now," and I gently pushed the furry lump once more. This time he slipped to the floor with a thud. At last I was free of the dog for the night, but the romantic mood had been stifled. It got worse when we both heard hard nails scrambling on the floor. Suddenly, this dog returned from the end of the bed, like a huskie romping through the snow (a lingering image in our minds) and landed between us, even delivering a few kisses to Becky, as if to say, "I forgive you."

"Get down, Buddy!" and I pushed him again. We heard him hit the floor, but soon there was the ticking of nails on the hardwood again, followed by the flying Wallenda circus act, and the dog landed squarely between us. End of game.

"Larry, I like you and I like your dog. But I will not go to bed with you while Macbeth is with us. Now, is it him or me?"

Geez, why did she have to make me choose? My hesitation cost me dearly, and Becky got up and quickly threw on her scattered clothes.

"See you later," she whispered. "Just remember that you were the first to quit. I don't blame you, but you did quit without much of a fight." No more words, just a quiet exit. I could hear Becky quietly say, "Good night, Mr. Johnson." So now the old man was definitely onto us. Without the nasty drama going on, my dog slept comfortably on the side of the bed that Becky has just vacated. All of the on-the-bed, off-the-bed activity must have really worn-out my dog, and he unintentionally but happily drooled on her pillowcase. There had to be a solution, but where?

Surprisingly fast, once Becky had forgiven me and after spending a few nights at her place, we thought we'd stubbornly take a stand and jointly exile Macbeth to his dog bed, now located in my living room. I had moved his bed as he had inquisitively watched me. We filled the spot where his bed had been with our clothes and our scents, which may have thoroughly confused him. Soon, Becky and I were snuggling in the bed when we felt the dog landing on our feet.

"I've got this," I proclaimed as I got out of the bed, picked up the intruder, scolded him with a malicious, "No!" and carried him over to his bed in the living room. I hadn't even made it back to our bed when Macbeth darted in front of me, leapt onto the bed, and started to settle into my place.

"No!" I menacingly scolded again as I picked him up and returned him to his designated spot.

Two more repeat performances and Becky thought she'd help me give banishment a try. This time we took a united stance and formed a human wall at the end of the bed.

Macbeth jumped up but was greeted with four forearms, causing him to fall back.

"No, Macbeth, no!" I continued.

Two more tries with the same result, and he reluctantly returned to the couch in the living room. His bed was not used that night. Becky and I lay in bed, grinning over our victory. We could hear restless activity, but were grateful that he couldn't do much harm, other than ruin the romantic mood.

When we got up, it was clear what his unseen activity had been. Becky's blue panties were shredded as though some insane demon had been seeking some revenge. This maniacal retribution was executed four more times over the next week, earning Macbeth the title of "Panty Slayer." We got his messages all right and soon learned to hide everything in the bathroom. The dog's bed was never used again in his entire life of fifteen years, only the front room couch or our bed without Becky.

Our sojourn in Pittsville lasted three years; to Macbeth and his owners, it felt like twenty-one years. Moving a Chicago boy to Pitsville for three years is more challenging than plugging a leak in the Hoover Dam with a kitchen sponge. The Pitsville excitement included Henry and Dee Vinehout winning the annual euchre tournament down at Dobby's bar for the second year in a row. If you don't think that's big news, the "coverage with pictures" was two pages long in an eight-page weekly called the <u>Pitsville Gazette.</u>

My lifestyle and rumors about Becky's and my relationship certainly gave the Midway Diner ample material for gossip and extended lunch get-togethers. I did not make the paper, but I was fortunate not to be executed, or as I referred to it as "mercy killing." One Saturday Becky and I went to a nearby town called Loganville to check the Loganville Furniture and Appliance Store to buy a bedroom set. We both agreed that it was time to replace old Mr.

Johnson's "comes-fully-furnished" antique (way past its usefulness) bedroom set with one that someone had not died on. Pitsville Furniture had nothing that would interest a couple under 180 years-old, such as a complete bedroom with laminated "oak" dressers, a "down" mattress, solid engraved frame, and more for one low price. Despite the local folks' hard sales pitch (Buy from us or you'll die!), we decided to shop around. The Loganville store was much more accommodating with information and discounts, so we purchased their set. We got a complete real oak furniture set built by the Amish, which cost more but would last longer than three weeks.

Unfortunately, delivery was not available for several weeks, so I had to borrow Rick Pauli's pick-up truck to get it home. Rick, a high school art teacher and rebellious colleague, had no problem with helping us move it all, but getting the high dresser and bed pieces into the back of the open pickup truck was like a free moving advertisement for Loganville Furniture and Appliance Store. Driving down Main Street in Pitsville was like driving through a gauntlet with merchants on one side and fiery citizens who actually whispered and pointed at us on the other side. I think that if I had been listening closely, I might have heard, "Traitor!" and, "Let's run 'em out of town on a rail." I began to really appreciate the mob-storming-the-castle scene at the end of <u>Frankenstein</u>. Macbeth even cowered in the back of the truck.

Fortunately, Iowa Becky did not go with us. She listened intently to our story, not in the least questioning its validity. She, too, hated the tedium of the burg and living with the most hated man in Pitsville history. One night after a bottle of local wine – Ralph's rose August – made by one of the janitors who enjoyed making it and giving it away, Becky and I surreptitiously made plans to leave the inferno at the end of the school year and to move-in together in Madison. I don't know why we kept it such an overwhelming secret from a town full of prying, detestable busybodies, except that it was a kind of sweet revenge to drop a few misleading, vague hints that something special was about to happen, and only we knew what it was.

Getting our new bedroom set into the apartment had been a challenge. Once Ralph and I got his truck to our place, we removed the old bedroom set to the basement and set-up our new one. Old Mr. Johnson watched us closely, lest we scratch some of his decrepit heirlooms. I did not know a man could shake his head in disgraceful admonishment at us for that long. I thought that perhaps he was suffering from some kind of a seizure or palsy and I politely asked if he wanted me to call a doctor, but he missed the sarcasm and went back into his upstairs half of the house. Macbeth, of course, was the first one to try jumping on the new mattress, even it was for just a short time. For helping me take away business from the local economy, poor Rick Pauli became the second most hated man in Pitsville. He also resigned at the end of the school year. Coincidence? I think not.

With the kangaroo court trials over (never quite sure who was on trial – them or us). Becky and I jointly brought our brief resignation letters to Superintendent Erickson, who did not seem surprised or disappointed, but did add a semi-sincere, "Good luck to you both." Maybe he was a shackled but true romantic.

One great advantage to teaching in rural Wisconsin school in 1973 was the early-release at the end of the school year. It was a customary and liquid rule that school ended by the end of May in order to allow students to work on the farms. Fortunately, the powers that be pretty much ignored the dwindling number of high school seniors who still actively worked on local farms. Maybe Macbeth could have gotten a job herding sheep, but he wasn't fond of working, especially in Pitsville.

Although school ended on Friday the 25th, I assumed that I would be able to stay in my apartment until the 30th. Wrong! Old man Johnson (may he and his entire family rest in the other hell, the one lower than Pitsville), interrupted our dinner with a firm command, "I want you out of my house the day after school ends. I'm tired of your sick jokes and immoral behavior. If you're not out on Saturday, we'll put your new furniture out on the lawn, your dog in the pound, and new locks on the door." Slam!

Whoa! I guess old man Johnson must have overheard some of our nasty comments about his age and dying soon, much like Pitsville. They weren't meant to be heard outside of the room. And there might had been a few noisy nights after we got our new bedroom set, but maybe senility had obliterated his memory of youthful activities.

At the old man's attack Becky did not move, her jaw touching the tops of her shoes. I guess she had never been yelled at like that. Neither had I, but who was he to threaten to impound my dog? It was the most piercing threat he could have made to me. Old man Johnson had two "special" sons – toothless Clem and slow Elmer, both married to first cousins, I was sure -- who could easily move out my furniture and change locks, but there was no way that they could take away my dog. I felt positive that the old man could not legally carry out all his threats, but common sense told me that it was not the best road to take.

Quick plans – Rick Pauli was willing to use his truck again to move us and our furniture, if he could drive it up and down Main Street past the house of Glen and Ellen Thompson, owners of the Pitsville Furniture Mart, representatives of the Pitsville affluent, and the runners-up in the annual Pitsville Euchre Championship, still a sore spot in the social hierarchy. We agreed if he allowed us to ride in the back with the furniture, and we held signs that read, "Purchased at Loganville Furniture and Appliance Store," Even Macbeth barked in agreement.

Step 2 was to find a place in Madison for the furniture, my dog and me. Iowa Becky had made plans last March to share an apartment in Madison with three of her high school friends who were attending the university, and they welcomed her to share the rent while she formulated her master plan. I was obviously not on the same program, but I would tag along to Madison, and if needed I could sleep in the car with my best furry friend.

So we did. Before we left my place in Pittsville, I encouraged Macbeth to pee in every corner of the house, which made no sense to him after all his training not to. The taunting mobile furniture display was a smash; almost everyone in town, except Father O'Leary, gave us the finger, and I'm sure that the good father was just wiping something from his eye. With a long honk of the horn, we left Pitsville, headed up Route 78 and towards Madison, all feeling that an enormous burden had been lifted and was burning in the hell we left behind us.

In Madison Rick drove us to one of many storage facilities to be found in college towns, where we stored our bedroom set in a damp and musty unit, locally referred to as the "Black Hole of Madison," without the luxuries. I vaguely thought about staying in the storage unit for a few nights, but I was not the kind of dog owner to subject my pet to that kind of misery.

The next few days sound like heaven, but they ended too quickly. Becky's former classmates and current roommates welcomed us to stay/hide in their place until I could find a dwelling of our own. So, for two days Macbeth and I stayed with four college girls. Even Macbeth smiled constantly. I cleaned and cooked while the co-eds worked and/or attended classes. We only had hamburgers and spaghetti before our world imploded. Some selfish moron, probably the druggie neighbor or the mayor of Pitsville, who lived in the other half of the rented house, reported us to the corporate Nazis for having a dog, apparently a felonious assault on Madison landlords' contracts. I had until noon the next day to vacate or else . . . Deja' vu all over again.

So we hung my clothes on an adjustable pole across the back seat of my Chevy Malibu and spent a couple days driving around the city. Macbeth had his head out the window with tongue happily flapping. We went to parks where dogs were still welcome, and he drank water out of a Cool Whip container. As a treat, we would stop at a McDonald's for a dish of soft serve ice cream, which left his black snout covered with white, another brief flash to the past.

At night we had no place to go, so the first night we attended an all-night horror movie marathon at the four-screen Sky-Hi drive-in movie theatre, occasionally grabbing some sleep. The dog slept in back while I nodded off in the front. The next day we did sneak back into the apartment for an hour to shower and to take real sustenance. After unsuccessfully searching another day for an apartment that took dogs, we again sneaked supper with the girls, then the two banished inhabitants tried sleeping in my car on busy Johnson Street. Could have probably slept better on the fifty-yard line at a Bears-Packers game. Macbeth readily slept in the back seat where only half of my clothes filled his space, and I curled up in the front seat. I think newborns probably have more room in the womb. Le Chez Johnson Street; Macbeth didn't seem to mind.

The third day brought some fortune. A block east on Johnson Street, I saw a new "For Rent" sign in the lower left window of an old brick house that the owner had split into four apartments. First chance I got, I sneaked back to the girls' apartment and phoned the number on the sign. A gruff old voice informed me that the place was for rent in two days at an unbelievable price of $145 a month, plus utilities. And yes, I could have a small dog (35 pounds qualified) and I could live with my girlfriend if there were no noisy parties and the rent was paid on time. Quite an improvement from old man Johnson of Pitsville.

I didn't care if I was caught and incarcerated for life, but that night at Becky's apartment, I made some Hungarian goulash, (one of Becky's favorites) to celebrate our first good fortune. As vagabonds, just one more day to kill. That night we decided to park the car in Tenney Park in order to avoid another busy main thoroughfare.

Macbeth and I were curling, cringing in a deep sleep when a loud machine woke us both. I quickly picked up my head to see the cause of the commotion. Ten feet from the front of my car was a giant auger used to dig holes for telephone posts and power lines. I quickly gained my senses and moved the car to the other end of the parking lot by the lagoon, lest they decided to put a giant hole in my aging Chevy. Once parked, I opened the back door so that Macbeth could get out and relieve himself. Glory Be! There was a large flock of geese walking out of the water in front of the crazy dog that needed his exercise. My best friend barked and chased the large birds back into the pond and did not quit until he thought he had given them all heart attacks. Macbeth must have thought that he had died and gone to dog heaven. The poor dog that had spent most of his life on a leash was free to chase geese. I really did not have the desire to disrupt one of his most glorious moments. Even the men who had been digging the holes pointed and laughed at the canine extravaganza. After a five-minute assault, Macbeth dragged his spent body back to the car, where I had his Cool-Whip bowl waiting. He had almost finished drinking it before watering my back tire.

Beck had Thursday off from her part-time cashier job at the corner "Beer Depot," which sold everything, even dill pickles from a white plastic tub. Now that we had our own apartment, we realized that we needed to furnish it with more than our lone bedroom set. We had some savings, but could not be lavish with furnishings. Perhaps the Pitsville Furniture Mart could give us a deal. The old Montgomery Ward store on State Street in Madison seemed to be our best bet, according to Becky's research. It was three doors down from the Fur, Fin, and Feather pet store, where we had purchased Macbeth.

They still had a litter of unknown breed puppies in the window, but now the sign read, "$15.00." I lifted Macbeth to see if he had any recollection of his time there and if he might still hope to see his brothers and sisters. He merely craned his head back and forth, so we never could tell if he was ignorant or sad that the litter mates were all gone. Dogs won't tell you anything unless a treat is involved. Then come the soulful eyes for your interpretation. Becky and I took turns going into the department store while the other stayed outside with the dog. Within an hour we had purchased a complete living room set – couch, love seat, chair, two tables and lamps for $600.00, including delivery to our new apartment, which became filled upon arrival of the new furniture. Probably not the best quality but certainly better than old man Johnson's antiques; plus, the fact that we were eager to set-up our home and play house.

Surprisingly, the three of us stayed in our new cramped Johnson Street apartment for 4½ years. I got a job teaching English at a rural high school about twenty miles west of the city, and Becky immediately took a job teaching home economics at Madison East High School. Guess there was more need for home ec. teachers than for English teachers. Best news is that we both had steady jobs, insurance, and cars. The years passed quickly and all was happy and serene. The only glitch that constantly bothered me was that Macbeth was limited to the tiny back yard on a ten- foot chain and collar attached to a stake. We would take him to run on our days off, but he was never able just to exit the door to a vast, half-acre yard. I'm surprised that he didn't run away, but there was plenty of love to share between the three of us. It's not like he had to live outside in all kinds of weather while chained to a crudely built doghouse. He knew we were trying.

One breakout day was a Sunday when we were leisurely reading the big Sunday newspaper. We had been looking for months for the perfect home once we had realized that rent gives no return other than a temporary place to live. The home economics teacher, who had agreed to marry me and my dog (package deal) two years ago, was teaching a unit on family living -- figuring bills, budgeting, interest payments, and taking care of your first child, which was represented by a raw egg. I guess that if you dropped it, his/her brains would splatter.

Becky realized that we had spent $15,660 plus utilities, in our occupancy of the small Johnson Street apartment. That would have gone a long way towards owning our own home. Amazing! That Sunday we found a listing for a 3-bedroom ranch about two miles from our current location on the western edge of the city. It took us only twenty minutes before pulling-up in front of an "Open House" sign on Lorraine Drive. The house was an off-color green, but had a nice front yard and looked solid to an eager young couple tired of paying rent.

We put Macbeth on his leash and anxiously made our way to the front door. From the side of the house, I could see a weathered picket fence. The realtor, Lynn Mahoney, greeted us and made us sign over our first born just to look at the place. I asked if I could let my dog loose in the back yard, and she assured us that even though the back yard did not have a complete wooden picket fence, that there was an old chicken wire wall across the back. "The owners also have a dog," she seduced us. Ten steps through the kitchen, out the back door, and Macbeth did his best imitation of an ICBM as he fired through the yard and too soon reached the chicken wire wall at the back. He soon realized that he was not wearing a chain and was free to run anywhere he wanted. For a dog it was as close to paradise as ever dreamt. Becky joined me and watched our dog enjoying his freedom, not ignorant of what this all could mean for our future. Our eyes got misty as we became magically entranced by the canine follies and our own euphoric destiny.

Becky nudged me and whispered, "We have to buy it now, Lar. I am not going to tell Macbeth that this is just a short visit." She was more sensitive than she let on. After a brief tour of the house, including the full, unfinished basement, with furnace and water softener, we gathered on the first floor.

"Let me get your dog some water; he looks bushed," cooed Lynn in a soft, melodic, salesperson voice. She took a bowl from a cabinet and filled it with cold water, then put it outside on the back stoop.

"Here, boy," she called, and my best dog ever ran over to her and started slurping before continuing his back yard exploration at a slower pace.

No need for any transition, just right to the point. "It's only $35,500 with a $5,000 down payment." Realtor Lynn Mahoney tried to gauge a reaction, but Becky and I had discussed not to fall for inducement like low closing costs and the obligatory warning that other people had already looked at it, and that the house was very close to being sold. "We do have two other couples who have shown interest, one putting in a counter offer."

"Sure you do," I scoffed silently. I remember reading not to accept the first bid, but what if another couple had bid more than the asking price? Besides, $5,000 down payment was not a major problem for us. Lynn gave us a stat sheet and assured us that the house came with an owner's guarantee, which would cover major repairs in the first year.

"Can we have a minute?" Becky asked. We had agreed not to jump into anything too soon.

"Sure," replied you-can-trust-me Lynn as she walked to the backyard to play with our dog. Always the realtor reminding us of what we could have there.

"I think that we should just accept the asking price right now. We have the down payment," Becky aggressively whispered, keeping her excited voice muted. I was stunned that she would agree so readily; it was a nice home, and Macbeth had already cast his vote.

"Miraculously" our bid was accepted and we agreed to meet at the realtor's office the next day at 1:00. Macbeth had not wanted to leave his wonderful yard, and I had to lift him out of the yard and back into the car, as he continuously craned his head to get one last look at "his" yard. He had looked the same way as when I had taken him out of the pet shop window and he had stared at his lone remaining brother, wondering if he would ever see him again. He seemed sad when I drove back to the apartment, but in another three weeks, we would be able to move-in and eradicate his melancholy for good. If only he had understood.

By ownership day Macbeth had completely forgotten his sadness as we drove back and he did remember the place; he ran and joyously barked at squirrels. He often stopped under the power lines crossing the back yard and jumped and warned the birds perched there, looking down at this possessed demon beast, fearful of how high it could jump. This routine was repeated daily, even through the bitter Wisconsin winters, when snow grew to two feet mounds, and the dog would briefly vanish for a while until he could dig his way to freedom. Macbeth clearly wanted to let all the fauna know that it was his yard, and no one else was welcome, now that there was no chain to withhold him.

In the warmer months, Macbeth would nobly lie like the great sphynx, looking over his land and guarding it closely, even barking at humans who dared to trespass on his street. He was proud, wondering why he had not done this his whole life, and Becky and I were happy to give him the opportunity to make-up for so many years shackled on a chain. It's not how dogs should be treated.

Of course, this tranquility could not last forever. Life happened. Spring, Summer, Fall, Winter. Sleep, work, relax, then repeat. Monday through Friday, Saturday, Sunday, repeat. Appointments, shopping, holidays, visitors. Birth, childhood, adulthood, death. Almost everything we take for granted peels away before reality sets in.

We lived in that home for fifteen years, and Macbeth grew older. Much of his black fur slowly turned grey. He quit trying to jump up to the birds or racing after the squirrels and chipmunks that frequented our yard, much to their pleasure and willingness to share. My first dog seemed healthy; he just moved much more slowly. He didn't seem to mind the change, but he had to sense that something was coming for him.

One beautiful Wisconsin day in September, we were all invited on a houseboat excursion with our best friends, John and Mary. The boat was docked about thirty miles away in Spring Green. We would spend one night on the boat after mooring on a sandbar in the Wisconsin River. One and a half days on the river -- scenery, playing cards, drinking beer, and enjoying the slowly passing shorelines of surrounding hills, trees, occasional deer and other such mysterious sounds and movements whenever we came close to shore. Our dog was welcome, and he spent much of the time lying on the boat's flat front, basking and barking in the sun as his black/gray fur absorbed the heat. It was glorious.

We kept his food and water in the kitchen. If the back door was closed, he would race outside along the one-foot-wide border leading towards the back of the houseboat. It was as if he had done it his whole life, running without fear of losing his balance and toppling into the dangerous current of the Wisconsin River.

Later that evening we were moored and playing euchre. Macbeth was dead tired and slept near our card table to keep an eye on us. Suddenly he got up and came to me and Becky, licking each of our hands, then did the same to Mary and John.

"That's weird," said Becky. "What brought on a round of dog kisses?"

"Just thanking us all for bringing him on an adventurous trip on the river," I replied. "I don't think he's ever seen a river before. Plus,

I think he's whipped after keeping watch and barking. It's not like he has a lot of room to run on a houseboat."

"I'll take him for a good, long run along the shoreline tomorrow. I usually jog in the morning. I think he'd like that," volunteered Mary.

Early the next morning before we unmoored, Mary and I led Macbeth off the houseboat. As soon as his four paws touched the ground, off he raced down the shoreline. He hadn't ever run on sand, and it was amusing watching him race like a snow dog down the beach, making a few quick diversions into the water. We yelled his name, fearful that he might go too far or angle into the woods. He usually stopped and waited for the slowpokes. He was like the anchor in a relay race. As soon as we reached him, Macbeth looked at us like we were the slowest species on the earth, and continued his heat-seeking missile mode and almost flew away. Push–leap-fly-repeat; push-leap-fly-repeat.

Sand and sun

Last day on boat

Chapter 4
Rainbow Bridge

"Dogs lives are too short, their only fault, really."
(Agnes Sligh Turnbull, American Writer, 1888—1982)

...Push – leap fly-repeat; push-leap-fly-repeat. Freedom was mine. Maybe this was what Rainbow Bridge was like. But I could hardly race anymore, even when I heard a welcoming voice call my name. Gratefully, I stopped and waited for a human to catch-up. My body was weak, so I stopped and waited for them to rescue me as they always had.

"What's the matter, boy?" Larry asked. "Wanna' run back again?"

I thought he might have lost his mind, so I just looked up at him and panted, never making an attempt to stand again.

"You okay, Buddy?" he stooped and stroked my side. "What's wrong, Macbeth?"

I had spent all my energy for the day, maybe longer.

"I'm going to carry him back. There's something wrong here." So Larry lifted all thirty pounds of me. I had grown thinner over the past months, adding to my weakness. He walked slowly along the beach, as I got a people-height view of the ground that I had just covered, but I was too tired to keep my eyes open.

When we got to the houseboat, Larry put me on the couch and brought my water bowl. Royal treatment. I slept the rest of the day and, surprisingly, all the humans decided to leave early. Short trip, but I was ready to go home.

Monday came and I could sense that there was something major about to happen. I felt worse than ever in my life, including that time as a pup when my sister Lucy and I drank that strange liquid that caused my sister never to return. Despite my weakness, once home I was able to jump into Larry's favorite chair and curl-up.

The next day they were both leaving for work, and Larry kneeled beside me to scratch my neck and ruffle the top of my head, his most frequent sign of affection. I looked up at him and suffered the feeling that I would never see him again. Brown eyes to brown eyes, forever bound. I felt his tear drop on my forehead and he said, "See you after school, Buddy. Rest up. You'd better be ready to play when I get back."

But the mere fact that he said that made me realize that he knew I would probably never run again. We met eyes once again as he went through the door. As soon as I heard his car leave, I coughed, and blood was on the chair.

'Sorry, Lar,' I thought. But I was exhausted and needed a deep, long-lasting sleep, so I did.

Various dreams permeated my peaceful rest. Everything was dark, like when I was first born and I could sense the presence of my brothers and sisters and the mother who had tended us. Even though I was too drained to bark now, I remembered my first yelp. "Leader of the pack," the people had called me.

They were good people, even after I bit the little girl Lucy. The human kids and my litter mates played all day in the field. My name was Duke, and I had grown dizzy, like I was now, from drinking the liquid that brought death to take Lucy. It took such a long time to learn so much.

I never completely understood why Samuel and Johan had separated the pups and loaded us into cages for a long truck ride into such a busy place like a city. The other pups leaned on me, as we snuggled together in a store window with only a single light shining above us. Frightened but helpless, one by one the pups vanished from the window during the days and went away with strange people. They all cried for me to help them, but I was helpless.

One day a man (Larry) took me out of the window and carried me outside, and I, too, looked back at my last remaining brother, Sammie, to plead for help. I was too scared to cry or yip, but Sammie just looked up and a tear slipped from our eyes. Five minutes later I looked back for the last time at my only remaining canine family.

A woman (Becky) joined us and we rode in a car, and I wondered if we were going back to Johan's again. Maybe there were new puppies to play with and I could teach them the rules of the games. We drove for a short time, and the woman held me. I was scared, yet felt safe and nice for a change from that store window, strange people, and my missing litter mates. For a few days we lived part-time with four nice girls who had briefly joined our family. They took turns petting me. Don't know why, but Larry and I slept in the car parked on the street and in parks, but as long as Larry was there, I felt safe. One night we were parked in a place with a big screen and Larry watched some silly movies, but at least we shared popcorn, which was good. We rode around most days, and one morning I got to chase geese by a pond. They were lucky that they could fly, because I was fast. Great time! The fun days were fewer as soon Larry, Becky and I move to our own small place (they called it an "apartment."

My freedom there was limited because I was attached to a staked chain in a small back yard. Occasionally when we all drove around. I would see other dogs running free in larger yards behind fences. I wondered if I would ever experience that much fun. Most every day was the same routine – alone for long periods of time in our small apartment, outside still on a short chain and occasional wonderful short trips with extended exercise. Although the apartment was right for us, I always wished for a bigger field someday.

So much time had passed before we left the city and moved to a small town (Pitsville) and a bigger apartment, but at least I got a new chain that let me run up and down the same yard. Better than what I had had. The rooms were about the same size, and I settled-in quickly, but was still bored and would have liked the freedom to run without having to be on a chain. I don't think the old man who lived upstairs liked me either. How could anyone not like me? I know that

Larry and Becky did not like him at all. But at least the three of us made a family.

Larry may have felt that he was the boss, but after a long time, I wasn't so sure. Becky ruled that I had to sleep in a dog bed and that she got to share the big bed with Larry, an idea to which he seemed to agree after considerable tension. But I got some minor revenge for a few days as I shredded her under clothes.

Snow! I didn't know what it was, but we often played in it. At first it felt cold on my pads, but after a while I got used to it when I sunk far enough that my paws were covered. Sometimes the snow was so deep that it was chest high. Then I thrust upwards until I landed again. It may not sound like it, but people should try doing it. The first time we did I was exhausted from using so much energy, but I thought that it was probably the best day ever. I was getting bigger and stronger but was still leashed at the apartment. Why? Sometimes they would let me run loose in a snow-covered field. They called it "playing snow dog," but we were a happy mixed family of people and canine, like when I had lived with Johan, only fewer members of the family/pack. When the snow was gone, they took me to a big place with barns and strange animals that I later identified as cows, sheep, and horses. Big animals. Larry and Becky would throw a ball into a field, and I would get it and bring it back to them. After a while they got tired and the game was over. I was glad, because I could hardly run any more either. It's not easy being a dog.

Many months later, we all moved back to the city, saying farewell to our second apartment. I sat in the back of a big truck that had all of our furniture in it, even my dog bed. When we drove through the town, Larry and Becky rode in the back with me, holding signs and waving to the seemingly angry people lining the streets. After a long drive, we finally got to a city, like the first one that my canine family and I had visited. Were they going to return me after all the years we had spent together? I thought we had made a good family. My fanciful recollections were interrupted by another hard cough and more blood on the chair. Slowly I realized where I was, I still wanted to stay on Larry's chair, but I felt something kept pulling me gently away. It took a little time before I was able to find peace and return to the last chapter of memories of the best part of my life.

I was still leashed in a small back yard, but fortune changed on one reading-the-large-newspaper day, when they took me to a new home, where I could run free behind a fence like I had seen so many other dogs do. I could only hope that my wish had come true, but then they took me back to the apartment and I felt sad again when they put the leash back on my neck. A month later to my endless pleasure, we returned to stay at the big-yarded, leash-free house.

I had spent many peaceful days lying in the back yard while guarding our house. I would chase and bark at so many furry or flying intruders, and the man who brought us envelopes almost every day. I knew I was doing a good job, because when I saw him and barked, he immediately turned around and left. I could have been doing those jobs for years, if only I had had the chance.

It was a long time before I started to feel pain in my joints, and something inside me caused discomfort. A few trips to Dr. Erickson, some more pills, and I just grew to accept my displeasures as part of life. Eventually I stopped chasing the back yard creatures and just let them be there. I think that I had made my point, and they no longer bothered my home. I was still guardian there.

Then there was yesterday. We all rode on a houseboat (funny name) that took us down a river, where I watched the passing scenery and just basked at the front and tried to let myself enjoy a dog's life. Then Mary tempted me with one last challenge – run free along the beach. I hoped that we would spend a lot of time there. Push—leap—fly—repeat. Push—leap—fly—repeat. It was like I was reborn and at first, I thought I could do it all day. But that hurtful pain inside started to take its toll, and I just lay down spent.

Larry picked me up, carried me to Becky, and we soon drove home. I did not feel better, but I was too weak and I didn't know if I could ever return to my active dog life. They both seemed very sad the next morning as they left for work. Larry could feel the difference and we met eyes for what I felt was the final time. Finally, for the last time, I closed my eyes and lost consciousness.

When I awoke, I was following a few other dogs of all sizes, ages, colors, and breeds down a grass path. There were no leashes and everyone was running. We all felt great and all aches and pains were gone. We crossed a small, wooden bridge, and suddenly I saw Lucy and Sammie and four other dogs I felt connected to – Ginger and Suzie and Dexter and Zsa Zsa, who I magically recognized. They were all joyously barking at me. I ran to them and we jubilantly rolled together on the field, so happy to see each other. I knew where I was.

Macduff going home

Macduff at his best

Chapter 5
Arrival of the Border Collie

"The dog lives for the day, the hour, even the moment."
Robert F. Scott, British explorer, 1868

Macbeth's death was one of the saddest moments of my life and Becky's. Little did I know how often we would experience our first dog's death; the cause of death was determined to be cancer. At that time, I never even knew that dogs could develop cancer. I had a difficult time resigning myself that I had not been able to save him. I kept analyzing his health history. What if I hadn't taken him on that houseboat and allowed him to run as much as he could? He was having the time of his life – literally. Certainly, a dog's demise it not hastened because he had enjoyed life too much. Still, I was haunted by every decision I had made of missed opportunities. What if . . . I can never forget the day he died and had coughed up blood on my chair. He looked at me as if to say, "Thanks, it's been fun." The blood that he had coughed up on the chair was finally cleaned up two days later – a gruesome and haunting last reminder.

Becky and I lived an emptier life for the next few months, often checking the back door to see if he wanted to come in. Expecting him to follow us out the door if we went somewhere. We missed his ferocious barks at the mailman. Natural reactions from pet owners who had lost a companion and suggested a support group though I didn't think that was something that I wanted to join. As the Wisconsin cold of winter (finally learned what the polar vortex was) kept us prisoners in the house, we reminisced about how Macbeth had loved playing snow dog in our back yard. On one occasion I had gone to let him back in the house, but he had vanished. Panicked we had searched by boots and by car. Not to be found. We could not solve the mystery of how he had escaped a completely fenced-in yard. We found the spot from which he had made his getaway. The snow was piled so high that Macbeth had been able to jump over the picket fence. Luckily, he had not been impaled. After a few fruitless hours of searching, I called the shelter. Yes, the police had found a stray black and white dog on the west side. I could get him tomorrow when they opened at ten. A night in jail for my convict dog seemed fitting.

Becky and I repeated enough stories about Macbeth before I broached the elephant in the room.

"Do you think it's too soon to get another dog?" I asked hopefully with just enough begging in my voice. I could see Becky's wheels spinning in first gear, but at least she didn't accuse me of being "out of my mind," one of her favorite rhetorical questions. Slowly she reached where she knew I was going all along.

"I think we should wait until school's out so we can house train him and/or not lose him in the snow," she conceded. Was I and some other dogs in the world lucky or what? I hugged her until she accused me of brutality. I had planned a few questions in case things had gone my way.

"Have you ever heard of a border collie?"

She gave it some serious thought. "I remember a few people asking us if Macbeth was a border collie, especially other dog walkers on the square. Why?"

"I did some research on them. They look just like Macbeth, and they're supposed to be the smartest breed on the planet. They're popular in Australia, New Zealand, and Scotland, where the farmers use them to herd sheep. If a farmer wants three sheep for shearing or whatever, he holds up three fingers and the dog will cut out three from the herd and chase them to the waiting farmer. They're classified as 'working dogs.'"

Miss Snark, "Good, are we going to get a herd of sheep, too?"

Something else was bothering her. "Are you sure you want a hard-working dog or one that reminds you of your first dog as an adult?"

I honestly hadn't considered that option. Perhaps Freud could tell us, but I could not sincerely answer that question, and Freud was dead. Maybe we could push this down the road. "We have a few months before school's out. Let's see where this road takes us. Besides, even if I did get a border collie, that's not such a bad thing. It's not like I'm getting a second wife to replace you."

"Or me a new husband. And where would you get a wife to replace me?"

"Iowa," I said with a straight face. "Maybe the state fair."

After she gave me the finger, we waited until June and that unknown road led us to a little farm in a village called Rio (Rye-oh, not Ree-Oh), and may you spend your life in hell or Pitsville if you should mispronounce it. Outside Rio lived a farmer named Andy Cole, who raised sheep and bred border collies, including a recent litter, which he had planned to sell for $150 each. That was a long cry from my $10 mistake, and I sure had gotten my money's worth there.

I had done extensive research on border collies. The local kennel club gave us information and even a phone number of a Scotsman in Virginia, a MacTavish, who was an expert breeder and trainer of the breed. I knew I was in trouble when he called me back and asked me how big my farm was and how many sheep I had. Fortunately, his brogue was so thick I could honestly pretend that I did not understand him.

"Ye doo nought want me dog for a hoose dog. It's nought fair to the dog or to yooo," he declared once we had established that I did, indeed, want a border collie. I felt like I was being scolded by an old uncle. I simply thanked him and it was the last time we spoke. I could feel his sense of relief over the phone.

Prices for purebred border collie ran about $350 and more, a little beyond our common-sense budget. I did find a few advertisements in the kennel club newsletter. Most certified dogs were about the same price for which MacTavish was selling his dogs, but there was one farmer in Rio who defied the standards.

On a peaceful Saturday we took the sixty-mile drive to Rio. We had called farmer Cole and agreed to be at his farm around noon, after his morning chores. As we pulled into his quarter mile long, dirt driveway, I was reminded of a teenage slasher movie – decaying outbuildings, secluded from the highway, a few scrawny sheep and cows, and I was sure that there was a chainsaw somewhere in the mix. We pulled in front of the "rustic" barn and got out. Almost instantly a middle-aged man dressed in overalls and without a chainsaw emerged from the barn.

I whispered to Becky, "Oh, Auntie Em, there's no place like home. There's no place like home," which was answered with a playful punch on the arm.

"You must be Larry," said a friendly voice. "I'm Andy Cole. Follow me and I'll show you the puppies."

No handshake or acknowledgement of Becky. I suppose he had to get back to his creation of blood sausage from some ignorant college kids. I grabbed Becky's hand and pulled her to the barn. About six feet from the doorway was a cardboard box lined with an old wool blanket. Inside the box were five of the cutest black and white puppies to be found.

They were in full puppy mode, yipping at each other and trying to climb out of the box. Most were whining for some reason.

"Pups are going a little psycho. I should put a burlap bag in there, but I thought that wool blanket would bring out the border collie instinct in them. Also, their mother is out in the fields working the herd, so maybe they're missing her a little," explained Cole.

I thought, 'What herd?' Why is the mother not here with her pups? What kind of moron would put a wool blanket in a box full of border collies? That seemed kind of cruel, like making a maze for a rat to run with his tail on fire and all the exits blocked. Shouldn't this guy have a license or something?' Maybe I was being a bit suspicious, of what I had no idea. My first time buying a pedigree was confusing.'

"And you say these are purebreds. Do they come with papers?" I asked as knowledgeably as possible. I should have talked to a couple dog breeders.

"Nope, no papers. Lost the blood line a while back, and haven't been able to trace the dogs' origins. That's why I'm only asking $150 for them pups. I'd need to get an expensive license and everything. But most people I sell to only want a good house pet and not a working dog. I can assure you that if you want a border collie,

this here litter is the place you want to be. They're a real bargain."
Not exactly breeder MacTavish's view.

I looked at the imprisoned puppies and wanted to take them all
home, perhaps to save them all. When we got Macbeth, he was in a
State Street store window and didn't seem in any stress. Maybe I
was being too critical. Everything farmer Cole said was true, but I
just sensed that something was too curious; too many questions and
vague answers.

"Beck, let's step outside a minute. I want to get your opinion," I
said as I grabbed her hand and led her away for some privacy.

"Do you feel that something's not quite right here?" I coaxed,
looking for an affirmative answer, an old teaching technique.

Unfortunately, she did not agree. "I don't know what you mean,
honestly. The puppies seem to be playing like normal puppies
would."

"Yeah, but they seem more desperate than playful. And Hillbilly
Jim there isn't even licensed nor does he seem to know much about
the border collie pups."

She gave me a shake of disbelief. "Do you think he stole them?"

"No, no, no. He just doesn't seem to know that he's selling a dog,
not a head of cabbage. He has no seller/owner license. The dogs
have no papers. And he gives them wool to sleep on. It just doesn't
add up."

"Look," she replied impatiently, "he's just a farmer trying to make
a few bucks by selling dogs. They all seem healthy to me, wool or
not. What do we know about anything, other than the fact that we
want a dog that looks like Macbeth? (Ouch!) He's got a whole box
full of them in there. You're the one who did all the research. Now,
do you want one or not?"

Becky was right. They were playing like puppies. And
subconsciously I guess I did want one that looked like Macbeth. So
what? Who needs papers? It's not like I'm going to buy a farm and
raise sheep. He won't be in any dog shows. I hadn't even looked at
the puppies all that closely.

We went back and checked the puppy-filled box. All but one
seemed to be active –maybe the runt of the litter? The loner, merely
exhausted, looked cautiously at my approaching hand. I picked him
up and looked into his sad brown eyes. Like Macbeth had done, he
started to pump his little legs to get his freedom. Soon, Becky was

holding him and smiling like a demented clown. Her smile was quickly replaced with a cry of disbelief, as the pup relieved himself on her East High School track t-shirt. I quickly took him and put him on the ground to see if he wanted to escape or if he would be mad at being separated and just wanted to return to his littermates. He stayed.

"Guess he doesn't like bossy women," I joked.

Farmer Cole thought it was funny and decided to make up for his indiscretion.

"Tell you what," he said humbly, "you seem like nice folks, so I'll give you that dog for one hundred dollars. It's a male anyhow, and females can be bred to raise more money for future puppy sales, kind of like crops. Sound like a good deal? I take checks, no questions asked."

Now the whole transaction really bothered me, but Becky saw it as an opportunity to save fifty dollars, even if the pup had peed on her. And the dog really was cute. Maybe we were rescuing him.

Suddenly he seemed to want to run free, but I picked him up and looked him in the eyes.

"What do you think, Ralph, wanna' go home with us?"

"Ralph, we're not naming him Ralph. I have a distant cousin named Ralph who won the 'biggest Moron' blue ribbon at the Iowa State Fair." Why did that not surprise me?

My mistake. "Okay, shall we select this little guy who belligerently peed all over your new pink track shirt?"

Becky nodded and smiled. I wrote farmer Cole a check and off we went, a new family. I still couldn't help but feel that we had saved this dog from being part of Cole's secretly blended blood sausage jerky chews.

On the road home Dog X (as I now referred to him, since Ralph seemed to hit a sensitive spot), squirmed and twisted in Becky's arms, wanting back his short-lived freedom or the only family he had ever known. I scratched his head, but he shied from me

"Put him in the back, Beck. I don't think he wants to be touched yet."

She reached in the back and put the little dog in the back seat of our Malibu. He seemed to feel better, less fearful as he walked around and explored, no cramped and steep box or hands holding him prisoner. Finally, he came to rest on top of a Dunkin' Donuts box, which we had purchased three days ago. No problem – he was so lightweight that he just perched and drooled like he had just finished a three-day trek through the Sahara.

An hour later we let our new family dog into our backyard, where we immediately proclaimed him "insane." It was like the first time he was completely free as he dashed in a circle like an uncontrollable carrousel that had lost its moorings. How he never fell onto his side as he raced at such speed and angles that had never been explained by any laws of physics.

We sat on the back stoop and watched that dog fly endlessly. Finally, I broke out of a hypnotic spell and opened the back door,

"Dog," I yelled, "come in the house, buddy." He saw the open doorway and raced through it, as if wondering if it might lead to more freedom.

Becky quickly filled a Tupperware bowl with cool water and placed it on the floor. Without hesitation he went directly to the water and consumed half of it before heading towards the other rooms. Apparently, he had not done well with his etiquette lessons, because he dribbled all over the kitchen floor and into the living room.

Thirst satisfied, like he had never had a drink, he sniffed at everything, as we waited for his approval. Unfortunately, I guess he did not like everything he saw, because he proceeded to lift his leg on the corner of our coffee table, unofficially christening his new home. Worst part was that he seemed to be smiling while he peed on our furniture.

"Can't ignore that," I announced loudly to the dog, as I scooped him up with one hand. "Sorry, dog, but you have to learn to go outside to pee."

Much to my chagrin, I took him out and he reenacted his first ten laps around the yard, and he was enjoying it even more. In his mind he probably thought he was being rewarded for his marking action. It was going to be a long training season.

"Well, I see you've mastered housebreaking 101," remarked Miss Snark with a grin. "You know, it's probable that he's never been in a house. Everything new looks so inviting. "

"I know," I conceded. "It's going to take patience. Let's take him inside and give him a name while he explores his new digs."

Again, he raced through the open doorway and tentatively returned to the scene of his scent. Becky and I sat on the couch and encouraged him to jump up with us, but he hesitated, not sure if he should or what we were up to. Finally, I just picked him up and held him high with one hand again. He just turned his head as if scoping out the land, but I felt that he was beginning to trust me more.

"What are we going to name him, Lar?" a demure probe.

Immediately, I replied, "What about 'Psycho' or 'Crazy Dog?'"

She pretended seriously to think about it, then said, "Only problem with those names is that if I was calling them, the neighbors wouldn't know if I was yelling for the dog or you."

"Ha, ha, Miss Iowa farm babe. Careful or we'll end up with another Shakespearean name."

"Something equally evil, like Macduff?" she misspoke.

"The evil hero's name was Macbeth. Macduff is a whole other character," I answered smartly.

She shook her head, "I know that. Even we Iowa farm babes have read Shakespeare. Both were Scotsmen like our border collie, or whatever breed we got that is supposed to be Scottish."

"You mean that you don't think our new dog is a real border collie?" I accused.

"Show me the papers. Plus, the whole deal was like buying a used car from Slick Eddie, the used car salesman."

"Well, I have faith in my fellow man, and I choose to believe that farmer Cole was a good guy with a litter of top-notch puppies. You were the one who seemed eager to take the pup now," I threw back at her. "And I'll consider your name offering of Macduff overnight and get back to you."

Fortunately, we were home all the time and were able to take the dog outside as soon as we saw his back leg begin to rise. He seemed to learn quickly, "a trait of the border collie, extreme intelligence." I kept inundating Becky with positive canine reinforcement.

"All right, you win about name choice," I proudly admitted at lunch the next day. "We'll call him Macduff."

A look of awe hit me between the eyes and really hurt. "How did I win?" she asked incredulously.

"You're the one who suggested it."

Becky barked, kind of like a dog, "I said it facetiously!" Macduff cowered, wondering if this crazy lady was stable. He was a very intelligent dog.

"Sorry, I missed the irony there, and I'm an expert at irony."

She saw this argument going nowhere slowly and relinquished with the worse sportsmanship. "Okay, but you're the one who's stuck with the decision, not me. You missed my sarcasm."

So Macduff joined our little family and we embraced his company. He would spend hours in the yard, nose to the ground, sniffing every foreign object possible, often ignoring people walking past him ten feet away. One of his most enjoyable activities occurred when he sat on the back stoop and tried to herd ants. Those little paws kept swiping at an escaping ant until he had it going the other way, back to its "pack" of ants. I never had the patience to see if he ever got them all in a circle, but he really seemed to enjoy the challenge and he slept well from the exercise, or was it tedium?

Unfortunately, the teachers' summer passed much too quickly, and our next task was to keep this puppy-no-more become more domesticated when we left him in the house alone for the day. It was as if we had a teenager who promised not to party if we left him alone for the weekend. So much for that adolescent promise.

The first day after school we learned that Macduff did indeed have a party, apparently with every drunken, drug-addled dog in the city of Madison. He must have been planning for weeks, rounding-up every homeless canine in Dane County. I couldn't help wonder if the city had a program for dogs like this; they did for teenagers.

We had a difficult time believing that one dog could cause so much destruction. Four shoes from different pairs must have served as rawhide chews; they were almost unrecognizable, except for the eyelets; three of them were Becky's, who started to support court-mandated lifetime sentences. Various odd dirty clothes, which we often left piled on the floor by the bed, had found legs to the living room where several pieces could pass for rags used at a high school car wash. He had relieved himself from both ends, including diarrhea, on our couch. Most mysteriously, the dog had knocked over a pole lamp next to my chair. Why? How? It was like he had lost his mind.

Of course, we yelled at him to no end, and Macduff had shied from us, not at all aware of what he had done. I ran to the back door and scolded him to go outside, which he did with the proverbial tail between his legs, head hung low.

It took us about an hour to get matters back in order, which wasn't all that long because most of the debris on the floor composed of unrecognizable clothes and shoes. Lucky me – I usually only wore one pair of shoes and one pair of jeans, not much to lose. But you would have thought that Iowa Becky was the prom queen and had lost her membership to the one percent.

"What are we going to do, Lar?" she beseeched, not vaguely knowing how to handle everything.

"I honestly don't know. We haven't really lost anything that can't be replaced. Tomorrow we'll try locking him in the kitchen. He can't really do anything to the linoleum. Put his dog bed out there with a few toys and rawhides."

Unexpectedly, there was a sharp bark from the backyard. In an attempt to clear the chaos, we had forgotten the dog. I let him into the house, where he immediately drank half a bowl of water, then jumped onto the couch as if nothing had happened, except he put his head down exhausted, instead of jumping on us for the usual affection.

"Do you think there's something wrong with him, Lar?" Becky discreetly asked, no sign of anger.

I didn't give the question much thought. "I think it's just his first day of complete freedom and he got bored" I answered honestly. The only thing that really bothers me is the mess he made on the couch. I thought we had him housebroken, but he just seemed to have lost it, like he was possessed."

I got a 4 x 6 piece of leftover paneling from our partially completed basement finishing project and brought it to the kitchen to make a barrier between the kitchen and living room. We braced it with two matching end tables between the opening (there was no exit, just an opening) and it held. The next morning, we stocked the kitchen with dog bed, water, food, treats, toys, including a Kong stuffed with peanut butter, which should have occupied the better part of his day. Fingers crossed, we could still hear some barking as we left for school.

Eight hours later I got home first and was greeted with jumps and kisses as I entered. Our barrier was open on the left side, where he apparently figured that his constant jumping on one end of the artificial wall would eventually push out the thin barrier and enable his escape. I saw no other damage, though I expected to see the television on and tuned to the White Sox game. I didn't see any beer or popcorn either, so was that a victory for us?

Becky got home an hour later and turned into a mental patient as she rocked on her chair and repeated, "How did he get out? How?"

Not sure if she was pondering how he got out or how we were going to keep him locked-up. At least there was no doggy mess this time, but what about next time?

Almost the same results for the rest of the week except for various items of clothing that he had added to his conquests – my socks, Becky's blue panties (just like Macbeth), and an old Iowa Hawkeye t-shirt. Still, no diarrhea or other major messes. With the weekend coming up, we decided to develop a full-proof plan for the next weeks.

By Sunday night we had decided to lock poor Macduff in the basement. Becky and I had partially finished a section of the basement with some tacky, crude red-brick paneling. I don't think desperate hookers would have been caught in our bar, but nobody had to see it much. We added some Goodwill furniture to make our own Ehrhorn makeshift bar. It also had a closeable door that we could lock. He had his own dog world with his usual bed, toys, water, etc., same as the kitchen, which he seemed to ignore. We even left a radio somewhat loudly playing hits from the 1960's, so what could go wrong? Other dogs would kill for such a spa. Nothing to ruin either.

When we got home on Monday our new kennel with attached bar was basically intact. The door had countless long, deep scratches, like someone trying to claw his way out of a sealed coffin. His eagerness to get out emphasized his desire for freedom, despite his seemingly futile work. Only a few times had he gone to the bathroom. What was odd is that instead of only going in one spot on the floor, he seemed to scatter his waste all over the floor as though he was out of control. Despite the morning drudgery of getting him downstairs and locked in his new plush digs, time passed fairly fast until Christmas break finally arrived.

Our little puppy was growing up rapidly (in dog time) and he reacted to his first snowfall the way I suspected most dogs do, wondering what the white stuff was all over the yard. And why was it so cold? We repeated Macbeth's first snow dog mode whenever Macduff went outside. The deeper the snow, the better.

One afternoon we looked out our back window and watched Macduff rolling on his back, thrashing around like he was fighting a bear. We both thought it funny at the time, until he limped into the house, physically exhausted like he really had been fighting a bear.

Ten days later we were watching the news and Macduff started quickly to circle the living room, accompanied by a few disturbing barks at nothing in particular. Suddenly he jumped onto the couch and Becky tried to snuggle his head under her arm, as though he was craving for affection or hiding from a monster.

"What's this all about?" she asked me as though expecting an intelligent answer. He had been extremely restless the last hour, very confused but aware that something was amiss.

"I don't know. What's the matter, buddy?" He looked blankly at me like I could help him. Without warning he leapt from the couch and began contorting on the floor. It was like the routine he had experienced in the back yard, only this time there was no snow to serve as a cushion.

Immediately I went to the convulsing dog and reached for him. I was met with a few staccato bites at my hand. Becky was greeted with the same defensive attack.

We pulled back and hoped this scene would soon run its course. He seemed to calm shortly, though it seemed an eternity. But not before cracking his head several times on the table and floor. Forgetting his snapping jaws, we instinctively tried talking softly and petting his rear quarters. It was like he didn't know us but felt grateful for some comfort. Then he collapsed and just lay there, panting like he had just run five miles, and closed his eyes. If we hadn't just seen him have a fit, we may have thought that he had died.

"Lar, get a towel. He just messed all over the carpet," directed Becky. Without thought I got a beach towel from the closet and proceeded to wipe the carpet and dog. By this time, Macduff seemed to be recovering and to had visually returned to us. His eyes were still glassy and he stumbled when he tried to get down from the couch, but he eventually approached normalcy except that he was too tired to move much. I couldn't help but think of Linda Blair in

The Exorcist—something possessed my dog, followed by a long period of confusion and deep sleep.

We started looking for a new vet immediately – it had been a few years since we had needed one, and our former vet for Macbeth had moved to Green Bay, too far to travel, so we checked the usually reliable yellow pages. We looked for the biggest ads instead of checking names alphabetically. Aardvark Veterinary Services just sounded too desperate. We settled on a non-descript clinic called Wisconsin Veterinary Services. According to their quarter page ad they had six veterinarians and were able to treat everything, including inoculations to prevent heartworms, whatever that was.

The three of us were in the vets' office at 3:30 on Monday. After filling out enough papers to establish ourselves as residents of the planet Earth, we were called in to the examination room. Dr. Valasatera ("call me Dr. V., it's easier") was a young doctor in his early thirties with UW Vet Clinic diplomas covering his walls. Okay, local. As we told him of the incident, his forehead furrowed, as if looking for an answer in the wrinkles of his brow.

"Did he consume anything that would be stressful to dogs?"

"Not that we saw," I answered as Becky nodded in agreement.

"No chunk of chocolate or some anti-freeze that may have dripped on the garage floor? These things can sometimes be fatal, especially to younger dogs," he replied hopefully, not sure if he was hoping that the dog hadn't gotten into something toxic or that he might think of a plausible reason.

"We don't even have a garage," I offered lamely, as I could see his brain swimming for a lifesaver.

"Has he ever done this before?" I was still searching but taking it seriously.

"Not that we've seen, but there have been signs – upset lamp in the living room, poop and pee scattered in the house, exhaustion and things we may have missed. This last incident lasted less than fifteen minutes," Becky responded as though rehearsed; she had thought seriously about this problem.

Dr. V. thought, but he clearly had no quick answer stored in his experience file.

"Let's check him, shall we?" and the doctor performed the perfunctory exam – eyes, ears, teeth, ribs, tail, anal glands, etc.

Macduff kept turning his head, as though to ask," Who's the pervert?"

Ten minutes later Dr. V. gave us his profound analysis. "I can't find anything wrong with this dog. But I do know a canine neurologist at the UW Vet School. I'll give him a call tonight and get in touch with you tomorrow. That seems to be the best plan for right now. Is that okay with you two?"

"I couldn't help but notice all your diplomas from the UW Vet School hanging on your walls here. Shouldn't you have some idea yourself?" I semi-attacked.

"Yes, but this canine neurology area is advancing quickly. I have a feeling that my colleague may have something new in his analysis." Dumb ass!

That was our dismissal, so our hope for immediate answers was at an end for the day. Hoped our buddy would be stable for another day.

The phone was ringing the next day as we both got home, anxious for an analysis from a colleague who had never even seen our dog. Macduff made it through the day without any obvious signs of another incident.

"Mr. Ehrhorn," Dr. V's voice sounded foreboding, "Dr. V here. Could you come to the office? I have a further diagnosis and some pills that should ease the condition."

"What kind of condition?" I jumped, trying to get some information immediately, and avoid another trip to his office.

"It appears to be some kind of seizure, but I can give you more information in the office. We're open until six," replied the still uncertain voice of the veterinarian.

Ten minutes later the three of us were in the office. Macduff wanted nothing to do with the waiting St. Bernard and some kind of terrier. I wondered what kind of communication transpired between dogs in a waiting room. 'What're you in for?' 'Getting any shots?' 'Hope they don't clean my anal glands this trip.'

Half an hour later we were escorted into the inner sanctum of Dr. V's diploma-ridden office. The other dogs had already gone by 5:45. Probably had a litter of puppies. Why didn't Dr. I-know-everything-but-not-just tell us to come at 5:45 instead of making us sweat while waiting for the answer? I guess I was subconsciously making a case not to like this guy.

"It appears that Macduff has been suffering from seizures. Hard to tell how many because you only witnessed one, but it's likely there have been more."

"What kind of seizure?" I interrupted.

"My colleague thinks epilepsy," he replied, careful not to place blame on himself in case. . .

Becky stated the obvious to us. "I didn't know that dogs got epilepsy. I thought it was a people problem."

"Oh, no," Dr. V. replied smugly, as though he knew this all along and was surprised at our lack of knowledge concerning our dog. "Epileptic seizures are not rare in dogs, but often go undetected for too long."

"What causes them?"

"Oh, a number of things," He took a legal pad from his desk, probably notes from the colleague. "Lyme disease, kidney failure, liver disease, brain tumors, toxins, strokes. Most likely an inherited genetic problem, too often found in puppy mills and inbreeding. You did say that Macduff was a purebred, right?"

I looked at Becky, her eyes wide, and knew that she was thinking the same thing. "We were told that he was but we never got papers."

"Then I'd go to the party that sold him to you and insist on those papers," Dr. V strongly suggested.

Accepting defeat, Becky played the optimist. "But he can be treated and cured, right?"

Dr. V seemed to be grasping our reality. "I'm afraid that epilepsy is not curable. We do have some drugs that may mitigate the seizures, but nothing specific that will cure anything like this. There's always hope."

'Hope I can find a better vet,' I thought as I reloaded my brain for helpful names of vets.

"I have some diazepam and phenobarbital tablets which could help. Doris has some pheno tabs for you at the front desk. Call me if it gets worse. Sorry I don't have better news," and he retreated behind his desk as Macduff gave a low growl.

I really hated Dr. V, not just for his negative diagnosis, which may have been entirely accurate, but for also for relying on an outside person who had never even checked Macduff. It would be like having your podiatrist tell a patient, "Sorry, but I think you may have lung cancer." Dr. V's bedside manner rated right down there with Biff the car tire guy, "Sorry, but I think you need a new engine."

We stopped at a Mac's on the way home and got two soft-serve cones and a dish. Just like Macbeth, Macduff finished his fast and emerged with a white snout. He deserved it; Becky and I did not.

Time passed in school-calendar stages – football, Thanksgiving, Christmas break, basketball (now both boys and girls), the long unbroken stretch through winter to spring break, spring sports (baseball, softball, track), the endless month of May, graduation, summer. Macduff had a few seizures, about one a month, and they were horrifying to watch. I always called Dr. V to tell him what had happened, hoping that he had found some new relief, but his only advice was to increase the dosage of his meds.

"We'll try a cocktail," he said. "Add some diazepam to his phenobarbital after each seizure, and we'll keep track to see if the seizures lessen." Not promising anything, but at least doing something. Of course, I couldn't help but wonder if he was giving the wrong treatment. I also wondered about the other border collies that farmer Cole had sold. Same seizures and prognoses? I thought about calling him to ask if he was running a puppy mill, but all he'd have to do is to deny it, and claim that he never could find the official breeding papers. 'The dog's or yours?' I thought. Farmer Cole might be the offspring of first cousins, married or not.

Come December the three of us went to cut our own Christmas tree. Macduff sat in the back and really seemed to enjoy the new rural scenery. We pulled into Barnes's tree farm, and let the dog run loose. Becky and I walked the long rows while Macduff stayed nearby, never straying out of sight or voice range. We cut down a seven-foot pine and dragged it over to our car, the border collie romping in the snow. He loved that outing.

After tying the tree to the rooftop, we began our journey home. Trusting the dog to deter any tree thieves, Beck and I decided to stop for a beer at a hidden rural gem, Rookies' sports bar, that only locals frequented. The neon Pabst Blue Ribbon window sign beckoned, so we left MacDuff in the car while we indulged in a beer and a shot of something called "Cherry Pie." It was good and apparently popular with the other faithful patrons watching the Badger basketball game.

Feeling refreshed without the buzz, we left the bar about four o'clock before darkness fell. At first, we could not see our dog in his usual watching spot behind the wheel. Panic-stricken, we ran to the rear windows and saw Macduff thrashing uncontrollably. He had thrown-up and relieved himself of all his bodily functions, creating a mural from hell. I threw open the door, called his name and risked being bitten as I grasped his head and tried to console his wracked body. A minute later he was almost sleeping, still panting in a semi-hysteric fashion. Becky brought a blanket from the trunk, and I wrapped-up the dog that seemed almost lifeless.

We got home and carried his body inside. Any neighbors watching would have thought I was carrying a dead dog, his head just hanging. It had been a long seizure, and Macduff looked like he had just lost a fight to fifteen, vicious pit bulls. We placed him on the couch. Becky washed the dog and I took care of the car.

"What are we going to do, Lar?" Becky asked in a whisper, as though wanting to "let sleeping dogs lie."

"I don't know. I suppose we'll have to call the vet on Monday morning. Dog looks like hell. Hope he's not suffering, and we both got misty-eyed as we held each other over the helpless border collie.

Macduff seemed better on Sunday, though still lethargic, as though asking, "What just happened?" Dr. V saw us at one on Monday. The doctor had now opened two other vet clinics in town during the past years. Someone seemed to be doing well, just not us.

After his thirty second check-up, he looked at us and asked suspiciously, "Did you say that you had him running through a Christmas tree field right before he had his seizure?"

"Yeah. Why?" I still did not trust him as a pet owner should trust his vet, but Becky and I had agreed that we had too much invested in Dr. V to start over with someone new.

"It's possible that he may have an allergy."

Stunned at the possible diagnosis and of the man's sudden turn to a new solution, we gawked like kids being told that there is no Santa Claus. "How can a dog be allergic to trees? There wouldn't be any place for a dog to go."

"Not all trees," came the smug reply. "Perhaps to balsams or spruce. If there was a field of trees, it would be hard to detect."

Voice of reason. "So what do we do now?" Becky answered with the same disbelief.

It didn't take the doctor long with his shot-in-the-dark answer. "We could run a complete battery of allergy tests to find if anything could be triggering the seizures. A complete scan might be a little costly, but he's your dog."

Guilt trip. Every time we saw this guy, I disliked him a little more, but we really had invested so much, unknowingly contributing to his new vet clinic expansion in the city.

"Ball park figure?" I asked boldly to show that I would not be intimidated.

"Somewhere around a thousand, I would guestimate."

'Hit me in the head with a frying pan,' I thought, a quaint saying taught to me by Iowa Becky.

"Wow, that's a lot," replied the dumbfounded real Iowa Becky.

"May seem like a lot, but, like I said, 'it's your dog.'"

I could picture the size of the print in the local headline, "LOCAL VET FOUND SLAUGHTERED IN OFFICE! Suspect pleads 'justifiable homicide.'"

"We'll get back to you," I said abruptly with as much rudeness as possible. I stormed out of the office, Becky following confused.

Macduff seemed relieved that we got home untouched, as he watched us downing our Whopper sandwiches, holding out for that last bite, and listening as we discussed his future.

"We've got the money, Beck, if we raid all of our rainy-day fund. What do you think?"

"I think if we don't do anything and these seizures turn fatal, we'd regret it the rest of our lives."

"That's true, but I just don't like this vet. I wonder if we could find a second opinion. This guy had to ask a friend, who never saw the dog, for a prognosis. Now he comes up with tree allergies. Did a friend suggest that, too?"

"But we'd have to start all over again. Besides, Dr. V hasn't really misled us. Who knows how much worse Macduff would have been without his treatment so far?"

She was right, of course. Isn't that what a rainy-day fund is all about? If there was a chance. . .

"Okay, we'll make the appointment on Monday. As if on cue to help our decision, Macduff followed us around all day on Sunday.

It would be another five weeks before we could get an appointment at the UW Vet hospital for the dog's allergy tests. I thought Dr. V had an inside man, but maybe only if it was for his benefit.

During the five-week wait, Macduff had two more seizures, and Dr. V suggested that I double his phenobarbital dosage. On test day we dropped off Macduff and were told to return in four hours. Of course, we did, but the results would not be completed for at least another week. Ten days later when we finally returned to the vet's office, not the hospital, for the test results and suggested treatment, I meditated for an hour to calm my inbred distrust for this guy.

"Well, we have some good news and some bad news, "he smiled as if setting us up for a joke. If only he knew what I had in mind for a punch line.

"I got the dog's results back, and the good news is that he has no allergy to trees. However, he does seem to have an allergy to two things. Ready for this?" he prompted.

Everything but a drumroll as I imagined a shotgun in my hands.

"It appears that Macduff is allergic to feathers and wool." Big sardonic smile.

Unbelievable! "You mean I have a border collie, a Scottish sheep dog, who is allergic to wool? I flashed back to farmer Cole's woolen blankets for the puppies; they had all seemed uncomfortable."

"That's right. I know it seems impossible, but the tests don't lie. I even had Steven double check the results."

Steven? Is he the inside man?

"Who's Steven?" asked Becky with venom and curiosity.

"Oh, I'm sorry. I thought you knew. He's my friend who works at the hospital and gave us the initial diagnosis of epilepsy. He's also my business partner. He's very good."

An inside man – as a hospital vet and a business manager. In a sense he had controlled much of the clinic's incoming money. Never able to completely verify my malfeasance, at that moment I decided the road to take for all of us. "Come on, Beck. Let's get out of here and go find a real vet. This city and its number of veterinarians is second only to its number of lawyers. Send me my bill Dr. Quack. We won't pay a single cent until I have all records – complete medical and itemized bills. Not a single cent!"

We rushed out of the office ignoring our awaiting bill at the desk.

"Mr. Ehrhorn, your bill, please," yelled Doris the witch.

"Dr. V knows what to do with it," and we were gone, allowing Macduff one last chance to lift his leg and water the clinic garden.

A couple of Becky's teaching colleagues highly recommended a Dr. Erickson on the east side, so the next week we decided to drive the extra cross-town traffic to avoid the Dr. V aura.

Dr. Erickson listened attentively, not guessing at any diagnosis or cures, before he said that there was very little research on epilepsy in dogs, but it sounded like all the right symptoms for treatment given to people. Ironically, we felt better about the confirmation of Dr. V's guestimate. We decided to adhere to the current treatment, but giving pills only after a seizure instead of daily.

So passed the next four years; it was the best of times, it was the worst of times (English teacher metaphor). During our best times Macduff seemed to love life and the three of us shared much joy. Of course, Becky and I were rather apprehensive about any sudden quirk the dog made. We never knew if Macduff only experienced the minutes leading up to a seizure, or if it, too, was always present in his mind. Border collies were supposed to be the smartest breed of dog, but were those smarts for aptitude in training or for complete brain storage, never forgetting anything?

One hot July day we decided to go forty miles to a town called Platteville, known for its state college, engineering school, Chicago Bears training camp, and annual dog trials. I had heard about dog trials from the agriculture teacher, Gene Carter. At first, I thought he was teasing, so I asked him what the judges did if they found a dog guilty.

Gene suddenly got very serious, "I guess they shoot it."

I didn't know how to reply, but he took me off the hook. "You don't know what a dog trial is, even though you own a fake border collie, do you Lar?"

So, I patiently listened for the next half hour and learned that a trial was really an international skills contest for border collies, the summer Olympics of canines. "Not a dog show," he emphasized because, "You could have a dog so ugly that it would scare your mother-in-law." Inside farmer joke, I assumed. As Becky and I drove down the Lafayette County roads to Platteville, I tried to explain what Gene had told me.

In a large field, perhaps the size of two football fields, a handler signals his dog by voice and hand gestures only to "fetch" a specific number of sheep from a small herd at one end of the field and to drive them the entire length of the field and into an open pen. Why anyone would do this will always remain a mystery to me, but it is a serious international event, and Platteville held one every year.

"Why is it called a trial?" asked Becky while Macduff seemed all attentive with his radar ears rotating as needed.

"Because if they find the dog guilty, I guess they shoot it," I replied smugly.

"What?"

"Just kidding. I have no idea. Probably a real trial for the dog."

Much to my surprise, the closest parking we could find was about a half mile from the fairgrounds. Action was in full swing as Macduff pulled hard on his harness, wanting to be part of the action. I started to realize that we were somewhat cruel in bringing a leashed border collie to a trial. Like bring a five-year-old to Disneyland to watch all the other kids ride and play.

We stayed about an hour, trying to pacify Macduff with treats and water. It was an eighty- degree day and all the canine participants ran to a waiting steel trough of water where they could immerse themselves for a few minutes. Poor Macduff looked at us with the deep brown pleading eyes, wanting to know if he could at least jump into the tub. Each trial took between five and ten minutes, and although we weren't sure of all that was happening, we had to admire the skill and fortitude of all the participants, including the human handlers. I sensed that the heat, jealousy, and non-participation were all frustrating Macduff. It was our only dog trial together, but I had to think that he had fun, too. Maybe not.

Macduff supplied the worst of times, too. It seemed that his seizures were occurring every couple of weeks. I was tempted to go back to his daily pheno dosage, but Dr. Erickson, our latest highly recommended veterinarian, warned that the meds the dog was currently taking were very hard on his stomach and other organs.

Macduff's energy seemed to be waning. The only spark of eagerness occurred on Sundays, when Becky and I had a traditional steak on the grill. Part of the meat went to the dog. One Sunday he didn't wait for us to cut it on the plate before putting it on the floor. Unexpectedly he leaped to the edge of the table and grabbed the entire plate, steak, and all. We got it back, no major argument about it. "You're the worst dog I've ever had," I gently told him.

It was a Wednesday evening when he had the seizure to end all seizures. His thrashing and convulsions would not seem to end.

When they finally halted, we put him on the couch to sleep, while I slept nearby on a recliner. About two in the morning, Becky joined us and slept on the floor by the dog, who did not move.

"Couldn't sleep," she explained without need. I smiled and started to weep as I joined my wife on the makeshift bed.

Macduff was still breathing but exhausted the next morning. I carried him outside, while Becky arranged for a substitute teacher so that she could take the dog to the vet. I had parent-teacher conferences and risked penalty of death for not being there.

"I'll see if I can get a sub; I should be there to handle this, too."

She grasped my arm. "Why, Lar? He's my dog too. We'll see you tonight."

I hugged her as my eyes teared up again. I had a feeling that this was my last look at Macduff, just like the last time I saw Macbeth.

"Call me," I said halfway through the door. Not sure why I said that, but it seemed right.

The morning dragged. I hardly heard any of the conversations with the parents, but "the show must go on." Some parents could tell that I was preoccupied but there were good people and let me be.

About noon Joyce the secretary came over the public address system in my room, "Mr. Ehrhorn, could you come to the office for a phone call, please? Miss Hess will keep an eye on your room, too."

Like a prisoner going to execution, I trudged to the office, where thy instructed me to use the private phone in the principal's office. Shaking, I picked-up the receiver.

"Hello."

A tearful voice responded, "Macduff died, Lar."

Macduff in basement prison

Macduff guarding table

Chapter 6
My Side of Epilepsy

"If there are no dogs in Heaven, then when I die, I want to go where
they went."
Will Rogers, American humorist

*I do not remember much about being a puppy. Just some other fur
balls and the big dog we referred to as Mom, though the humans
called her Julie. Mom nursed me and bathed me and pretty much
taught me where to go and when. I really don't remember much
about puppyhood, except that the other pups seemed to learn things
faster, important things like being first to nurse and escaping
through a reappearing hole in the box that we called "home."*

*The blanket the people put in our box was warm and fuzzy, but it
sure made me itch. When my littermates tried to chew off one corner
of the box, I was getting pretty intense scratching my neck. One day a
pup freed himself through the hole they had all created in the box. It
didn't take long before my siblings were right behind him. Naturally I
was last, but it felt so good to run free and see a new world. My
previous world had consisted of high brown cardboard walls, over
which none of us could see until the man occasionally picked up one
of us for a short time. It was a boring life and sometimes the man
would gruffly put one of us back as if he was mad at the pup. Too often*

a sibling never did return, and we all wondered why and where it had gone.

Most all days were the same: sleep, scratch, stretch and twitch. I seemed to be the only one who would need and could sustain a lengthy scratch. While I was scratching, my puppy mates worked on chewing another hole after the man had covered the first one with some grey tape. We got some time in the barn to relieve ourselves, but it was dark and the fresh air outside beckoned us. Our blanket was rarely changed. Mostly we just laid there and absorbed as much as our developing brains could hold, so we were innately semi-educated on life's basics – colors, numbers, emotions, hunger, etc.

One day was a little different for a short time. A different man looked into the box and picked up a puppy. They were gone for a brief time, followed by a short yelp, and the pup was returned, favoring his left rear leg. One by one we all went and returned. I was the last one chosen, and soon found myself flying high above the ground. If I hadn't been so scared, it would have been fun. I lost sight of my home and landed on a litle table where a sharp needle and other stuff were waiting. Before I knew it, I was being firmly held wih one hand, felt a cool liquid rubbed on my leg, and yelped as a sharp needle jabbed me for about two seconds. It was fast but very unpleasant. Then I flew, via hand, back to my box of awaiting family. We each received some kind of treat, bones from other animals. They didn't have much taste, but they were something different to occupy our tedious days.

It took many days before there were only three of us left, four having vanished with other strange people. Of course, I always had this desire to run and run and run; I was lying there one day lost in a wonderful dream when I was interrupted by a hand from above, raising me, and soon I was looking into another man's eyes as though he couldn't see me close enough. Sensing freedom, my litle legs started to run, but I got nowhere. Soon a woman, not the usual one, had hold of me in the same manner. Whoops! I had forgotten to pee when I had the chance that morning, so without warning I let go all over her pink shirt. Suddenly, the first man grabbed me from her and placed me on the ground, not angrily.

I wasn't sure why he put me there, because I had just peed, but I sure was overjoyed to get a little extra time of freedom. Who were these people? I started to race towards the open barn door and towards some patch of grass and what appeared to be doggy paradise. Didn't get far before I felt myself flying again. This time I wasn't afraid. The new man put me at his eye level again and started to talk, but he never shouted the only word I usually heard," No!" He didn't seeem upset like the man who had helped raise us, and he didn't smack my bottom and throw me back in the box either. The new woman also came over and smiled as she talked to the him. She, too, showed no anger, even though I had peed on her pink shirt. Already today was the best day of my life.

Both talked to the man who always made me cower, and I hoped that I would never see him again. The new people took me to their car and we all got in. Were they taking me with them? Was I going to start a new part of my life? Could my other two siblings come with me? What would happen to them? I wanted to ask if all of us could go, but I did not know how. I had never felt guilt before this time and our canine family never met each other again. Still, I felt so excited that I jumped on the woman and instinctively began to show my joy by licking her face all over, which she quickly stopped and gave me to the man, who I assumed wanted the same treatment.

They put me alone in the back seat and I wanted to jump in front to be with them, but I was too unsure of what to do. After all, they took me away from that dreadful farm and gave me all the space in the back. I explored my new surroundings, which were far bigger and better than my old box. They had put a bowl of water on the back area. I could't believe it – no sharing, no slobbering. Just cool fresh water. I had almost finished the whole bowl when the man took away the bowl, but I had had all I could wish for and smiled.

Soon we left my birthplace, which I would never miss or see again, except for my family. I snifffed around the back seat until I stumbled across a small box which emitted a wonderful, smell. I had never smelled anything so pleasant on the farm. Suddenly my mind felt busy and unbalanced and helpless. I fell onto my side, still twitching. I was a puppy; how bad could this excitement be? Today was busy but adventurous.

Time passed quickly, and before I knew it, I was being lifted and carried to a large grassy area, which they called a yard. Best of all I was free to run as far and as fast as I wanted. Circle after circle I raced, until I finally quit from exhaustion. Little did I know that it was actually my first of many days with my saviors.

Finally the man opened the back door and I heard him yell, I think, for me to come in the house, where a fresh bowl of cold water awaited me. After having my fill again, I began to explore the other spacious rooms. The odors were all new and beckoning. I found a table with wooden legs and I was grateful for the chance and place to pee, so I smiled at them in gratitude and let loose on the leg.

As though rewarding me, the man lifted me and immediately returned me to the yard where I had first run in circles. Even though I was exhausted, I repeated the performance that they seemed to have enjoyed. Soon I felt myself floating back to the room where I had peed, hoping they weren't expecting a repeat performance there, too. My little tank was empty.

They sat and gestured for me to join them. Afraid I might earn a beating for being someplace I shouldn't, I just looked up at them until I was lifted to their level, and the man lifted me high over his head so that I could see everything in the room. I sensed that these people were nice but just a bit odd.

I learned quickly that they wanted me to pee outside, which I faithfully did, except for the few times when I seemed to lose myself and fell to my side and began jerking and drooling. It didn't hurt much, but it was scary, and I could usually sense when the fit was about to occur. It was when I really wanted to be close to my humans, but they were often gone and usually misunderstood me and set me in the yard, where I had to experience my commanding spasms alone and feel frightened without anyone to help.

But life was good, also. I learned that they had people names – Larry and Becky. They also gave me an odd name – Macduff. I had never heard of any people with my name, but I quickly learned to respond to it.

One afternoon after time spent trying to herd some black bugs into one spot while my people watched and laughed to no end, our family seemed to change. They left me alone for the day, and I could not get out to my yard. I tried not to pee in the house, but there was only so much a pup could do.

The first day was the worst. Being used to having complete outdoor freedom, I sensed a similar prison-like atmosphere like my old farm home box, only this was bigger. Mostly helpless to get outside, boredom forced me to entertain myself. Luckily, they had left some footwear at my disposal. Some of them tasted awful, and some tasted like special treats. They were tough, but I had no place to go, so I chewed them for a long time until I was able to get them into smaller pieces. Also, there were odd pieces of clothing scattered about the floor of their bed, and they were scented, soft, tasteless and too easy to rip apart. I spend the whole day entertaining myself; it had been a decent first solo day.

My fun day ended when I heard the front door open. They were both there with astonished faces. Voices roared, and I instinctively cowered and ran to the back door, which they opened for my quick escape. The words "bad dog" kept filling my head, a bad memory from days on the farm. I didn't know what I had done, but I felt frightened. Why? Instinct?

They seemed to have forgotten me, as I felt shame and panic alone in the back yard. Finally I barked to tell them I was there. Soon Larry opened the door and I raced to my water bowl, then up on the couch.

My people talked for a while, often glancing at me, then brought what I thought was a new dog bed; it was beautiful and plush and comfortable. I had never had one, only an old blanket. They put it in the kitchen, which confused me, and I didn't know how to react. Who punishes a dog by getting him a new bed, then putting it in the kitchen?

Becky put me outside and turned on the back light. I was afraid that they were still angry at me and would leave me outside all night. Without my brothers and sisters, I was afraid of being alone; I never had been. Shortly, Larry picked me up, turned off the light, and put me in the new bed. Grateful to be warm and safe, I tried to sleep, but I kept experiencing involuntary twitches, which no one else could see. I must have fallen asleep and out of my new bed, because it was day when I finally moved.

Soon Larry called me to go out into the yard to do my morning business, while they scurried about the house. I hoped that they weren't going to leave me alone again. Unfortunately, I was wrong and sadly watched them leave. This time they left my toys accompanied by my new bed and water bowl in the kitchen. Only now there was a wall where the doorway to the front room had been. I couldn't get out at first, but when I jumped to see over the new wall (I was a great jumper!), I could see two of their small tables holding up the piece of thin wood across the doorway. Naturally, I took a running jump to try to clear the height, but I fell far short. I hit the wall with good force but fell back onto the floor.

I had succeeded in moving the wall a little. Not seriously hurt, I thought I'd try it again. After all, I had all day. So I tried it again and again and again. The last jump pushed the wall over and into the front room. I was free and soon enjoying the liberty of the house. But I thought of how I had changed their mood with yesterday's playful destruction and restrained my impulses. It was quite dull not chewing on shoes and other pieces of clothing. But I was going to be a good dog, so all I could do was sit on the couch and peer over the back out the window.

For a few minutes I threatened a man in a blue uniform who carried a big bag, which I bet would have been fun to chew. He came to our door, and I was pleased that my threats were enough to frighten him away. The same thing happened for several days, but he must not have been too smart, because he kept coming back for more scolding. At least Becky and Larry would be pleased that I was guarding the house.

Many hours later when the door opened, I whimpered for joy as I jumped on Larry in welcome. He ruffled my neck and immediately pulled out that wood/wall that he had installed. He opened the back door for me to escape my prison and I ran circles and the fresh air felt so good.

Soon I heard Becky come home and felt the need to jump on her, too. I stood by the door and listened to them talking, somewhat tensely, but probably happy that I hadn't chewed anything else.

Again, after a congenial night, all seemed back to normal. However, my people had spent a long time downstairs, looking up at me, as though planning something sinister. Also, they had arranged all my toys, water bowl and kibble neatly in a row. I wasn't really concerned until the next morning.

After a lengthy time outside, Larry lifted me and carried me downstairs, where my upstairs belongings awaited me. He put me in my dog bed, pet my head, and told me to be a good dog. Then he left, tightly shutting the bar door behind him. Oh, no. I was beng punished for some reason. I could hear them leave and tried to figure a way out of solitary. My only life-like companion was some awful music coming from the radio, some song about getting physical, and I couldn't stop it. So I lie there, head over the edge of the bed and contemplated. They had left me nothing that wasn't already mine, so maybe it was something upstairs that I should not have touched.

Slinking out of my bed, I went to the door to see if it was slightly ajar. Nope. When that click had sounded, my fate had been sealed until they released me. I started to claw at the hollow door, but I created no sign of an escape route. So, I scratched harder and faster until the door showed deep nail marks, but the door would not open or even show any signs of opening. I wished I had paid more attention to my litter mates who had managed to create a breach in our old box. But I persisted, for how long I do not know. In fact, I lost track of all time and grew so weak that I fell on my side and convulsed, slamming my head on the legs of an old sofa that they had put there for me. I tried to wave my legs back and forth, like I had seen some dogs do in deep water, but it was futile. Chewing my tongue seemed to be a new reaction, and I began to drool on the floor.

When I finally calmed enough that I almost felt normal, I looked around my enclosure, unsure of where I was. No damage was evident, except where I had unknowingly gone to the bathroom in several spots. The smell and the waste was reminiscent of my early days on the farm. Still, there nothing to do but wait until my people came home to take care of me if . . .

Eventually, Larry did release me and before he picked me up, I shot up the stairs and waited for the back door to open or I'd scratch the daylights out of this one, too. No need; Becky was there to open the door and I felt some new strength surge back into me as I ran "crazy dog" circles.

That night was rather quiet. They did not seem to blame me for anything but were not their usual familiar, entertaining selves. I don't know if I had caused their moodiness or if it was something else, but they kept looking at me lying on the floor, wondering if I was okay. Occasionally, I responded with a tail wag, which seemed to help with smiles and neck massages.

And we repeated this routine for days on end, except weekends when life went back to normal. Normal, except for this cold, icy water that fell from the sky; they called it "snow." I had to wait patiently every day for them to allow me outside so that I could play in this snow by running and leaping. They frequently referred to me as

"Snowdog." I didn't think that was a breed, but I didn't care. Best of all was that some days so much snow fell, that Larry and Becky stayed home with me all day, and I did not have to miss any outside adventures. They even joined me in playing, Becky often hitting Larry with a ball of snow, then Larry doing the same. Of course, I was not skipped, but I was way too fast to hit. I could even catch some of their snowballs. Impressive.

Sometimes they would lie in the snow and move their arms and legs, after which I would pee or poop in their newly cleared areas. I appreciated that, because although I was getting bigger, it was still very challenging to squat in the shallow snow spots.

These days passed quicky, and the snow never left. I worried if I would every get my yard back, because I was getting tired of the snow. I think Becky and Larry really enjoyed the warmer weather, grass and leash walks at night, but it looked like those days were gone for now, but for how long?

There was a time during the heart of snow season when my people were home for many days in a row. This joy crashed one day when, for some inexplicable reason, when I was exploring the snow, my head started to hurt and the pain was the worst I'd ever felt. I had felt this before when I was locked in the basement, but they had never seen me suffer this. I fell onto my back and my legs began pumping again so hard that my back left the ground and I slammed back into the deep snow. Because I was bigger, the snow began to cave in from the sides, and I seemed helpless to myself. No idea how long that lasted, but my legs finally stopped their thrashing, and I slowly rolled to my side and tried to get up, stumbling several times.

For some reason Larry and Becky were laughing, as though they had just watched something funny. My front legs gave way, and I hobbled my way into the snow, heading towards the back door. Their laughter had stopped as suddenly as it had started, and Larry kept asking if I was okay. Staggering inside I went to my bed and collapsed, exhausted but relieved to be someplace safe.

Other than my complete fatigue, Becky and Larry did sense something different about me, but I doubt that owners ever feel their dogs' headaches, unexplainable actions, or confusion. Maybe some mood changes from new diets or periods of loneliness, but what if I really had something wrong with me that could not be detected by humans, no matter how good people were and meant to be.

Days later I was almost feeling normal again. However, I could feel my head becoming buzzy right before I developed another headache. I grew anxious, so I started to clumsily stagger in the front room. Becky knelt and stroked my back, and I instinctively felt like I was in a safe place, so I leapt onto her chair and pushed my head under her arm, trying to hide from the invisible fear that I felt was coming for me.

Larry said something to me just before I snapped. I jumped to the floor and immediately twisted and cried, even lashing out at Larry's approaching hands. It wasn't voluntary, just uncontrollable, and I was not in terrified. I also bit Becky, who was frightened, but did not seem angry at me. At the time I did not even try to understand what was happening. I could only recall that sense of terror that had been following me for so long.

Normalcy gradually returned, but not before I had convulsed once more and slammed my head hard into the table. I was aware that It hurt though, and soon Larry and Becky were speaking softly to me and petting my rear quarters. I just lie panting and drooling, closing my eyes, and hoping for a little sleep. I saw them moving as they cleaned my mess, which I had not even realized that I had caused. Eventually I struggled to my feet and looked at them through glassy eyes, caused by tears of disappointment and/ or my seizure. That night Larry slept on the couch and Becky lie on the floor with a big, warm quilt, a perfect place for a frightened dog.

Five days passed without incident. My people seemed to be mysteriously talking to other people, as though they did not want me to hear. They seemed content; I think it may have had something to do wih me. Finally, we went to another place where I could sense the presence of other dogs, even cats. It was called a vet's office.

A man in a white coat led us to a small room, where he put me on a shiny, cool table. Larry helped me stand, not that I needed any help at the moment, while the man in the coat prodded, shined light in my eyes and ears, and even stuck a finger where I did not like it. If Larry hadn't been holding me, I think I would have bit that man.

They released me and I eagerly headed for the door, but Becky had put a chain around my neck that choked and stopped me from leaving too fast. After more extensive talking, we left the building, and I could sense some anxiety in the three dogs waiting in the lobby. As we left, I felt this horrendous need to pee on some pretty flowers outside the door, but Becky pulled me away to some plain, old grass. I felt great relief, but I'm sure those flowers would have made me feel even better.

Several days later we returned to the office, where a big dog and one my size were keeping the anxiety level high. Surprisingly, the man in the white coat did not crudely handle me, probably because I was ready to retaliate. Instead he talked extensively to my people and we left. Other than their increased tension, it was a simple appointment.

When we got home, they began to feed me little pieces of something. One at a time, they put them on the back of my tongue, then slammed my mouth shut, holding my snout closed until I swallowed. I had no choice, and it was a bitter pill to swallow. This process continued for several days. They called me to the kitchen as they often did to give me a treat, but instead substituted a pill. I fell for this lure a few times, but within a couple of days they were ganging up on me and one forced me to take a pill while the other held me tight. Not fair.

I never knew the purpose of the pills, but they tasted awful! One time when Becky was talking to Larry, she tried to put the pill on my tongue, but missed and I felt it in the back of my mouth, but not on my tongue. I worked the pill over to my jowls, where it remained hidden until I could spit it out in the back yard. I was able to repeat this trick about every third day. I actually felt more tired than I had during my seizures, except for the days when I was able to avoid swallowing any pills. I thought I was rather clever and wondered if all breeds were.

One day during their winter break from work, the snow filled the ground, and we decided to take a family outing. We did not go far before we came to a place with rows and rows of trees. I thought how wonderful it would be to lift my leg on all of them. Surprise – Becky released me to run up and down the endless rows of trees, as long as I came back when they called. For this much freedom in such a wonderful place, it was easy to obey and stay close. We even cut down a tree and tied it to the top of our car. I found this to be an unusual custom, but then I had heard them mention the magic of Christmas. Sadly, our day of adventures did not end well. We stopped the car and Becky and Larry went inside a small building called The Pabst Blue Ribbon. I could see the front door, but I had to wait alone inside the car. It seemed like they were there for a long time, and I worried that they had forgotten me, or worse, that they had left me for good. This time the spell took me quickly, and I was tossed into the back seat, smashing my head on the door handle. I don't know how long it lasted, but I was ready to die.

Next thing I can remember was that Larry had wrapped me in a blanket, and Becky held me tightly until we were finally home. She took me in the house and bathed me in a nice, warm bathtub. Unusual, but I felt safe again.

Although I did not have to return to the vet's office, Larry and Becky made some phone calls, and they began to give me more pills, some in different colors. Unfortunately, matters grew worse as I saw the world through a hazy cloud.

Life continued with more fatigue but a little less trauma. One day for a brief time, I felt like a new dog and grabbed a whole steak on a plate from Becky's side of the table. Unfortunately, they quickly caught me, but still shared some with me.

The last happy day of my life was a real paradox. We all went to a big field full of border collies, running and herding sheep. I wondered if any of them were my brother or sister. I thought I was going to gag because I pulled so hard on the choker chain leash in an attempt to play with my kindred, but the leash only went so far, and neither Larry or Becky were about to completely release me. Why did they even bring me? The time seemed interminable as I got excited every time Becky or Larry moved, wondering if they were going to take off the chain. Try as I might, I lay fairly still and hoped for a miracle. An unusual and rare whimper emerged from my throat and my eyes grew wet. Let me go, I pleaded with my mournful eyes. Finally Larry must have sensed how awful this must have been for me. I wholly agreed that this could have been fun if. . . I don't even think that they enjoyed the outing, but I could do nothing.

My strength and desire slowly ebbed and I had no desire to do anything except sleep and sleep some more. Not even the loving, coaxing, and attention from my owners helped inspire enthusiasm in a seemingly lifeless dog. One night I had a tremendous seizure that I thought might end me. Becky and Larry were up all night trying to give me water and food, even ice cream, but I craved nothing except peaceful sleep. It was my last seizure at home.

The next morning Larry left for work. He got on the floor and scratched my neck. He was crying, which started me crying. I deeply sensed that for some reason we would never see each other again."Enjoy Rainbow Bridge, buddy. Say 'hello' to Macbeth. He'll take care of you." Then he broke out into a heart-wrenching cry and bolted to the door as though trying to escape death.

Becky was also crying and brought me out to the back yard, where memories of good times relived themselves in my mind. I was grateful for their care of me and the fun we had experienced. Soon, Becky lifted me and carried my dead weight to the car. I could feel her tears fall on my fur. She carefully placed me on the front seat next to her, not my usual place in the back. For my last ride, I was in Larry's seat.

We pulled up to the vet's office, and several people were apparently waiting for our arrival. They immediately led us into a room in the back and placed me on a warm blanket on a table.

Becky stood, scratching my neck and tears continued to run down our faces. Everyone spoke soothingly. Suddenly I felt a little prick, which almost immediately made me want to close my eyes. Their voices faded. Then a second deeper pain struck my back left leg and the voices slowly vanished and I had no more pain. Only a single dog voice from across a beautiful, overhead, bridge.

"Macduff, cross the bridge and I'll take care of you now."

Dicken's First Day Home

Dickens Ready to Show

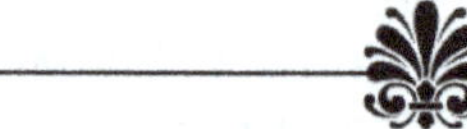

Chapter 7
The White Ribbon Winner

"When a dog looks at you, he is not judging you"
Lindsey Bijas, Environmentalist

Eleven months passed before I was forced to fill the void that was present when I returned to an empty home from school and tried to adjust to the absence of my border collie greeting me. That fateful morning, I had left my dog, knowing that it would probably be our last contact. I can't image what Macduff had felt – did he know that we were finished forever? Did he know why? I had tried not to cry in front of him, but I had to cut our departure short before I had accepted his fate and my selfishness in trying to save his obvious painful and unhappy end of life again. I just wanted him to know that no matter how contrary it appeared, I was doing what I honestly felt was best for him. Good old dog.

Thank God for Becky, who had the fortitude required to do what had to be done. Did Macduff know why she had taken him to the vet for a final rest or for more useless agonizing treatment? Who knows what a dog thinks when human sorrow is present; instinctively, he seems to share our sadness without knowing the cause; it just wasn't right. His eyes probably revealed the uninterpretable thought, but who can read that deeply?

Becky had risen from the couch and ran to me as soon as I had walked in. We held each other while our tears flowed. When we finally separated, we went to the kitchen and I drank three fingers of Jim Beam over ice for each of us and we toasted the memory of Macduff – the worst dog ever.

Pain and sadness lessened slowly with the habitual glance at his varying sleeping spots -- his tartan-patterned bed, our bed, the porch, and freshly mowed yard on a summer day or how hard we played sled dog during the winter. Particularly noticeable were the missing water and food bowls. All of his history, including toys, I stored in a black tote; I don't know why I kept it all; I would never give it to another dog. It just seemed respectful.

Christmas marked a turning point in our path. More difficult to have a merry holiday without our beloved border collie, but family and general holiday spirit seemed to work some magic, except for that insistent question from everyone, "When are you going to get another dog?" I don't know why people ask such a personal question.

After the seasonal merriment had passed and less mournful memories had ebbed, we decided to go for broke. One cold and snowy January afternoon as we were absorbed in the encyclopedia-sized Sunday newspaper, I saw a picture of a litter of German shepherds in the classifieds, which triggered a non-expectant blurt.

"Beck, have you seen all these ads for dogs in the paper?"

Smartass never quit. "Seems odd to me; dogs can't read. Who would place advertisements for them?" It's another reason why I loved her.

"You're a riot, Alice." Still, she did not immediately dismiss me, and what was that innocent former farm girl doing with my brain? Pretending not to see where this scenario might lead, I nonchalantly looked out the picture window. "Might be a snow day tomorrow if this keeps up."

"Yeah, maybe," not returning to the dog issue. Restless moments passed in silence. Again, time for the elephant in the room.

"Have you thought about getting another dog?" I asked pointedly, no chance to hide our real thoughts.

"Yeah, maybe a little," she smiled with a glint in her eye, the little shrew.

Window's open. "Any particular kind?" I innocently pursued.

"No, what about you?" Ball in my court.

"Just looking through the paper and they had this neat picture of German shepherds," I volleyed.

"You already mentioned that. I don't think I want something that big. Let's go smaller like our last dogs."

The discussion was open; now I just had to barge through the semi-invisible barrier, careful to watch for her well-placed land mines. She probably already had a white poodle hidden in the basement or knew someone whose dog had just . . .

"When I was a kid, my ma had a basset hound, Miserable Dexter, that she took to downtown Chicago hotels for dog shows. It's one of my fondest memories, except that I was naively proud that Dexter had finished third out of three contestants. Still, it was really cool and a lot of fun."

She paused as that picture developed in her brain.

"Really? You want a show dog?" without too much attack mode, but questioning my sanity.

"Sure, why not? There's another ad in the paper for a fresh litter of cocker spaniel puppies. They're cute, you know, like Snoopy."

Rapid and rabid response to the moron. "Snoopy was a beagle, Lar, not a cocker. And you want to go pro?"

I honestly did not know that he was a beagle, but I couldn't let a little mistake change our discussion now. I was determined. Damn beagle!

"Okay. Either breed would be good for me. Forget the German shepherds." Flashbacks to Mr. Carter, my former principal, asking me if I wanted to coach the high school debate team. Of course, I declined, but I had to confess that I was good at twisting logic enough to get what I wanted or rejected. Or had Iowa Becky outfoxed me again?

Anyway, this discussion was held before the rapid evolution of everyone-at-home-has access to the internet, so although we had a computer because it was the thing to do, we were not fully versed in its use and how simple the task would be to look for pictures of dogs for sale at our leisure. Like so many parents at that time, we were far behind computer knowledge than the kids. Instead, Becky and I would eagerly spend the next four Sundays perusing the <u>Wisconsin State</u>

Journal, spending extra time on the classifieds. Another ad for cocker spaniels demanded our attention.

"Here's another ad for cocker spaniel puppies in Middleton. Three hundred dollars," my eagle-eyed wife announced after a furtive glance; it was the first thing she spotted and readily shared with me.

"Remember, Macbeth only cost ten dollars. My ten-dollar mistake we used to call him. Do we have a budget on this one?" It was a lot of money, but certainly doable. We weren't rich, but we were certainly better off than we had been at any time in our lives. Idea!

"Maybe we could skip all Christmas presents for your family and buy us a dog," I tested. "It could be their gift for us, and they won't even have to shop."

Her wheels turning to develop a smart-ass reply. "Or we could give the dog to each other for Christmas and no other presents."

I wasn't sure if she was kidding or not, one problem with being married to the queen of the absurd.

Time to test the water's depth. "Would you be okay with that?"

"Of course not, but I would be happy with half a dog and a twenty-dollar limit present for you and no limit for me under the tree. And, a two–hundred- dollar prom dress if we have to chaperone this year, but not due until May."

I didn't know how to react, so I did what any truly grateful man would do – I jumped her and covered her with kisses, moving to more advanced foreplay. She didn't object. She meant it. We were getting a dog.

We called and made an appointment to see the puppies for Wednesday after school. The breeder lived in a nice home on Lake Mendota. "Classy puppy," remarked Becky with a sharp elbow to my side. In the kitchen awaited a large basket with four puppies sleeping, at least for now. Their mother watched us like she'd kill us if we took one more step closer.

"Is that lone black dog a male or female?" asked Becky meekly, probably afraid that the mother could understand English and may decide to mutilate her.

"That's the only male left. His two brothers left last night," replied Ken, the owner. From his tone of voice, I wondered if Ken meant that they left in a Rolls Royce or just took a bus.

"May I hold him?"

Ken went straight to the basket and plucked him out of the sleeping pile. No one seemed to mind except the mother, who immediately returned to sleep. After all, she had already lost two of her kids in the last twenty-four hours. Puppies. Becky cradled him and was glad that this dog did not pee on her, instead giving her a sandpaper lick on her cheek. Smart move, little guy.

Four pairs of brown eyes looked beseechingly up at me.

"What do you think, Lar, since we can't take them all home with us?" I couldn't help but remember an old cliché – "there's nothing cuter than a basket of puppies, unless it's Meg Ryan."

"I think he's just fine," I smiled.

Much against our mellow and receptive aura, Ken took back the pup and returned it to the basket, where it proceeded to nudge his way back into the fur pile.

"How would Saturday work for you folks?" he asked as if we should know what was happening. I think right now would have been easier and more fun.

By that time, your check should have cleared and we'll have all his papers ready:

health records, lineage, AKC documents and so forth. Saturday okay?"

Disappointed that the blanket and box we had in the back seat for immediate transport would not be required right now, we just nodded affirmatively, wrote a check, and left the house empty-handed, with our tails between our legs. It wouldn't be the last lesson our show dog would teach us.

We felt that the week's wait was worth the disappointment, after we realized the paperwork involved with a purebred. Of course, the dog was thrilled to be at a new home, but we weren't sure if he was overly fond of us, with a whole new world of grass and the lack of a basket full of furry siblings. His first trip to the backyard, where for the first time in his new life, he was free to run like an escaped convict from Cook County Jail, proved to be anti-climactic. Being so small, he didn't cover the ground of Macbeth or Macduff as fast, but I wondered if we would ever stop comparing our current dog to prior residents. Then I thought that by the time that he acts like our former dogs, he won't be a puppy anymore, so there goes that lovable puppy phase of a dog. He was small enough to almost fit between our pickets, but, hopefully, he would relatively soon grow too big to squeeze through them. Buy a puppy, get a dog.

Of course, because he was a puppy, neither of us could help stop chasing him or picking him up for puppy kisses. Too damn cute. All black with a white chest, brown eyebrows, floppy ears, which soon developed an unpleasant odor, and puppyness.

He was quickly house-trained with the usage of "pee pads," a new staple, like milk and bread. Neither of us had ever heard of such a product—a two-foot square scented cloth pad that lures the dog to pee on it. Prototypes must have been beer scented because that's what happens to me.

We still had that void of a nameless mutt; I mean purebred dog. We had pretty much run out of characters from <u>Macbeth</u>. Who wants a dog named Banquo? Still, clinging to at least a literary name, fate intervened the following Saturday. We were playing tug with this flat, cloth garden hose, so much the craze for gardeners, certain canine breeds or any puppy with needle-sharp teeth. I was pulling this puppy all over the yard, even spinning him in the air, when he went flying as the cloth ripped apart from the nozzle.

"He tore the hose?" Becky laughed in disbelief as she watched him retreat with his spoils. "Remember when Macbeth used to chew-up your underwear? This is similar, and who needs a twenty-five-dollar hose, anyway," I tried to justify. "Boy that dog is full of the dickens." And then it hit me.

"Dickens. That's his name. Dickens."

Becky tried to bring me back to Earth. "Larry, what are you talking about?"

She still couldn't see the hand of destiny.

"I wanted a literary name, and the dog brought one to me. "That's his name – Dickens, as in 'full of the Dickens and Charles Dickens. Get it now?'"

She was staring at me, mesmerized, wondering who this psychopath was that she had married. "I knew that I should have married Graham. Besides owning his own pig farm, he also was of sound mind."

I might have been hurt by that comment under other circumstances, but the thunderbolt of having the dog's ideal name delivered to me was so striking that I could not reply. But the thought that she would have been better off by marrying a pig farmer? That really hurt.

It took a day before Becky realized that I was sincerely committed to literary names, in particular Dickens. Ready to register him with the American Kennel Club with Dicken's lineage records and official affirmation of his pedigree in order to qualify him for dog shows, we started to fill-out the paperwork.

Becky, whose handwriting was neat and legible, did the honors. "They want two names for the dog. Should I put Charles as the first?"

It took a while for that bit of information to be digested. Why two names? Memories of Ma telling us that Dexter had to have two names, thus Miserable. Not wanting or able to fight city hall, I quickly analyzed Becky's obvious choice of a first name. "No, too simple, but what about Chuck?"

"Chuck Dickens? The working man's dog?" Slight sarcasm from Iowa.

"Something like that. We can't be too pretentious."

So, the dog was probably confused as he grew older. Becky always called him "Dickens" while I always used "Chuck," the working man's name.

Chuck Dickens grew-up in a normal Ehrhorn canine household -- big fenced-in yard, daily walks, plenty of treats, comfort, warmth, and safety. Nothing unusual happened until our serene and orderly world was hit by a tsunami. Chuck was going to have a human sibling – a real live human baby due in May. I knew that we should have stopped alcohol consumption at my last birthday, but I was happily resigned.

For the next few months, Becky and I painted the future nursery yellow and added a Disney character wallpaper strip around the middle. We made 2.3 million trips to every store in the city and surrounding counties looking for furniture, supplies, and sanity medicine, often prescribed by our good friend Jack Daniels. We were happy about having our new addition, just overwhelmed. Dickens sensed that something was happening, as he often got left at home alone and did not engage in all the shopping activities, feeling somewhat neglected, I'm sure.

By the time of the actual birth, a new semi-relaxed tension permeated the house. Becky and I did buy a book of baby names (ridiculous purchase) and a book about cocker spaniels, which included interesting chapters of preparing the breed for a show and a chapter on their relations with newborn children. We breezed through them both while our dog slept between us on the bed, lest he miss something.

"Says here that cockers make excellent family dogs," Becky read joyfully.

Time for a little levity, "Forget dogs, but what are we going to name our kid? Banquo? Shylock? And what if it's a girl? Lady Macbeth? Juliet? Seems like all the good names have been taken."

She wouldn't bite. "Growing-up we had a prize pig back in Iowa. How about Chester?"

I could see where she was going with this. For every Shakespearean character I mentioned, she was going to counter with a gross pig, cow, three-eyed cousin, or small-town derelict in order to keep my mind off my humorous suggestions. And I thought naming a dog was rough. After having gone through every other baby book ever written, including a few foreign-language versions, we were "ready" to enter the hospital without a chosen name.

One Saturday night Becky and I took Chuck for our evening walk-and-talk after having devoured a double order of French fries and a Gritty Burger, a local favorite-- beef patty covered with special, mystery "Gritty Sauce," rumored to have been a concoction of thousand island dressing, pickle relish, garlic, onions and the mysterious special ingredient.

Halfway through our stroll, Becky clutched her belly and said, "This may be it, Lar." We tried to hurry home with Chuck pulling us like a sled dog. By the time we got home and she had rested a few minutes, she felt fine. Dickens did not appreciate the shortened but faster exercise, until about an hour later, when Becky suggested trying another round with the dog.

"Are you sure? You didn't make the last one."

"Yes, I'm sure," she snapped. "I think some exercise will help occupy my mind and get the body parts moving. Let's go!"

As I grabbed Dicken's chain, he went crazy with joy, like winning the daily double of two walks in one day. Becky just went out the door without us, as I remembered a piece of advice that Pete, the gym teacher and a father of six conveyed to me, "Don't ever argue with a pregnant woman. She's right." Now I understood.

We barely made the whole circuit and Becky assured me that it was time

"To hospital." (a new verb, but don't argue with a pregnant woman.)

I let-in Dickens, closed the drapes, threw down some dog treats, turned on the tv for some canine company, and grabbed Becky's suitcase. We got to St. Mary's around nine and checked-in. I was still limping from a hamstring injury that I suffered the past week, while playing in a faculty/senior fund-raising basketball game.

"Sir, do you need a wheelchair?" asked a nurse from behind the front desk. Stunned, I had all I could do to not fall. "No, but my pregnant wife here might need one."

After a thousand apologies, they wheeled Becky to the birthing room, me limping behind. I could have used a ride, too, but I had already made two rounds with the dog that evening, and proven myself worthy of martyrdom.

Seven hours later came the expulsion of all the gritty sauce from the hamburger (her fault; she should have known better than to order that cardiac-intimidating burger.) I hoped that our unborn baby could not hear or understand the language that passed from its future mother. Never one to be fond of watching childbirth "educational" films (I had once been forced to watch one on PBS, while my wife sat on my lap and bounced to assure my attention), I elected not to be present for the real big show. Thankfully, her sister had agreed to attend prenatal classes and attend the actual birth for me. Becky was sensitive of what a coward I was around blood and did not object that I did not attend the live birth.

I was the only man occupying the fathers-to-be waiting room, which allowed me to watch the Los Angles Thunderbird roller derby team in action. Unfortunately, with the score tied and an important jam about to commence, I got the call from a nurse standing in the doorway.

"Mr. Ehrhorn, you have a son that's calling for you in the delivery room. Please follow me." It was a command, not a request, and it was time for me to "man-up."

After donning an unusual paper suit, complete with booties, I entered the room. Dr. Kamnetz held something in her arms while Becky lay exhausted in a bed. I cautiously walked over to them and looked at my son. Tears emerged from somewhere, and everyone except the baby was smiling. The doctor took the baby to a butcher's scale and recorded its weight. Nine pounds. Eventually, the time came that we had been planning for months but that we had never finished.

"What should I put down for his name?" asked Dr. Kamnetz sweetly but all business-like.

Larry," replied Becky without hesitation." We're going to name him Larry after his dad."

More tears flowed from that same somewhere as I grasped Becky's hand.

"Larry or Lawrence?" the doctor asked, not wanting to interrupt what appeared to be a "special moment." Hell, I thought we'd name him Walter, after the mailman, an ongoing joke between us.

"Make it Laurence with a 'u.'" Too many with a 'w,' and I didn't want him to go through all the confusion every time I had to use my given name, such as during the military enlistment physical that so many of us with low draft numbers had to experience. "Real name!" some uniformed moron yelled at me. We were already scared; no need to add any more anxiety.

"Larry is my real name!" I snapped back, emulating the "soldier," but he would not concede to his error.

Anyway, Laurence Allan Ehrhorn, brother of Chuck Dickens Ehrhorn, entered our familial world.

People always warn about how much a baby would change one's life. Becky and I were adults; we made a baby so we must have been grown up. Good logic. A major worry was about the effect on the dog. Dickens would no longer be "top dog" in our household. Other people had felt the need to relate disturbing stories about Australia and the dingoes, wild dogs that were accused of stealing babies. And, of course, they were glad that Dickens was not a pit bull terrier, the bane of all households with children.

Becky and I read every possible bit of literature about dogs and babies now that preparation was too late. We even found some of the same articles in both magazines, <u>Dog World</u> and <u>Modern Baby</u>.

Most every source agreed that most dogs were infant friendly, except for dingoes, pit bulls, and black cocker spaniels. On such a cautionary atmosphere, we began the raising of our son. At first the dog seemed friendly, once Dickens had finished his mandatory one thousand sniffs test. Never any aggression, just curiosity, of course. The baby disappointingly was not yet walking by six months, and with luck, he would not start until the age of fifteen.

When we sat on the couch, cradling the baby, the dog would jump up and lie against our legs, which was his usual behavior. Sometimes he would lift his head up for a quick check, sigh, and return to resting position. So tranquility continued for six years before Dicken's first sign of aggressive behavior appeared. Unfortunately, the black cocker spaniel had bitten the neighbor boy

Little Larry had recently started a six-year-old's social life with Robbie, a neighbor's son. They would often play catch football or ride bikes on the sidewalks in front of our houses. I didn't actually see the bite happen, but apparently the ball went over Larry's head and Robbie tried to get to it first, playfully pushing my son out of the way. That's when older dog/brother attacked Robbie, biting at the fallen kid's arm. Fortunately, Becky was in the front yard planting flowers, and was almost as fast as Dickens in getting to the scene of the incident.

She did not see any blood, but thought that Robbie was scared to no end. They had played catch and fetch with the dog many times and they were unprepared for an attack. Becky picked-up Robbie, as I grabbed Dickens, scolded him and threw him in the house.

The Thompsons felt it best that they take Robbie to the nearby emergency clinic to have him checked. Becky went with them. Two endless hours later, Becky walked through the door. I awaited the verdict. Like most dogs, Dickens had no idea that he had done anything wrong. She glared at the dog as she spoke.

"I guess Robbie's okay. No broken skin or bones, just scared. Hope it doesn't carry over to adulthood, but the Thompsons seemed okay with everything; they didn't sound like they were going to sue us. According to the doctor who saw us, this was not a rare occurrence, especially with a black cocker spaniel. However, it takes some kids a while, if ever, before they get over their fear of dogs."

Turns out that Robbie was okay, but Dickens' actions would stay with the boy for a few years. I have not mentioned one seemingly unimportant fact – the Thompson family members, including Robbie, were black. In that progressive decade, race was not supposed to be a factor to normal human beings. Unfortunately, my black dog was not a normal human being and developed a permanent sensitivity to black people. He barked and snarled at every black person he saw, from mailman to pedestrian, no matter age or sex. I hate to admit it, but my future show dog was a full-blown racist! I was almost shocked that my insurance man suggested that I also purchase insurance for pet owners, in case of a future lawsuit.

Gradually, life ran its course, as the son and dog grew older together. Eventually, Robbie and Larry were playmates again. Larry and Dickens were best friends during those formidable years, but Becky and I started to warn visitors not to make eye contact with the dog, because he was nuts and highly unpredictable, so they usually withdrew their hands unscathed. Sometimes people would ask if they could pet my dog, something I usually do out of habit. I think dogs can sense fear in people. I don't think that Dickens bit Robbie because the kid had shown fear, but, instead I believe the dog felt that he was protecting his human. If Robbie had been white, the dog still would have bitten the kid. Unfortunately, it was Robbie's black skin that made an impression in the dog's brain.

I always remember that classic joke: A man and a dog were waiting at a stop light. Another person joined them, smiled, and asked, "Does your dog bite?"

"Nope," replied the man, so the stranger bent down to pat the dog's head.

"Grrrr, snap!" was the dog's response as it struck like a cobra, just missing his target. "I thought you said he didn't bite." The first man looked at the almost victim quizzically and replied, "Ain't my dog," and the light changed.

One lazy summer afternoon, I casually muttered to Becky, "I think we should enter Dickens in a dog show."

The immediate vexing facial reaction was quizzical. "What? You would have thought that I had suggested we have eight more kids.

Pause for calmness. "I think it might be fun to turn Chuck Dickens into a show dog. It's sort of a <u>My Fair Lady</u> thing. He's a purebred, very handsome, but without proper formal training, and I have fond memories from my childhood of attending shows in Chicago."

Don't-even-think-about-it mode. "Lar, you just don't buy a book and change an eight-year-old nut job into a show dog. You wouldn't even know where to start."

"You start at the very beginning," popped in a little voice, from a boy who had recently seen the movie <u>The Sound of Music</u>. (I had considered doing the high school musical at some point in my teaching career, secretly hoping to sneak in a field trip to Austria, after I had listened to the soundtrack too many times.)

"Larry, did you hear what your dad suggested?" replied a stunned mother.

"Yeah, he wants to put Dickens into a show," said the now thirteen-year-old, who was suddenly becoming way too old.

"Did you hear what I said? It's an idiotic idea!"

"Everyone starts somewhere," Confucius said. I wasn't sure if it was Bill Confucius who managed the Pizza Hut or the ancient Chinese philosopher, but I had a feeling that Iowa Becky was not going to attribute that quote to a local.

After a full minute of silence, I thought I'd try a peaceful renewal. "How about if we consider it for a few days, and I'll check the library for how-to books?" the fool of the realm suggested, secretly cowering before his overbearing queen.

Major role-reversal appeared three days later. One afternoon when Becky had gone to complete some errands, Larry, the prodigal son, revealed a whole new world to me – the internet! Of course, I knew about computers and their major effects on the world, but as a humble, small town English teacher, I had no extensive use or interest in this phenomenon. Why would Hester Prynne be on the computer? Why discuss "semicolon vs. period"? That's why we still used textbooks. During one in-service day at school, I had been forced (at gunpoint) to learn word-processing, which in more advanced cultures had taken the place of the typewriter. After years of trial and error, I got to like and to use it as I gained more skills, and it was good!

But enough was enough. There were strong rumors that the following school year, all staff would be required to do attendance and grades on the computer. I felt sure and somewhat hopeful that I would be retired or dead by then.

So, what specific world did Larry open to me? The world of dogs! At the mere click of the correct keys, I could find all the information I needed in life. Farewell to Border's Book Store, Kroch and Brentano's, and the countless used book stores that were multiplying everywhere, places where I could spend endless hours while writing copious notes, or, better yet, I could photocopy pages for only ten cents a page.

With this scientific advancement, the computer, I could stay at home, play with my cocker spaniel, and learn all I needed in order to prepare for a dog show at the Kendall County Fairground in Yorkville, Illinois, which had a competition on a Saturday in four weeks. Also, after the Kendall County fair, on the following Sunday was the DuPage County dog show at my old stomping grounds in Wheaton, Illinois. It was Kismet – two blue ribbons in a single weekend. What were the odds? All information was supplied to my home by computer world. And Becky would never need to learn how much actual time I had spent on my preparations.

We had four weeks until the shows, plenty of time to get Dickens indoctrinated to the canine arena. How hard could it be? Even though the experts supplied me countless useful steps and tips, the computer itself did not actually do the hands-on training. So, after a few weeks of semi-intensive instruction, we were ready to head south to Illinois. A few days of practice runs in the back yard of display for the wife, Becky was impressed, not knowing how often I was actually doing anything constructive. Ole' Chuck and I put on a pretty good show, and I think he may have learned a few major moves. We were smart, good-looking, and performed well as a team.

Becky was pleasantly pleased that I had seemed to be taking serious action to attain my goal, and that I was not treating it frivolously. Of course, son Larry and I had a secret pact: he wouldn't tell mom about my shortcuts and I would reward his silence with a new Nintendo game for the next three months. No qualms about blackmailing his own father. I think he got that from his mother. Expensive but worth it.

So the Ehrhorn family, including the purebred dog, braced ourselves for the challenge. We were able to get a room at the Highway 30 Skyline View Motel, looking out over endless acres of cornfields, and there was always a skyline view somewhere. Highway 30 was a major truck thoroughfare that went straight west to Iowa or south to Missouri; also, the natural landscape created a great auditorium for enjoying the symphony of "jake brakes" twenty-four hours a day. I found the motel courtesy of the internet, of course. Becky was shocked, but somewhat surprised and pleased that I was learning about the cyber world. This was before web sites solicited customer reviews, but it was a family outing, and they took dogs, so we were not going to allow anything to curtail our festive weekend.

One crisp October afternoon, we drove the seventeen miles from our "suite" at the Skyline to Yorkville and the Kendall County Fairgrounds. My memories of the opulent Bismarck hotel, big wide sidewalks, city noises and urban smells were replaced with truck air horns and the constant aroma of animal waste. Sidewalks were replaced with narrow paths between stacks of straw and hay. So much or reliving a fond childhood memory and trying to give my family the same experience. Almost all local lodgings had been filled weeks ago in anticipation of the fair. Live and learn. The fair was typical of small, rural counties -- few rides for kids and a large assortment of various sized tents, smaller ones to be used for the judging of baked goods and 4-H projects, larger ones for housing most farm animals. She didn't say, but I think Iowa Becky was feeling a bit nostalgic. Maybe she was hoping to see her old flame, the one who owned a pig farm.

No idea where to go, I asked a man dressed in a neutral-colored sport coat and a dog-patterned tie, or maybe it was the other way around. Either way, ironically, I thought it was a bit formal for a warmer than usual October day in a farm field, but then, it was my first county fair and dog show visit. He kindly pointed in the direction to the far end of another field covered with Airstream silver mobile homes and colorful pop-up trailers attached to pick-up trucks. The field looked like it was a longer way than I had anticipated, so we packed a constantly tugging Dickens back in the car while an already bored Larry wandered off to see all the city-boy novelties. It was his first fair, too.

We drove down a county road lined with all sorts and sizes of vehicles until we found a small opening for our exotic Chevy Chevelle. I dragged out an eager Chuck, and he immediately started to lead me through a chaotic group of people and dogs gathered in small cliques, exchanging boasts and points of showmanship. Stranger in a strange land and not knowing what to do, we eventually found our own elm tree near the show tent. Becky sat with a still hyper Dickens and started to brush him, pretending that we belonged and knew that it was best to brush your dog hours before a competition.

"I'll go check us in," I said authoritatively but shakily.

The entry table was at the side of the show tent, and I marched to the first table, where I gave my name, the only thing I was sure of. I had already sent all the information and was soon given an arm band with the number "26" and a manila folder of mostly meaningless papers, but I did find schedules. On the way back to our tree of knowledge, I looked closely at the surrounding displays. There were several small tents for washing and grooming, a company called Ring

Craft that sold various educational training cassettes, souvenir trinkets with the dogs' names engraved. From the looks and demeanors of these people, I had a feeling that pets (particularly dogs) comprised a very lucrative business.

By the time I returned, Becky had changed from brush to comb, probably to give the appearance of "not-my-first-rodeo" display. Chuck just tried to escape his stake in the ground. His Cool Whip water bowl looked out of place for a show dog, but he didn't really seem to mind as long as it was wet. So much for a condensed course in effective dog show appearances.

"What's up?" I asked the groomer-in-command.

"Nothing, really. A few people walked by and gave some sympathetic, side-wise glances. I think they're all kind of snobby, Larry," said the Iowa farm girl.

"Beck, think about it – most are all dressed in nice clothes, in the middle of some northern Illinois farmland on a beautiful October day. What does that tell you? This is obviously the highlight of competitive dog season, and this is where they choose to be. We're still learning."

Without hesitation, Iowa Becky snapped, "We're here, you know."

"Yes, but it's our first time, we didn't know any better, we'll never be back, and we don't have to be here now. We can leave at any time, but other than our pride, what's to lose? This is the social event of Kendall County. "

"Losers!" she directed to anyone within earshot and breathing. She was back and nasty, all intimidation gone. "What did you find out?"

I shuffled through the cluster of papers they gave me until I found the schedule. "Tri-color cocker spaniels at 3:00 for judging."

Under a list of contestants was "Chuck Dickens," followed by my name, breeder's name and the names of Chuck's canine parents, including the history of their breeding. Apparently, someone else, probably the people from whom we bought our pedigree, gave out that information, because I had no idea where it came from. I guess that made us official members of Snobarama. They should be judging the dog, not the ancestry, right? I bet old Chuck shows them all up, though I had about a million doubts.

"We still have two hours. What now?" asked a lost-at-sea Becky.

Quick with the quip, "Well, did you bring your cherry pie and apricot preserves, Mom?"

"Smart ass!" and she punched my arm. Hard.

We let Dickens lead us, and we found Larry in the large animal tent, where he was talking to a cute, stereo-typical farm girl minus the blonde pig tails and blue gingham dress. Instead, she was brunette, wearing a DeKalb high school baseball cap and a barn-worn jacket adorned with a Farm and Fleet logo. Every memory of farmer's daughter jokes flew out the window, but that was probably safer. Too young for romance? Junior high school?

God, did the schools even teach about the opposite sex to innocent twelve-year-olds? She had probably seduced him into her stall, where they were petting some big cow. "Holstein" said the entry card on the front of the stall. She looked like such a nice girl that the term "slut" barely crossed my mind.

The feminine side whispered and teased, "It looks like Larry found a girlfriend. Did you have the talk with him yet?"

"Of course, not. Isn't that the job of the public schools and their playgrounds? He's not Catholic. Besides, she's just a friend who's a girl."

No time to ponder. Stunned at the sight of us, son Larry took the lead. "Mom, Dad, what are you doing here? This is Patty Simpson. She was just showing me her 4-H project -- this cow." Quick thinking, Lar.

"Holstein," corrected Patty, trying to sound professional. "Nice to meet you," she replied pleasantly. Smart, cute, well-mannered, and probably a young gold digger who had noticed my elite arm band. Was our son worthy of such a girl?

Sensing my awkwardness, Becky took over. "Nice to meet you, Patty. Larry hasn't really seen many farm animals. This is our first fair. We're showing our dog at 3:00 and were just going to get lunch at one of the food trucks. Would you care to join us?" Holy shit, talk about backing your son into a corner. Whose son wants to take a girl to lunch for the first time with his parents? If I had said that, I'd be in big trouble. How do women know how to handle these situations with grace?

"I'm sorry, but thank you. I really have to attend my animal until the judging later this afternoon," she replied honestly and probably relieved.

"I think I'll just hang around here, too," said Larry before I could say anything else awkward, "if it's okay with Patty."

"Sure," she said immediately. Oh boy, in ten years is this chance meeting going to grow into something? Stop, Larry, both of you!

Becky's turn, "Patty, can you recommend any of these places for their food?"

Patty furrowed her brow, deep in thought, trying to please the future in-laws?

"Actually, if you drive back along the highway for a few miles, chances are that you'll find some roadkill, maybe even fresh."

We were startled. Shockingly, that was damn funny, and we both laughed to show our appreciation for her humor. She smiled. Dickens just stared at all the unusual animals.

Actually, there is a truck that serves good quarter pound hot dogs; it's called Big Frank's. Great freshly cut French fries, too. Fair food is not just a passing fad; it's an institution. Really can't go wrong."

More smiles and Becky and I and Dickens left in search of Big Frank's. I don't think the kids even knew that we had gone.

Big Frank's lived up to the culinary expectations and critique; the French fries were choice, the perfect blend of grease and salt. So, we bought two more orders and brought them back to the probably starving young people. We approached stealthily.

"Mom, dad, did you get lost or what?" challenged a startled son, looking up from his own bale of straw.

I had a feeling that he was embarrassed – helicopter parents, returning in twenty minutes. "We thought you'd like some hot dogs and fries," as I extended the greasy bag.

"Patty made some sandwiches; we were just eating," he replied accusingly, like it was our job to mess up his early flirtation.

"Thanks, Mr. and Mrs. E, I'm sure they're a thousand times better than peanut butter and jelly," jumped up Patty from a different pile and gratefully snatched the bag. "I was getting tired of day-old sandwiches."

I really, really liked this girl. I'm sure she could do better than our son.

"Good luck on your showing," she wished as she returned to the seat.

Unfortunately, her wishes did not affect the outcome of my lack of preparedness. I had assumed that a leash and a decent bath and combing would be sufficient for a dog show. Right? Not even close, but we would never see those people again, so it was a life lesson for an outsider. I tried to recall those tips and pointers that Chuck and I had learned and practiced – trot with the dog's head up, right front leg moving first in coordination with the other legs. whatever that meant. Dogs must remain on the exhibitor's left side, treats are fair usage and you can "show" the dog's teeth to the judge, rather than risking a nasty bite when the judge lifts the dog's lips to check its teeth. No braces? There was nothing I did right that day. I was grateful to the judge who checked Dicken's teeth. She sensed a possible problem, probably from my tension and not the dog's, and I honestly think that Chuck sensed her hesitation/fear, so he bit her hand. Flashback to Dexter's debut and judge biting. Thankfully, no blood; just shock from everyone in the tent, possibly the state of Illinois. But the judge was a professional, and I had a feeling that this wasn't the first time that she had been bitten and escaped with only a minor bite.

With only three dogs in our division, at least I was guaranteed a white ribbon for third place. Wrong! I noticed a nose-in-everybody's-business dog exhibitor pointing at us and talking to a judge, who nodded his head in agreement. He seemed hesitant but asked Chuck's judge and Mr. I'm-a-special-dog-owner something. They assured the judge that something furtive had occurred and turned away.

Shortly, the chief judge announced, "A disqualification has been requested by a contestant. Number 26, Chuck Dickens, is disqualified for incorrect registration. He should be registered in the 'black cocker spaniel' category, not the 'tri-color' category."

I always thought that Chuck had a rather regal air about him – a shiny black coat with a white chest and two brown eyebrows. Apparently not up to AKC standards. My fault. I had assumed that black, white, and brown would put the poor guy into a multi-colored class, not black. He was the workingman's spaniel not Charles Dickens.

I gave one of those incredulous nods at the judge, then a piercing glare at the mentally challenged dog's owner. For Christ's sake, the joker was wearing a Madras sport coat, and he protested that Dicken's not pure black coat was inappropriate. Mr. Madras turned his head to avoid eye contact. Of course, he won first prize and denied me of my first ribbon, even if it was for third place. He returned to the ring to claim his laurels and proudly showed the blue ribbon to anyone who cared. Being the graceful loser that I was, I walked up to him and extended my hand, which he surprisingly shook without making eye contact.

"Dipshit," I enunciated clearly in his ear so that no one else could hear. He seemed nonplussed as he rapidly exited. I wish that I could have barfed a Big Frank's quarter pound hot dog with all the fixings on his almost as putrid sport coat.

Becky gave me several words of sympathy as we returned to the dairy tent where we had stored our son. Patty felt about as sad at the result of our first dog show as she was about saying goodbye to Larry. Never found out how her cow did. Blue ribbon, in my books. Wondered if they had planned a farewell kiss. Ironically, Dickens could sense that I was sad and shared his tongue with my cheek. Unlucky dog, unlucky son, rotten dad.

We had one day to prepare for our next root canal at the Wheaton Fair Grounds. No fair, livestock, crafts, or baked goods, just judges. Pretty much the same people, including Mr. Madras, who was still flaunting his ribbon or having a hissy fit that some ingrate had been rude to him. As we arrived, I again turned down an offer for Ring Craft classes. Someone must have witnessed yesterday's performance and thought he might help me prevent another disaster with a single class. We just bumbled our way through the next ordeal with more confidence, but no more skill. Becky didn't even bother brushing and combing Dickens. We changed the registration category to "black cocker spaniels," and won a third-place ribbon, out of three dogs, or course. That story grew to eight dogs before my shame stopped me from revealing the truth. My days as a proud dog show participant changed to the days of wine and roses.

I looked Chuck Dickens squarely in those soulful eyes that most dogs have as I held up his chin and told him, "That's the end of my dog-show-owner phase and the end of your chance to be an official blue-ribbon champion, but I don't think I'd want to be a member of those snobs, anyway. No more pretentiousness for me, buddy. Although you didn't help my life-long dream come true when you bit that judge; she seemed nice. Did you really have to do that?" He tilted his head as if to say, "Who? Me?"

"Anyway, you're the worst dog I ever had. Let's go home, Chuck."

The only one in the car who showed some excitement was Larry. He and Patty had exchanged addresses and promised to keep in touch. If only he had known that the fair was the first and last time that he would see her. A few letters came and went, but within months they had faded, and that was a hard life-lesson weekend. Larry learned that as exciting as a brief flirtation can be, no matter what age, it often doesn't travel over time and distance. No heart break, just disappointment. And I learned not to dawdle where I have no business. Can't swim the English Channel before learning how to swim. And Becky? Becky learned to be an even more patient mother and wife who gave help where and when needed. Larry never grew-up to be a chauvinist, and I never learned how to change the oil in my car.

Chuck lived another eight years, two more than he really had to suffer. Chuck did not age well, and I should have had the courage to end his pain sooner than I had. I knew that dogs did not live forever, but I thought that my thoroughbred show dog would last another three years or so. He had occasional bursts of energy, so much that I had to drug him before taking him to the groomer and tell her just to do her best. I was never fond of having someone else groom my friend, especially because psycho dog had to be drugged before she was even willing to try. Cleaning his floppy, rancid ears posed another drug-induced coma. His last two years digressed into loss of motor skills, and he would often fall for no apparent reason other than old age. The joys of a casual walk through the neighborhood and growling at anyone who passed had vanished along with Dicken's desire to do anything, even live. He didn't want to go in the car anymore. Son Larry's efforts to play fetch or tug with him gradually came to an end, too, leading to endless questions like, "What's wrong with Dickens?" by a suspicious but saddened human brother, who probably knew but was in denial. Dickens was, after all, like Macbeth had been mine, his first dog of many, I hoped.

The first week of October, he refused food and rarely drank. I had to carry him outside for bathroom duties, but usually he just fell in the cool grass and waited for me to carry him back inside, where I would carefully place him in his dog bed. On Saturday, I called the vet for a consultation. Dr. Patterson knew the problem and told me to bring him in when and if I was ready, a tone of finality. We knew what he meant. There didn't seem to be anything that anyone could do to help ease his age and pain, except the obvious.

"I'll take him," said Becky, knowing the outcome of Dicken's last journey and how incapable I was of doing it.

"I'll go too," offered Larry with tears reluctantly running down his cheeks. "I want to hold him in the car," he suggested practically.

Choking-up, I countered, "Larry, why don't you stay here with me? I could use some company."

No hesitation. "No, I want to be with my dog in the car. Ma needs me too."

Maybe he had more courage than I had. He chose his dog over his dad, but I fully understood his decision. I would still be there tomorrow.

"Okay, I'll carry him to the car. Larry, you go settle in and be ready to rub his neck and belly." I turned to my worst dog, looked again into those soulful eyes and muttered, "Goodbye, buddy. Thanks for the trip."

I watched the car as it turned the corner and I closed my life on another dog chapter. Two hours later, Becky and Larry returned, their eyes red and damp. At least, they got some of the anguish purged. I just sat on the couch and full out wept. No sense in even trying to "man-up."

Dickens Stands Guard

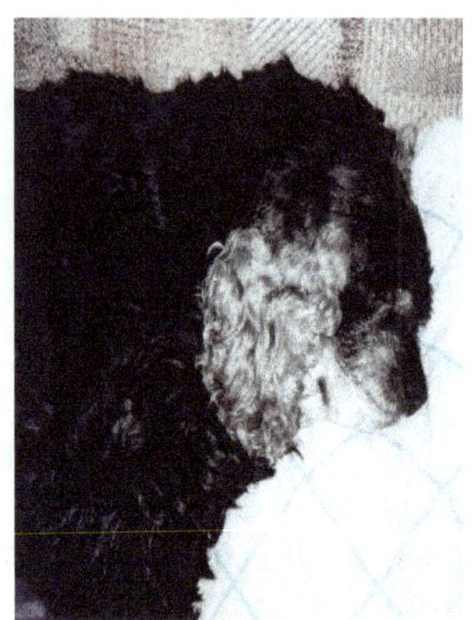

Dickens Getting Old

Chapter 8
I Never Sat on a Cow

"A dog is the only thing on earth that loves you more than he loves himself."
Josh, Billings, American humorist

When pondering back to my first lucid thought of puppyhood, I was snuggly sleeping amongst my mother, two sisters and lone brother; the other two brothers were no longer with us after a short stay; lacking a sense of time and space, I had no awareness of where or how long they had been gone, just a vague memory. One day I felt a hand lift me straight up like I was ascending to the sky, but I wasn't scared. I had seen it done with my siblings. It was much later that I learned about fear.

Soon I was quickly handed-off to someone else – a woman, I thought from the different smell, my best sense. Fortunately, I had just peed in the basket so I didn't have to spray this stranger like I had sprinkled the last one, because that misstep had changed the mood from fun to serious. Funny how fate plays a role in one's life,

114

even as a puppy. If the first woman hadn't been peed on, she might have taken me home and I would have had a completely different life, for better or worse. This new woman held me close to her face, and I instinctively licked her cheek. I sensed that it was already a better reaction than if I had peed on her. She seemed nice and safe and smelled good. Suddenly I was taken from her and placed back into my sleeping place. Oh well, time to return to normalcy after the day's excitement had come to an end.

Much later, I'm guessing days as my awareness of time and space became more finely tuned, I again was lifted from my mother, brother, and remaining sister. Only this time I would never see them again. We all looked like we were giving our last farewells as we yipped in unison. Maybe I would join my other puppy siblings. At least we had experienced this parting before, but nobody knew what happened once a puppy left our safe bundle of fur. The only positive side of the situation was that I remembered the scent of the lady who had held me before. Again, she lifted me to her face, so I felt like I had to lick her again; same taste, same reaction.

Then a man grabbed me and held me high above their heads. But I felt his firm hand and believed that I was safe. When he lowered me to his face, I assumed that he wanted me to lick him, too. We seemed to form a bond quickly, unlike with my current owners, who only provided us with basic needs, and no fun or anything else that I could feel.

This time was different because I went with the new people and left everything I had ever known behind me. Was this the start of a new life in a new place, with these strange but nice people? Why couldn't my mother come, too? After a long car ride cuddling in Becky's (I had learned their names quickly) arms so that I could see my new world, we stopped in front of another place to live (home) and we all got out of the car and went inside, through the house, and straight to the grassy yard in the welcoming backyard.

Much to my surprise and delight, Larry placed me in the cool grass and set me free. I had experienced this with my siblings and mother at the other place, and, at first we felt that it was fun, but being returned so soon seemed to be punishment. This time Larry wanted me to run, so I did and the two people tried to catch me, but I had the feeling that they were letting me escape, time after time. Soon I became too tired and just stopped and rolled in the grass. No one followed me or picked me up. They just stood near, smiling, and seeming to enjoy the moment.

After running back and forth, I realized that there were no boundaries here, other than a long white fence surrounding the yard. Still, it was the most open area I had ever seen for my usage, and it was all mine, I thought. Soon they started to laugh and to chase me again, but it wasn't fair because they were so big and I had such short legs. Maybe someday. Exhausted, I just did the normal thing any puppy my size would do—I decided to take a nap.

More laughing and Becky picked me up for more of those tongue licks, which she called "kisses" and handed me to Larry, who continued lifting me straight up an arm's height and made weird sounds with his mouth. I thought that I might get sick from all the air motion. I just wanted to sleep. Haven't you people ever seen a puppy?

We all went inside and Larry dropped me by something I finally recognized – a bowl full of cold, refreshing water, better than the old big bowl that I had to share with all my canine family. At the original home I was just starting to learn that the people wanted me to pee on an oddly scented pad, which in this home was located next to the water bowl. I didn't want to disappoint my new owners, but I was empty. I had left it all in the back yard. Still, I made a quick sniff and looked up at them watching me in hope.

They also showed me a big room where I was able to explore. It was so much bigger than the old box I had shared with my mother and siblings, and it was all mine, too. I wondered if they all had new homes that were as large as mine, or if they still lived in a box and saw each other or if they were all separated by now.

Much to my surprise, I was able to go into other rooms, too. Why had they so much space? I never did understand, but it was wonderful. In the first room there was a nice cushion on the floor, and since it was at my level, I stepped into it, curled-up, and immediately fell asleep.

I don't know how much time had passed before those bright flashes of light woke me, very different from the old place. Quite unpleasant! But when I opened my eyes, Larry and Becky were sitting on the floor with the flash makers (cameras) while they grinned and laughed. Other than the annoying flashes of light, I sensed safety and security and an instinctive twitch on my back end.

It seems that I used to have more to wag, but that was okay. Don't know who took my tail or when, but I was just fine.

It was time to eat, I guess, but who would feed me? They took me by two bowls, one filled with clean water, and the other had little pebbles with some water sprinkled on top. They called it "kibble" and called me a "kibble eater," like it was something bad. Larry would often say, "Hey, kibble eater, let's go outside." The water mixed with the kibble created little taste, which I somewhat enjoyed even though eating the kibble was like munching stones. Good thing my teeth were solid. Not much later in life they all fell out, some which I swallowed, but new, bigger teeth took their places. Made kibble eating much simpler.

When it was dark, there was a small light close to my pad (they called it a dog bed, which was fine; better than a kibble eater's bed, and I had it all to myself.) Although a little lonely, I did enjoy sleeping without being stepped on, but I still missed my mother's kisses of assurance. I slept the night through, but Becky and Larry slept in another room.

One time during the night, I had to pee, so I got up, waddled a few steps, and lifted my leg on the corner of a wooden structure, like a skinny tree. I later learned that it was something called a table and that I shouldn't do that. Bad dog!

Time passed slowly in dog years. Life soon became routine – get out of bed, a quick visit to the back yard, then eat some kibble and water, various treats tossed on the floor, then they left and I waited what felt like a long time for their return.

One evening after I was playfully spun in the air like a bird while I bit the end of a ratty cloth hose, and for some reason they began to call me "Dickens." I didn't mind and I quickly learned to respond to it.

Then Larry began calling me "Chuck," so I guess I wasn't Dickens any more, but that was still what Becky called me. To make matters worse, Larry called me either or both. I was so confused that I just responded to both. It seemed acceptable.

As I grew bigger, I was able to jump on the couch. Its back faced the big picture window, and with my new length and stronger legs, I was able to spend much time standing guard while I watched everything that moved – squirrels, chipmunks, birds, other dogs, and anything I could threaten. Sometimes my barking and window scratching frightened them.

Every day I scared a man carrying a large sack over his shoulder. He was bolder than the other creatures and walked up to the front door as though he was going to enter without permission. That's when I went into attack mode and started barking and clawing at the window. I was terrifying. It must have been quite a show, because the man with the sack immediately turned around and left. It was my job to guard the house. Never stated explicitly but understood. Except on weekends when Larry sometimes greeted the stranger and acted friendly. But I knew better. If Larry kept acting nice, he'd soon be talking to squirrels and other vermin. Standing on the back of the sofa, I eventually became so good that I learned to lie on top of the couch's back and observe life without having to stand and grow tired. Life didn't change much until one night Becky told Larry something that seemed to excite them both. After a while of hugs and kisses, they went to their bedroom and shut the door. No dogs allowed. Not even some extra dog treats.

Not long after this life-changing night, they began to spend more time away from home, even weekends, and they returned home with boxes and packages, mostly which they stored in the spare bedroom. In the evening they sat on the couch with me and endlessly looked at magazines and books. At least they kept scratching my neck and throwing me pieces of popcorn to catch. It started to look like Becky had eaten too much kibble and treats, as her belly developed a comfortable resting place for my head. Everything was good.

One night I got very lucky – two walks after supper. Becky slowed us a bit on our first mile-long course around the neighborhood. She seemed sluggish and often had to rest. I was afraid that she was going to throw-up her kibble. I did that sometimes, too. We all got home and rested for a short while, but then they got the leash and we started walking again. Beautiful evening, lots of smells, and another walk. Heaven.

However, this time when we got home, Larry rushed around, closing the front drapes, turned on the tv, changing the channel to a game that he seemed to enjoy watching but never played it with me. Rapidly, he filled my kibble and water bowls and added lots of treats. They seemed in a hurry but not worried. I got comfortable on the couch, watched the tv screen, and soon fell asleep, dreaming about chasing squirrels in our back yard.

Being in the house alone seemed like forever, especially in dog time. No one came back the entire night, and I really had to pee. I had distinct recollections that they did not seem overly angry if I peed on the kitchen floor, except that the era of pee pad training was long past. Still, I felt guilty as I left a puddle on the smooth floor. But then I easily returned to the whole couch and soon fell back to sleep.

The sunlight had begun to creep through the opening in the drapes and fill the living room. Should I worry or will they return as always to take care of me? Soon I heard the noise of keys in the door, and Larry swept in like someone trying to rescue me. He picked me up, ruffled my neck and said, "Sorry buddy, but the good news is that you have a brother. I'm sure you'll be the best of friends. Come on, let's go outside." From somewhere in my dog's brain, I seemed to recall something about a brother, but that was too long ago to remember clearly; I think it was good and bad.

Even though I had recently relieved myself, the outside felt wonderful – cool, slightly wet, and wide open. Much to my surprise, when I got back into the house, my earlier puddle had disappeared. Larry must have cleaned it without yelling at me. Maybe news of that brother had changed his feelings. I suspected that we were entering a new, uplifting phase in our relationship, not that it was ever bad. I hoped that my new brother wouldn't pee on the floor. But there was something missing; where was Becky? I always liked her. No sign or mention of her to give me a clue about what had happened? Did Larry trade her for a brother? Something deeper in my mind seemed to trigger a distant picture of my siblings going away and never returning.

Days later Becky returned to us. She looked exhausted but thankful to be in her home, so, naturally I gave her smacks until she had to ward me off. I was so happy that things had returned to where they should be. Except that Larry was holding another bundle in his arms. He slowly kneeled and showed me a little person in a blanket.

My 15,000 nose sense detectors could not detect any evil. It seemed innocent and was nothing that would threaten my wellbeing or those of the household. In fact, this new miniature person seemed to bring a happy aura to other people who met him. Larry whispered the word "brother," and I was surprised because I did not think that dogs could have human brothers, but I trusted that they knew what they were doing. The brother didn't do much, and I was glad that Larry had not traded Becky for him. There was something reminiscent about my litter mates. Becky almost seemed maternal, and I wondered if one day this new baby would be separated from his mother.

Attention shifted in the household, mostly dictated by "the little one," who I realized was also called Larry. This family seemed to have a problem with names. I still had several – Chuck, Dickens, Chuck Dickens, Buddy, kibble-eater, mutt, etc. Good thing that dogs can swiftly adapt to new names, especially considering all the words that various people used to acknowledge him – big boy, prince, hey you, sweet, kid, big one, looks-like-his-father, etc.

Time passed in stages. Unfortunately, Becky seems to have lost her wonderful, self-made pillow that I had so much enjoyed. New Larry would have liked it, too. At first, he had to be carried everywhere. Then he slowly invaded my domain on the floor, but there was plenty of room. Soon (long in my years), he was kind of stumbling across the room, while being closely followed by Becky or Larry. I did not remember them becoming that interested when I started running in the back yard. Maybe they did. At first, his trips were short. At times I thought he was going to fall on me, and I was never sure if I should escape or try to help. Usually, it was a combination when I mostly escaped his toppling body but still was able to cushion his head before it hit the floor. Becky and Larry praised me for my quick reflexes, and I developed this feeling that I might have a full-time job as guardian.

Eventually little Larry was able to walk upright, like other people, only with less grace. After a while, he even began to walk, then run. He seemed to want to play with me but could never keep up. After all, I had four legs. Not fair.

As I got slightly older, I grew to meet and accept more people, especially new little friends of the new Larry. They all seemed nice and friendly, and sometimes one of them threw a ball high, waiting to see if I could make a leaping catch. Or they would throw a Frisbee high above what they thought was my height, forgetting my great leaping ability, and I would catch or at least hit it with my nose, deflecting it almost every time. Unfortunately, my dominant skills soon bored the boys; it's no fun to always lose, especially to a kibble-eater.

One day Larry's friend Robbie brought over a very unusual ball. It was oval and did not bounce very high. It must have been hard to throw and catch, because at first the boys could do neither very well. I wasn't sure what my role was in this new game. Of course, I could not even carry the odd ball in my mouth or keep it away from them. And no one could bounce it very high, so I was resigned to watch from the sidelines.

I was in a half-sleep mode when I heard a shout, "I got it," and saw Robbie running after Larry, who had missed catching the ball that was far over his head. Then Robbie ran hard after Larry, trying to get to the ball first, which was common play for them. When he was almost even with Larry, Robbie pushed him from behind and Larry went tumbling. Instinctively, I went into my protector role and went after the two fallen boys. Robbie had his arm on Larry's back, like he was holding him down so that he could get to the ball first. I did not hesitate to free Larry by biting Robbie's arm, just once.

Before I realized what was happening, I was flying like a bird, courtesy of a very angry and scolding big Larry, who snatched me up and kept calling me a bad dog, while slapping my butt and he threw me into the house, before he returned to the boys. I thought I had done the right thing – protecting Larry from harm.

I could see from my perch on the couch that Becky took Robbie away in our car. As they drove away with Robbie and his parents, I though it odd that they didn't take me, too. Someone usually asked me if I wanted to go in the car as he jangled his keys in front of me, and I would respond with excitement tremors. This time no one asked, so I sulked off to my bed and tried to sleep, wondering what had happened and what role I had played.

It seemed a long time before Becky had returned and the Thompson family had gone home. Becky and Larry talked seriously while little Larry and I sat on the floor and watched some game using that oddly shaped ball, which I learned was called a "football." No one seemed to be angry with me anymore, at least not yet.

Over time I sensed that all people were discouraged from petting me or even greeting me. It was as if I had been put in a prison but I did not understand what I had done wrong. Sometimes I saw a person who looked like Robbie, and I quickly associated that person with my defense of Larry, which had led to my current treatment. I was still protecting Larry, but now I could only bark at the nemesis, not bite. It was not an easy task. Some detail was missing from the puzzle, but I never learned what it was.

Several cold seasons passed and little Larry grew bigger, almost as tall as his dad, and he grew the same height as Becky. I often watched Larry and Robbie, who had also gotten taller, playing catch with that football. I was eager to get out with them so that I could play, too, but Robbie never really came near me again. Occasionally he'd say, "Hey Dickens, what's up?" and start to ruffle my neck, but he always pulled away at the last second. I really missed that contact. I think we both knew that I wouldn't bite him again unless he tried to hurt Larry, but there was never going to be a return to our old behaviors; too bad.

One night for some reason, Larry and Becky brought home books and magazines, and I thought that maybe they were getting another baby. Normally, this activity would not be exciting, except most of these magazines had pictures of dogs on them. One even had a picture of me on its cover! At least, I think it was me. Now I understood why people spent so much time leafing through the pages of pictures. Unfortunately, I was not able to gaze through the pages without supervision. I couldn't turn the pages without using my teeth, which would have caused endless damage to the magazine and probably myself.

In addition to all the books and magazines, whenever Becky left, little Larry and big Larry spent much time sitting at a small computer screen in the corner of the living room, while they typed words and wrote notes by hand. They made plans of some sort, but I did not know what plans they made. As soon as Becky arrived home, they immediately turned off the computer, sat on the couch, and pretended to watch something else on the big screen. Big secret, but don't tell the dog.

"Who's winning?" asked Becky immediately.

Larry did not break his staring at the screen, trying to act unconcerned that she had returned home.

Larry, Jr. (another confusing name) lazily replied, "Oh, you know, same old stuff." His response seemed to satisfy her, and so the ruse continued. One thing that did change was my exercise routine.

Every day Larry put on my collar, which usually excited me; I loved to walk around the neighborhood. There were so many other dogs to greet with a hello bark; by their tone you could tell that they were always glad to see me, returning my hello. Other people who we passed also greeted us, though never bending down to pet me for some reason. They sometimes stopped to talk for too long – boring, let's move on. It's my walk.

Peculiarly, many of our neighborhood leash walks occurred in our back yard. Why would I have to walk on a leash in our own fenced-in back yard? Not only did we not get anywhere, but he kept repeating a short path, back and forth, with me always on his right side. The only trick I learned was to stop and wait when he stopped and said, "Heel." I eventually mastered the task because he would pull a small treat out of his pocket. It was okay but no big meat bone.

This endlessly walking back and forth was occasionally expanded to longer walks, and it felt good to see the old gang again. Every so often he would run his hand down my back and sometimes pull up my gums as if to check my teeth. It's a good thing I knew Larry, because if some stranger had tried that, I would have had a finger snack. It was an invasive action, reserved for Larry, Becky, and the rarely seen vet.

This daily routine lasted for too long until one day we all jumped into the car (they called it a Chevy), and drove for a long time, with my head hanging out the back window, whenever we slowed enough so that my big ears would not be ripped off my head. Just a road trip to nowhere, but it was wonderful.

Finally, we stopped at a large flat building. Thankfully, and much to my surprise, my back seat partner put on my collar, and I was out of the Chevy and pulling him to the corner of the building, which I watered with great relief. Then I was free to drag him onto the grass and walk around the area, where some people were eating at an oddly shaped table. One person about big Larry's size extended his hand to me with a bite of meat and bread.

"Is it okay if he has this bite? Got a dog myself," the man asked.

"Sure, answered Larry and I grabbed the delicious treat out of the stranger's hand, careful not to bite the hand that fed me.

Becky called us over to her and we went into a small room with two beds and cold fresh air. It felt wonderful after the long hot trip. With all our stuff in the room, it looked like we might be staying there, a very unusual activity. Little Larry flopped on one of the beds, called my name, and beckoned me. Of course, I jumped at the invitation, though the bed seemed higher than usual; everything was harder to do, but after two failed attempts, I made it. I guess that Larry and I were going to be bedmates for the night, a tradition that had faded over the years as he grew bigger and I gravitated to my own smaller bed on the floor.

The next morning everyone left for a short time while I was stuck with a bowl of kibble. At least they soon came back for me and even brought back something undefinable for me to eat. I actually preferred my kibble. I was proud of my affectionate title "kibble eater."

I even got to go back in the car, where I sat in the back with Larry, and I held my head out the window for as long as I could. It felt so good with the wind blowing back my ears like wings. Sometimes we went so fast that my ears made snapping noises. Little Larry had no such luck; his ears were too short. Eventually we slowed and drove down a road that was lined with cars. Between all the cars and trucks, I could see many people standing and running on a field. And dogs! I had never seen so many dogs in one place. Big, small, furry, hairless, neatly groomed, shaggy, but they all seemed calm and glad to be there. I could not understand how so many dogs did not go wild and start to roam and chase each other. Maybe they had mean owners.

Oh, and the smells! Not just other dogs, but other animals, the people, the cooking food, the undirected anticipation, the atmosphere. I could hardly wait to get out through the car window and join them all, but little Larry held me back. I would never bite him, but I really was aching to get out and join the fun. If they brought me here to play with all these other dogs, making me wait was a cruel gesture. Big Larry got out, holding my leash, so I jumped into the front seat.

"Easy, boy, take it easy. We'll get there," Larry said in a solemn, but not too serious tone. He almost seemed a bit scared, but I could not imagine what would cause him to grow tense. We were in dog land. How could it get any better? Just let me go. Soon I was on the ground and immediately began to pull him toward a group of other dogs and people. Unfortunately, he was much stronger and the chain around my neck began to choke me. I stopped and the chain went

slack so that I could breathe freely. Becky removed my chain and put on a new collar that went around my shoulders, but not across the throat. So, I started again and we repeated this cycle several times until I got used to it. I couldn't escape but at least I didn't gag. It felt like every dog was watching this struggle in awe, and most of the people just shook their heads in disbelief. I felt out of place. Neither the dogs nor the people seemed too eager to play with anyone, especially me. I let Larry lead me without additional conflict.

A short time later, much shorter than I wanted, we stopped under a tree. Larry twisted a stake into the ground and attached my leash to it. I guess that meant that I wasn't going anywhere with him or to play with any other dogs. Did all those dogs think that they were too good for me? I was a captive as I watched my master walk away. Becky took my brush out of her bag and began to smooth my fur, especially after all the tangles I now had from the car ride. After we both seemed to get tired of that monotony, she changed to that silver-toothed comb. It felt wonderful, but what I really wanted was to run and play. Maybe I could escape this stake for a little while, so I gave it a few strong tugs, but it did not move, and Becky quickly scolded me until I stopped. Big Larry returned with a sense of dread waving over him and onto us.

After a short discussion we took a long walk through more people and dogs and other strange animals. They all seemed to look at me like I had no business being there. Maybe the other dogs got lots of play time, but I still wanted to outrace them, just to show that I was special to someone and that I belonged.

We reached a place that was full of large animals in pens. I really wanted to rub noses and jump on them, but Larry decided to carry me. I knew that I could stand on the backs of some of the larger animals without causing them any harm. I thought that it might be fun to stand higher than almost any other animal around. Maybe later. We walked with Larry carrying me through the rows of pens. Later I learned that they were horses, sheep, goats, geese, and more. Surprisingly we found little Larry in one of the pens with a strange girl and one of those beasts that I wanted to stand on. It was too big to play with but it seemed friendly. I think the one in the pen belonged to the girl, and I was hoping she would offer me the chance to stand on its back. Larry, Jr. and his dad both seemed a little tense, but I don't think anyone in the family needed any protection. She

(Patty) talked freely with the family, and even rubbed my neck and said some nice things, I think. She did refer to the big animal as a "cow" and I hoped she'd offer me a ride on its back, if it really was her cow.

When the discussion was over, we left little Lar behind and walked outside again, Larry grateful to set me down. I couldn't have been that heavy; I think he was just getting weaker and sweatier. We made our way between several odd places until we stopped at one table where Becky sat with me and Larry left again. When he returned, he was carrying a wet bag, which he set on the table. It was food and I realized that with all the excitement occupying my tiny brain, I was hungry. But I didn't see any kibble, so I just sat in anticipation of any food droppings. Not to disappoint, Larry gave Becky some food, himself some food and I just sat, feeling my stump of a tail moving in anticipation. This maneuver and pitiful look always got them moving to my treat cabinet, but that was not there. Slowly Larry brought out something like people food, wrapped in paper, opened it, broke the round piece into smaller pieces and put it all on the ground. Best meal ever! Sometimes I got a bite of something they had left over, but this was all mine, bread and all. Becky set a plastic bowl of water next to it, and I was in heaven. What a day! If only I could run and play now. Or stand on a cow's back.

After a while we carried the other bag and went back to little Larry, big Larry deciding to carrying me. Little Larry was talking and laughing with Patty. The nervous tension still seemed present, but not as bad, and I did not feel any need to protect him. As soon as he saw us, he approached in surprise. Reluctantly he looked at the bag of food that they were offering. If he didn't want it, I'd sure take it, no hesitation. Patty came up to us, patted my head, and happily took the bag. Without offering the dog a bite, they both went back in the pen and started to eat. I still hoped that someone would either give me food or a lift to the cow's back. I just wanted to stand on a living creature and see something from so high. Was that asking for too much?

We left again without little Larry and the girl. Larry and Becky's attitude toward the girl went from "We're fun people," to "Let's behave ourselves; this might lead to something special" mode. It was so much easier to relate to people not by their words, which is rather limited in dogs, but by their tones of voice. Not even vaguely sure of what was about to happen, I instinctively was led on my unpleasant leash. I tried to ignore all those eyes that I felt were watching us, wondering who those intruders were.

All three of us got to an unusual room with cloth sides and a pointed roof. Once inside, Becky left Larry and me and went to sit by herself in some shelf-like seats. Larry changed my collar from the choker to the odd harness that we sometimes used in our backyard at home. When he attached the chain to the harness, I felt that this moment was the whole point of this trip – no running or playing, just whatever this was.

Soon I was walking on the ground the way that we had at home. It was simple – right, left, right, left, back again, just follow Larry's lead. After a few rounds of that, we stopped and waited. Then Larry lifted me onto a table, where he held up my head and grabbed my butt. I could sense that he wanted me to remain still, so I did. Good dog. Then this strange woman approached us. They talked briefly and without warning, she lifted my gums as though to check my teeth. My doctor sometimes did this, but this woman, who seemed harmless, was unknown to me. She had a little feeling of uncertainty, not quite fear, as though anticipating some unexpected reaction. Instinctively I snapped at the fat, probing fingers. She was quick to withdraw, and I was not certain that I got her, but if I had, not too bad. This action temporarily stopped the world, and all eyes were on us. I'm not certain if people liked the fact that I bit her or the fact that she had intruded into my mouth and paid the price. Bet she never did that with a pit bull. I had a sense that the other two dogs in the ring with me felt that I may be their hero or that they knew that I'd be gone soon. Never got to play together either. Whose fault?

After a few more prances and then showings by the three dogs with me, which I found quite boring, Larry was ready to leave, I could tell. I think I heard the announcer say, "Chuck Dickens." Feeling sure that Larry and I had won something, I was proud and eager to receive it, whatever it was. Instead, Larry led me away after a strangely dressed man whispering to a man who seemed to be in charge. I had never even seen a dog dressed so awful. Larry shook his hand and whispered something in his ear. Probably one of those "good game" exchanges that I had seen so many times after little Larry's soccer games. I was sure that it was not a compliment on the man's coat. Whatever Larry had said must have upset the man, and I awaited word for me to attack him. Heck, I had already bitten one person today; let's go for two. No such luck. Head held high, Larry took me outside with Becky.

After Larry talked to her, she started speaking in a loud and agitated voice. Her hands were all over as she yelled, and she even stomped the ground. I was afraid that maybe I had done something wrong, like biting that rude lady who had tried to look at my teeth without warning, but they did not acknowledge it to me. I felt lucky that Becky had not stomped on me, like she ever would. Maybe the guy in the funny coat deserved to be stomped on by Becky.

Just enjoying all the sights and smells, I followed them back to little Larry's pen. Wondered if the strange girl was showing her cow. She was still there and greeted us warmly, including another pat on my head. Maybe now she was going to let me sit on top of that Holstein. She seemed sorry to hear about something that had happened to us, but my canine senses were overwhelmed by the events of the day, yet I could not distinctly recall what had happened.

Eventually we returned to the car. Little Larry seemed sad, hung his head, and when we got in the back seat, I licked his face. Maybe he wanted to stand on that cow, too, but that girl hadn't offered. That face lick usually brought a smile, but this time he rubbed faces with me and he scratched my ears. That was a major reaction, and I could feel that his eyes might be getting wet. Anyway, I was dog tired and soon was sleeping on the car seat. Couldn't wait to get home – my bed, back yard, food, treats, and everything a dog could want.

Much to my surprise, when I was awoken, we were back at the same place that we had spent the previous night; too bad. I was hoping that we wouldn't spend the next day at the same boring place we had today. It could have been so much fun, but everything was so structured that there was no time for running and playing. The next day we drove a short time and pulled into a huge parking lot, where we all climbed a little hill and entered a different building that had the same atmosphere as yesterday. I even saw some of the same dogs with their same owners. Mostly they ignored me, but no one in our family seemed to care. Despite everyone's attitude I was still hoping to play and maybe see a cow.

Unfortunately, this place also lacked excitement or fun. There were only dogs, and none of the various strange animals that we had seen yesterday. Looked like no cow riding for me today. Larry and I repeated our routine from yesterday, minus the bite from my teeth on another new intruder/judge. I learned not to do that, and this time Larry got some prize. He seemed quite pleased. We saw the man with the ugly jacket again, and I was hoping that this time I would get a shot at him, but Larry ignored him, so I followed the leader.

After the event, everyone went back to their cars. I was glad to leave and again sat in back with Larry. Surprisingly, big Larry reached over the front seat, raised my chin, looked into my eyes, and said something. He didn't seem upset, at least not at me, but I could feel some disappointment. He had that questioning tone, but, of course, even though I only spoke and understood a few words of English, I seemed to learn more every day. So little Larry, who seemed to be in a more chipper mood, and I watched out the windows as we drove home. We were going faster than usual, but I thought I saw several cows. I barked hello at them, but everyone in the car seemed to disapprove, so I stopped. Just trying to be friendly.

Nothing much exciting happened forever after those travelling days. More snow, visitors, days alone and days with Larry, Becky and little Larry. He grew so much bigger and faster. I could not even run faster now that his longer legs would carry him so much farther with each stride. Most of the time I was just content to sleep, opening my eyes in reaction to some sound or presence. My body was just getting worn out, but in dog years that happens fast. Not much pain, just a weakening of everything vital. There was less and less joy to be found in the back yard.

Occasionally they took me to the groomer. Before I went, I took some other pill, only instead of lessening my aching muscles, it made me very tired. Actually, I could not stand on the grooming table, and one person held me up while the other washed me, even my ears, and cut my hair. I usually felt better after we got home.

Finally, Larry took me to the vet, who checked me and stuck a needle in my skinny forearm. Before we left, he gave us some more pills, which I took every day. I thought that the pills were supposed to make me feel better, but they really didn't. My legs often lost muscle control and I fell. Sometimes I had to go to the bathroom and I just went on the floor, too weak to run in circles by the door the way I used to. Larry or Becky often tried to catch me before I embarrassed myself. When they did, Larry usually lifted me to the cool grass and sat on the back step, closely watching me, his chin in his hands, and I think he was weeping.

Unfortunately, the pills did not help me. I still fell and ached all over. I often threw-up my food, even when they gave me special meat. I even lost desire to do anything except sleep and, I had a hard time drinking, so I stopped eating and drinking. I just wished that I could sleep all the time, and that when I awoke, I would be normal again. I just felt none of my old-time playfulness and desire to do anything anymore. If . . . only.

Finally, one day Larry lifted me and gently carried me to the car, like he had when I had first come to live with them. He spoke to me and I could feel his sadness from somewhere. Oddly, he passed me to his son and returned to the house. Becky drove us to the vet while brother Larry rubbed my neck. The petting did not feel great, but it felt reassuring.

When we got there, little Larry carried me into my usual examination room, where my vet was waiting. He spoke to me in a soothing voice while he patted my head and stroked my back. Then he put a large warm towel on the table, and brother Larry placed me on it, constantly rubbing my neck. I already felt better.

Then came a needle prick in my back leg. Slowly the muscles went numb, and then a long needle went deeper into my muscle, and it hurt a little more, but not for long. Soon I was so tired that I readily closed my eyes. The last things I remember seeing were brother Larry and Becky crying. 'Where was big Larry?' I wondered.

Soon I felt a breeze on my face and I was standing in a field by a bridge. All pain was gone, and I felt that I could run and bark again. I thought that I may have seen a cow and hoped that maybe now I could jump high enough to stand on its back. Before I got the chance, some other joyful and playful dogs called to me.

I'm so ugly that I'm cute

New Christmas gift

Chapter 9
Teddy to the Rescues

"Dogs are wise. They crawl into a quiet corner and lick their wounds
and do not rejoin the world until they are whole once more."
Agatha Christie, English writer

Sometimes you can search too long for the perfect dog and when you're exhausted and frustrated, usually a fortunate wind takes you to fill a hollowness that needs to be filled. Especially in 2005, when it was so easy to conduct a search for anything, anywhere, and not have to leave your own home. Besides the regular newspaper advertisements, note cards pinned to grocery store cork boards, friends who knew someone who knows someone who knows someone else whose dog just had a litter of the cutest puppies ever born, both purebred and mutts (not from the same litter, I trust). And of course, there were farmers' markets, crudely painted roadside signs with an arrow pointing two and half miles down Darcy Road to "while-they-last" golden doodles. That rudimentary sign made me think back to my first dog, Macbeth, and I wondered if he came from such an isolated farm before he ended up in the window of the Fur, Fin and Feather, pet shop in Madison, Wisconsin, ready to be given a good life by a young, newly married couple that was just killing time one afternoon; my ten-dollar mistake.

Of course, now there was the internet in my life, for which I have never forgiven my son Larry. I thought I could use it to hide my earlier dog show aspirations, but it enslaved me to the world of easy global access. Give me a few rare idle minutes and I'd browse the universe for dogs, even though I had no intention of buying one quite yet. It felt too soon after the loss of my white ribbon canine star of the DuPage County, Illinois fair. But I could still briefly look, not search, just in case I found the perfect dog; serendipity or fate? "Idle hands are the devil's workshop," my mother used to tell me, even claiming that she had created that cliché. When she died at the age of fifty-four from breast cancer, I never told her that I knew better. Still, I used her "creation" to justify any browsing I did on the internet, and any other time that it became useful. So, I surreptitiously, found a million dogs each looking for a home, while my subconscious mind kept nagging that I would be helping another canine-in-need, while satisfying my own craving for a dog.

Surprisingly, I was overwhelmed by the large number of rescue-dog organizations. There were resources for almost every breed, including many that I had never even heard of. In addition, there were large city services, county humane societies, and dog lovers' foundations, everyone seeking people to take one of their dogs to its forever home. Somewhere, someone not only had something that I wanted, but was actually searching for me. Serendipity plus! Of course, my other half would have to agree with me. She, too, missed Dickens dog, but I wasn't sure if she was ready to renew the responsibility of another dog, cute or not.

"Lar, have you thought this through? We've already had our hearts broken three times. I don't know if I can or want to handle another one."

I gave her my best disappointment look, as I stared at the floor appearing to be deeply contemplating the meaning of life and the size of the solar system. I was like a kid whose parents promised him a dog, knowing fully well who would end-up taking care of it, despite hollow promises. Still, I had no more weapons. Come on

Iowa Becky; it's not like I asked if I could start dating other women. It's a dog, and you've had experience. Almost a full sixty seconds later, she began to crack, probably intuitively contemplating my "other women" thought.

"What kind of dog would it be?" she opened the door, but not wide, just a peek to see who was there.

I lightened a little by ceasing my staring contest with the floor; the floor won. "Any kind you want. These rescue services provide any breed, sex, or age that you could desire in your wildest dreams." Put the burden on her shoulders.

Easy answer. "I don't want an old dog. Too soon gone," she wisely replied, as if considering the dilemma. She knew the importance of a dog to me, the only canine bleeding-heart.

"There's no rush. Plenty of lost dogs out there, praying for someone like us to give one a real home, destined for a better life. Just read the newspaper ads." Maybe I was pushing too hard, but what could I lose at this stage? When the door is open, crash through it.

"Are they like the ads that suggest that someone was selling the perfect used car?" Her sharp sarcasm was the right card to play, I thought she would just agree or disagree, not make me think any more. She squinted, hopefully trying to envision our good dog days.

Softly, she suggested, "Okay, but let's wait four more weeks. No rush, but let's see what the options are." It was an amicable but vague enough agreement.

We had enjoyed our "dog shopping" for a few weeks, laughing, pointing at pictures, fussing about possible bad literary names (Twain, Swift, Baldwin), always only half-joking. Then one Sunday afternoon, our world took a major curve in the road, over the guardrail and into the canyon.

The phone rang, and it was my sister Lynn, who sounded tremulous. Our father, Bud, had had a minor stroke, what the doctor called a TIA. He only lived five miles from Lynn in the Chicago suburbs, but he had just turned eighty-three years old and was showing major signs of aging – too idle, loneliness, less ability to take care of himself, and just listless. Perhaps it was time that we started to look for an assisted-living care facility for him. I know what she meant, but he had lived in his current home for forty years, buried two wives, and was rather attached to the place where he had spent almost half his life. For safety reasons and from observation, we had taken away his car keys several years ago, so other than the mailman and meal-on-wheels saints, he had little human contact.

Lynn and I agreed that we seriously should start searching. It seems that I was always searching lately. It would be comforting for him to stay in his own home and die there peacefully in his sleep. Horrible thoughts, but realistic.

A week later another angel, a DuPage County senior health advisor had responded to a call from Lynn asking if there were any county programs to help our elderly father, who was close to a shut-in. Lynn had explained the situation in great detail and asked if they offered any assistance for a case such as ours. Without committing to anything, the woman agreed to meet Lynn at Dad's house the next Tuesday to discuss the options in Bud's presence. Of course, Lynn was curious if Dad could possibly continue to live there without assistance. Good sister/daughter that she was, she had cleaned his house completely to give the impression that Dad did not live in a pig sty and kept everything in livable condition. Also, he was physically stable and only lived five miles from her. During all the small talk, Mrs. Witzel did a close analysis of the house, when she noticed a picture with Bud and Clancy, a golden cocker spaniel that he been one of his former dogs. She asked if he currently had a dog.

"Not for a couple of years now," he replied recalling his many pets.

Mrs. Witzel did not hesitate, "There may be several service dogs that you would qualify for." Like an eighty-year-old born deaf man who was hearing for the first time, he came out of his semi-coma.

"What's a service dog?" Lynn and Bud had asked in harmony.

Mrs. Witzel appeared surprised that no one knew. "They're specially trained dogs to help people; some larger breeds are trained to help the physically handicapped, but smaller dogs help senior citizens who just need some companionship to occupy a lonesome and idle mind. Most large breeds are trained to physically help the deaf or blind or wheelchair-bound people who still live in their own homes with the help of these saintly dogs. The general feeling amongst authorities advocating for senior citizens is that barring any major medical problems, the best place for the elderly is in their own homes, where they are surrounded by a comfortable and safe environment, just what dogs are seeking, such as yourself, Bud."

Lynn was still trying to assimilate all this new material. "To help all these people, wouldn't the dogs have to be large, like German shepherds or setters, something to deal with people needing physical assistance?" Lynn was apparently overwhelmed with the possibilities that she asked the question that Mrs. Witzel had just explained.

Patiently, Mrs. Witzel nodded affirmatively. "Many are large dogs, like you sometimes may see in the supermarkets, but they don't always need to be. For example, smaller dogs like beagles or terriers can detect an oncoming seizure and alert the victim to press the panic button for help. A well-trained service dog can detect a diabetic's needs and/or a prolonged depression."

"How do they find such smart dogs?" asked Bud, also stunned but hopeful concerning this information about dogs more than when he had first heard about computers and wondered if he should have one in the house to ease his boredom. Luckily, Lynn and I were able to change his mind on that pursuit, after telling him countless stories about computer scammers who feasted on lonely seniors who spent too much time on the internet or found other ways to victimize the elderly.

I still believe that one scam led to Dad's failing. How depressing to work for so long, spending a life of commuting during Chicago rush hour traffic for forty years and to be cheated of all that effort. No wonder he seemed so lifeless lately. Maybe a dog could work wonders. I knew how much he loved dogs and perhaps it would keep him occupied. Maybe that's why they were referred to as "service dogs." Mrs. Witzel was probably aware of all the senior citizen scams, but knew that rescue dog services were legitimate and safe foundations.

"Believe it or not, Bud, most dogs are very intelligent and are chosen from shelters for extensive training. Sites like 'Dogs for Better Lives' fosters their dogs for selective teaching. There is a Service Animal and Support Animal Registry (ESA). This all began in 1990 with the passage of the American with Disabilities Act."

Just what my dad needed – official-sounding alphabet soup. Things were sounding better by the second.

"Are these dogs housetrained?" asked a practical Lynn.

"Actually, most are. You could put up a small fenced-in area in that big backyard of yours and just open the patio door when he gives the sign, usually impatience or a few yips, that he needs to go."

"Can I walk him?" asked my getting eager father. Another door broken down.

"Sure, I don't see why not. You have a great back yard, and I'm sure you would both like a nice walk, a little exercise. Another reason that seniors have cats or dogs."

Everything seemed somewhat settled then. Some activity for an old man to keep his mind occupied and some physical activity for both of them. They were both prisoners in a way, and this living situation would, hopefully, satisfy them. It was the answer to all those rescue dog ads that we had read, "a perfect match may be waiting for you."

What Mrs. Witzel had neglected to tell us before she stoked our hopes, was the waiting list. I had assumed that there were several dogs-in-waiting. She clarified, "In fact, waits for some dogs could be a year or longer, usually 24-36 months, depending on the patient's needs. Dogs able to open refrigerator doors or other difficult tasks for people with more severe physical problems, were not easily trained or readily found. Dogs tasked with fewer physical tasks, such as those related to autism or depression should be easier to find within two years."

With all the anticipation about to implode our brains, we were resigned to play the waiting game. Not a day passed without Dad calling Lynn to see if she had heard anything. Also, he was constantly making plans for the new dog. Over the next couple months there were a few false alarms with dogs that had visited Bud in his home. Some were too big, about forty pounds, or too frisky, but that was Lynn's judgment, always acting the protector. Dad was pretty much agreeable to a few of them, but I think he would have considered a fire-breathing dragon if he could walk it and it could fit in his house and yard.

Becky and I decided to suspend our personal canine search until one was found for my father. It only seemed fair, because I did not want to show-off our new companion before he had one, so six months dragged on before we found a suitable dog for Dad.

One day Lynn called for my advice, which was silly, because she knew that I'd almost always go along with her judgment about getting a dog for Dad.

"Lar, he's only six pounds. I can't picture this dog being of much use if Dad needed real help."

"What do you mean by 'real help'? Like he wouldn't be able to dial 911 if Dad collapsed or tripped? He has one of those emergency bracelets to push in case of emergency. The dog is just there for company and to give Dad some exercise. It looks exactly like what we have been waiting for. I say jump on it, not the dog, especially if it's only six pounds."

"I knew you'd say that. They're coming for a visit next Tuesday. Could you come down, too?"

I wanted to help and knew that I had promised, but it was near the end of the school year and not an easy time to miss. Besides, there would be two adults. How tough can it be to choose a six-pound dog? I admit to being selfish at this time of my life, and not looking forward to the three-hundred-mile round-trip journey to Wheaton. Besides, what about my dog need? Like I said-selfish.

"I'd rather wait until Dad gets settled-in with the dog. See how it's going. Maybe in a few weeks. Lynn, you can tell if it's a decent match, can't you?"

Lynn was no longer my little sister in need of big brother's help. She, too, had inherited the dog-loving gene plus the twenty-four-hour-on-call care of the elderly parent.

"By the way, Lynn, what kind of service does this dog offer? Will it make Dad his usual martini at night? Does it cook, fetch the paper from the driveway?"

Long pause. "I'm not sure, but we pretty much agreed on a small companion dog, right?"

Even easier to choose then. Six pounds? "If they first meet and the killer dog goes for Dad's throat, not a good match. Then another potential problem crept into my pessimistic brain.

"How old is this dog, Lynn? We don't want him dying before Dad, or we'd have to start the process all over again." I knew as soon as I said it, that I did not phrase that properly.

"Geez, Lar, you want Dad to die before his dog does? Not too selfish."

"I didn't mean it like that, Lynn. I just don't want Dad to get up one morning and find his six-pound service dog lying dead in his slippers."

"Fine, I'll take care of it then, as usual, and you just don't worry about anything." Slam!

Little sister was pissed! And she was right. She was she only one who lived within five miles of Dad and the only one who took him shopping, to the bank, doctor, post office, etc. Lynn was the one who'd run over when our father had a minor panic attack and/or forgot something. Now we were adding another potential burden – a strange dog. Becky agreed with Lynn.

A week later Lynn called back. I apologized profusely and sincerely meant every word and emotion I could find to thank her. I vowed to do anything I could to help the transition.

I could detect an emotional reaction in her voice. "Anyway, it's done. We had to jump at the opportunity or it might have been another month's wait. So, we took the dog, and he seemed to take to his new forever home right away, like he had had practice. He jumped right on Dad's lap and began with the dog kisses. Of course, Dad was overwhelmed; I think he approached teary-eyed. Dad walked him on a leash around the back yard and all went well. The dog quickly found new water and food bowls in the kitchen, so Dad immediately rewarded him for such a discovery by giving him a small milk-bone. Did you know that they made small bones for dogs under twelve pounds?"

"I have to tell you, Lynn, I did not know that, but thanks for sharing. What kind of dog is it?"

"The paper says, 'poodle mix,' whatever that means. It has grey, curly hair, but to be honest, he's not very cute. He looks like a drowned ferret."

"Sounds like he should get along with Dad then. You mentioned a paper that declared its breed. I assume that it was just one sheet that served as a receipt for buying this mutt, a breed also known as 'Heinz 57.' In other words, he's short a few requirements to be classified as a 'show dog.'"

"Not funny. His name, at least for now, is Teddy, and he's about ten-years-old."

"Seventy in dog years. Perfect companions? Who else could they send to rescue a feeble eighty-year-old man but a seventy-year-old, six-pound poodle mix named Teddy? Like some old comedy teams: Laurel and Hardy, Martin and Lewis, Bud and Teddy. Where'd he come from? A circus where a little dog jumps from one horse's back to another horse's back?"

"The paper says that he was categorized as a 'service dog,' not a show biz dog. I don't know what that means either. You going to come down and see him soon?"

I had promised to do more to help Dad, and Lynn, actually. My pile of excuses had been exhausted, so I agreed to come the week after school ended.

Two weeks later, the best I could do, Becky and I pulled the old Malibu into Dad's driveway, ready for anything. We slowly got out of the car and cautiously walked to his side entry door, like Halloween trick-or-treaters about to enter a spook house. As usual, the door was unlocked. I pushed it open and almost fell backwards from just the heart-piercing sound of a banshee. At the same moment, I felt like I had been struck by a soft tennis lob off my shin.

"Teddy!" came the gruff yell of an old man, whose ferocity had vanished years ago.

I looked down and saw this gray ball of lint jumping up and down like a yo-yo. This had to be the new dog, unless aliens from an old Star Trek show had already landed and really liked my dad's house. Two puzzles raced through my brain: (1) could this little creature have created such a chilling shriek and (2) how long could he jump like that? Realizing that I was not being attacked by a miniature, rabid pit bull, I bent down and extended a hand in friendship, which he almost licked off. Friendly chap.

"What is that sound Lar?" asked a friendly voice from behind. I had blocked the door, and after that shrill screech, Becky had no idea what had happened, nor had she witnessed the perpetual trampoline exhibition.

"I think it was Teddy," I replied to her startled face.

Finally, my dad had captured the active nerf ball and carried it back to his spot on the couch.

Teddy was one of those dogs that was almost so ugly that he was kind of cute. The paparazzi used to write that Sophia Loren's appearance was composed of so many mismatched parts that she was considered the most beautiful woman in the world, like Teddy, but he was only six pounds, with a mouthful of rotting teeth, and legs like toothpicks, but all parts blended made him look like a drowned Chihuahua with a hint of cuteness and likeability.

Becky and I sat on the love seat opposite the two characters in question, and like a shot out of a cannon, only faster, Teddy was on my lap licking my face like I was covered with honey. Never saw him cover the eight feet between us.

"Teddy, Teddy, let them alone now. Come here," Dad cajoled. It was like the magic trick where the magician replaces his lovely assistant instantly. I wished we could have harnessed that speed. I don't know why, but somehow it seemed to be of some value.

"So that's Teddy," Becky said.

At the sound of his name, the gray flash was on Becky's lap, covering her face with small dog kisses, never her favorite demonstration of affection.

"How does he do that?" I asked Dad, hoping for some reasonable answer about his inexplicable speed, if one even existed.

"He likes anyone and everyone and wants to make friends. He's a good companion but I can't keep up with him. Luckily, I don't have to. He listens to everything and pretty much follows. Unlike my son." Not bitter but gentle humor like an eighty-year-old man might create for someone's entertainment. I didn't deserve that, but maybe he was talking about my teen years.

"Does he ever get out the front or side doors?" I asked, curious why he couldn't escape if he really wanted; it would be like catching Peter Pan's shadow.

"I walk him at least four times a day. We do two laps around the house. Takes about fifteen minutes. He's a good walker. Didn't pull too hard after the first few laps. He's a fast learner and senses the right pace, like a car responds to a gas pedal."

It looked like little Teddy might have been the right choice after all. Gets my dad to do some daily exercise, which I figured was just over a half mile, so that was one reason for Teddy's presence. And we could see the transformation in my father's attitude. He was actually smiling as he rubbed the belly of his six-pound living creature, which could pass as a stuffed animal in a toy store or a small prize at a county fair game. Teddy was enjoying his belly rub while he was panting with his little pink tongue hanging out the side of his mouth. He was glad to be there and so were we.

Dad continued giving us Teddy's credentials. "He has a hard time eating, though. I have to give him a half packet of soft food, like what cats eat. He can't eat kibble at all."

"That's odd. Think he needs dentures?" No humor appreciation.

"They thought he was about eleven years old, but no exact date. Hopefully, he'll be here longer than me."

Just what a person wants to hear from an aging parent. I did feel that Teddy would add time to my dad's life span. Right then, everything seemed more optimistic than a few months ago.

The next year went smoothly, and I was pleased when life returned to somewhat relaxed and enjoyable. I would make monthly trips to Wheaton to see Dad and his little companion. I even built a 10' x 10' wire fence enclosure, so that Dad could just let Teddy run loose for a while instead of always taking him on a leash, especially during bad weather. The snooty neighbor thought it was an ugly attachment to the house and that it would decrease property values for the entire neighborhood, but too bad, no building laws were violated

Becky sometimes went with me, but often I went alone to do the "manly" chores, so that Lynn could take a break and avoid complete burnout. Leaves got raked, grass got cut more often, storm windows got exchanged according to season, some rooms were painted, and minor repairs were completed, which often entailed several trips to the local hardware store, where workers got to know me by my first name as they educated me in the installation of a window shade, stopping a minor drip, and disguising some rather dark and chipped grout. As an English teacher I became more educated about real life than the surnames of Romeo and Juliet.

One weekend I was eager to get to Dad's because my weekly Wednesday call presented an interesting puzzle. I checked every Wednesday to see how he was and if I should bring any special tools, with me.

Calmly, he said, "I've got roosters in the house."

"Roosters in the house? Not likely, Dad."

"Yeah, they crow every day at 5:42. I've called the police, the telephone company, and the elderly assistance office of DuPage County."

I knew he wasn't kidding, which was really quite scary. "Didn't they suggest anything? Neighbors or tricksters? Ghosts of chickens past? You always did like chicken. Maybe it's the ancestors of all that fowl."

"No," still calm and ignoring any sarcasm I often used. "They're in the house. The telephone company sent a repairman, but after a half hour of checking phones and the power line, he couldn't find anything. Just said that he was sorry."

With working hours and a long drive, Becky and I weren't able to get there by 5:42 on Friday, the chickening hour, so we anxiously had to await another day before the demon roosters would dare to appear again.

Teddy was still as spry as ever and really enjoyed his walks.

"Where did he get the name 'Teddy' from?" I asked.

"He just came with it. The people said I could name him anything I wanted, that dogs adapt easily, but I decided just to keep the name he was used to. He's probably almost twelve plus years old now, and I don't think I could respond so quickly if you started calling me 'Ralph.'"

Tension built as it neared 5:42. We had no idea what to expect, except that there would be something. Dad didn't usually make up stories. One Sunday I called him and he said, "I'm not as pretty as I used to be. My two front teeth fell out."

"What do you mean that they fell out?" I asked as though I needed clarification on that simple sentence. Actually, it had taken him a long time to tell me that he was eating popcorn and the teeth had taken leave, as though to say to each other, "This is boring. We're out of here."

That incident led to the rest of his teeth being pulled and replaced with dentures, so any time Dad sounded like it was time to commit him because he made some outlandish statement, it turned out to contain at least a kernel of truth.

We awaited the last fifteen minutes in silence, except for Teddy, who hopped from lap to lap as though announcing, "Isn't this nice? Family bonding-time. We should do this every day."

Five, four, three, two one, "Cock a doodle doo!"

Becky and I immediately jumped up and raced towards the back room. I had converted a third bedroom to Dad's TV and reading room, with access to Teddy's back yard pen. There was no way . . . Not sure how long the rooster would crow, and not wanting to wait another day for a repeat performance, Becky and I almost knocked over each other while trashing the place. We could still hear the inexplicable morning farmyard animal of sunrise almost daring us to find it. It was exactly 5:42 p.m.

"It's behind the daybed," Becky pointed, not feeling silly in the least.

She was right, but I couldn't resist asking, "Do you really think there's a rooster back there?"

She looked at me like I was really obtuse, and wasn't sure that it was a wise decision to leave behind all those Iowa farm boys. "No, dummy, but that's where the sound is."

Then it quit. Dead silence except for the unspoken sarcasm in the air.

"Well, was I right?" asked my dad, smiling and holding an oblivious Teddy.

I shook my head in disbelief. "Yeah, I heard roosters. Now let's find 'em."

Forcefully, I removed the daybed's mattress, and I uncovered a treasure that only a six-year-old boy could appreciate – coins, comb, keys, golf pencils, crumbs, wrappers and some oddly shaped red plastic object. Upon closer inspection we could see that it was in the shape of a rooster with perforated holes serving as speakers, in the center. On the other side was a yellow decal thanking the owner for his contribution to the Hearing Health Foundation in New York. It was a rooster alarm clock that could be placed bedside or even "under your pillow." For some random reason it had been set for 5:42.

My father gave away too much money to causes that he thought might be worth his efforts, not yet aware about all the senior citizen scams. He still trusted people and gave away almost five hundred dollars a year to various causes, which, of course, sold his name to countless other charities; indeed, some honest, many not. Include a picture of a dog or other animal, and it earned a guaranteed donation. He had more notepads and calendars than Barnes & Noble.

Unfortunately he had already been swindled by one of the widest spread and most "successful" con games of the decade – the Canadian lottery. It only took one random mailing to his home, among twenty he received every day so that the mailman would often bind them with a rubber band to fit them all into Dad's mailbox. One official-looking piece of junk mail arrived and Dad was a goner. One piece of trash was soon followed by a phone call from a smooth talker who called himself Bob Stephenson, a safe-sounding white Anglo-Saxon name, despite the thick accent (Middle Eastern, Latino, Asian, etc.) Once the caller had made sure that Dad had received his mailing, friendly Bob would call weekly to check on his health and to give his sympathies on the death of his wife, Doris, who had died thirty years ago. My father was grateful for any outsider who seemed to care.

One day Bob told Dad that he had some good news, of which he should have final details the following week, which really sunk the hook. Sure enough, two days later a FedEx truck pulled into his driveway with a thick envelope, for which Dad had to sign. Inside was an official "Winners' Certification" letter, complete with a "real" Canadian Congressional seal on top. The old World War II veteran had finally had some financial good luck. Praise Be!

That same day, coincidentally, Dad got a call from Bob Stephenson, who wanted to extend his congratulations. There was just one minor obstacle: Dad had to pay fifteen thousand U.S. dollars total to release the money from the foundation, which included processing fees, Canadian taxes, etc. Please send it in the form of a certified check and use the enclosed postage-paid envelope.

Within the hour, he had called Lynn to take him the next day to the bank and to the post office. Standard procedure. He had planned on surprising Lynn after he got the money and had arranged for it to go toward his kids' generous inheritance. We never did learn how much Dad had "won," but according to Bob, it was in the seven figures. As frustrating as it sounds, he truly believed that he did it for his children. Neither Lynn nor I could be outwardly upset at him, but I seriously pondered the odds of hiring a hit man to kill Bob Stephenson. My father used to clip ten cent coupons to help him afford buying Chips Ahoy cookies, and then he gave away most of his savings to some conman who was hiding in Canada, gloating about his immoral exploits.

When my dad died, he was down to forty thousand dollars, not much for a long-devoted career and retirement. I wondered if he had had a dog, if his loneliness would not have left him as receptive to be victimized. How depressing to work for so long, spending a life of commuting during Chicago rush hour traffic for forty years and to be cheated of all that effort. Of course, once we finally went to the police, we learned more and became enraged at how wide-spread the scam was and how rarely anyone was actually caught.

Once we had exorcised the chickens from my dad's home and had a short visit, we left and instructed him not to tell anyone about the fowl incident. During the days we stayed, Teddy always followed his "best friend" (as my dad had titled him) wherever he went. At night he would go to bed when Dad did--8:00, early even for two beings whose combined ages totaled to about 150 years. Around ten though, Teddy would come back out and join Becky and me in the living room to watch the Channel Seven local news. He usually jumped on Becky's lap first, learning the routine that she would go to bed right after the news, so that just he and I could watch late night talk shows or movies. It was a bonding time for us; like I've said all dogs seemed to like me.

"We have to do something with this dog's breath, Lar. It smells like a sewer." Of course, Teddy sneaked in a few quick dog kisses, something she really did not appreciate, especially from Sewer Breath, a name with which she instantly christened the poor six-pound poodle-mix.

"I wouldn't worry. I doubt if he'll be dating anything, soon."

"No, but it may be a sign that there is another health issue somewhere. Besides, you don't know when he might catch the eye of some bitch."

After that parting shot at humor, Becky retired for the night, and I fully reclined on the couch, Teddy snuggled against my stomach with me rubbing his belly, and we watched "The Tonight Show." Becky was right though; he did have horrid sewer breath, and I wasn't sure of the cause. Did he eat the wrong food? Was he rotting from the inside?

Six months later we discovered the cause, but we paid a price. Dad had experienced a series of minor strokes, called TIA's, and he was going to spend an unknown amount of time in a senior rehab center for a complete physical and rehabilitation program.

One night I got a call from sister Lynn. "Larry, I have two cats now and the only time they met Teddy, they got along like cats and dogs. Could you take Teddy for a week?" Like there was any choice. The logistics did not quite work well. Although we had postponed the search for our own dog for a while, getting Teddy to Madison was a major challenge. My mind raced like a motorized rolodex.

Would Greyhound take a dog as a passenger? I'd pay full adult fare for a six-pound mutt. Amtrak? No. Hitchhike? Too short, no thumbs. All three of us had jobs and would have a difficult time making the four-hour round-trip journey. But on a Saturday we could each drive two hours to Rockford and make a clean hand-off. According to local news, drug dealers did it all the time. So, Lynn and I agreed to meet at the Best Western parking lot in Rockford, about half way for both of us.

I waited outside my car for Lynn's Bonneville to pull in and to accept my six-pound ball of responsibility. She parked next to me and immediately reached to the floor and found the ready-to-go package, including leash, soft dog treats, foil packets of food and a few special toys. It was like packing a sixth-grader off to summer camp for at least two months. Teddy jumped right into my arms, happy to see me, I think. Maybe he thought I was my dad. We did resemble each other; could dogs tell the difference?

After exchanging small talk, Lynn drove off to retrace the path she had just taken. Teddy really did not seem concerned, even after I had passed him to an awaiting Becky in the car. No turning back, but I think he was aware of that. He sat on her lap almost the entire seventy-mile trip back to Madison.

"He's still got sewer breath, Lar. And look at those nails. They almost completely form a whole circle. Guess he's been neglected for a while," Becky said sympathetically as she rubbed his skinny neck.

"That doesn't look good. My dad was probably busy and simply started to forget details. But I thought that the people at the groomer's would have noticed that Teddy was due and just do it." I always tried to deflect blame from my dog-loving father to anyone else.

"I never had much confidence in those groomers, especially after they gave us the wrong dog that one time." Teddy's usual groomer was located on a corner in downtown Wheaton. It seemed to follow that cutesy tradition of making puns for their establishment, like the Barking Lot, Lori's Pet Agree, of the Dog Haus (dogs of German pedigree only, I guess.) On one of our four trips to Wheaton, we brought in Teddy for his 10:00 appointment and were told to pick him up at 2:00. We returned and asked for Teddy. The counter girl, Amber, went to the back room and brought out a beautiful malamute and handed me the leash. No hesitation; my father had always prepaid for services.

"That's not Teddy," I barked.

She tilted her head to check the dog. "Are you sure?" as if I should rethink my statement.

The malamute was a real dog – blue eyes, athletic body and an intelligent demeanor. I briefly wondered if Dad would notice the change. This could be a major breed upgrade.

"Of course, we'd know our own dog!" Becky shattered my reverie. I couldn't have done it anyway. The real owners would have searched the earth to rectify the idiotic mistake. Poor Amber!

After Amber retrieved the right dog, she made an immediate return to the back room, I assume to hide and to avoid the need to apologize for her error, somehow trying to blame us. She's probably a Congresswoman now.

Back to reality and time to take control of this dog's future. "Teddy's going to be living with us for a while. Let's see if Dr. Erickson will take a look at the little guy's general health. Maybe he can tell what those quacks in Wheaton did or didn't do."

A quick and desperate-sounding call led to a 3:00 appointment for the next day. Dr. Erickson had been my go-to vet, until he finally retired to teach at the university level. At the time he saw Teddy, the good veterinarian had only taken care of Dickens in his last stages, and that dog seemed to require more care than the average dog. It was Dr. Erickson who made me come to grips with the reality that I was probably prolonging Dicken's suffering. His honesty earned my trust for my other two dogs, and still counting.

I had put Teddy on the examination table and was rubbing his neck when Dr. Erickson knocked and entered the room. I never understood why vets always knocked before entering, but I guess it just seemed proper manners when going through a closed door. Vet training 101? He immediately walked to the table and put out the back of his hand so that Teddy could sniff it.

"So, where did this little guy come from?" he asked in his usual soothing voice. I swear that he could calm an asylum full of rabid beasts with just a few words.

Becky and I together covered the whole story and explained Teddy's history. Dr. Erickson listened attentively as he pulled back Teddy's lips and looked at his teeth. Probably already knowing the answer, he still asked, "Does Teddy eat much? Kibble, Milk Bones, treats in general?"

"Not really. He only seems to like a soft food, some stuff in foil packages that my dad gets him. I don't ever remember seeing Teddy eat any hard treats."

Without pause of thought, he said softly but firmly, "I suspect that he's in too much pain to fully bite much. Even when he's not eating, I'm sure that there is constant pain, but like so many dogs, he has been able to adapt to his life changes. If only dogs could talk."

Beck and I looked at each other with sharp memories of the last "he's-in-pain" talks concerning Dickens.

The wife took the helm," So what are you suggesting, doctor? That it may be less painful and that it might be best that he be put down?"

"Oh no, not at all. Other than his teeth, his health seems good. It would be a very simple procedure to extract all those tiny, rotted teeth. He's probably swallowed some of them. He would feel much better without them. Trust me."

"How will he function with no teeth?" I asked, trying to absorb the good/bad news.

"He'll be fine. Keep feeding him the soft food, maybe with some table scraps as a special treat, and some soft treats – no milk bones, which are often encouraged to help keep the dog's teeth clean." The doctor offered Teddy a bit of liver-flavored something, which Teddy took but soon dropped. I'm still betting that the little dog rejected the offering because he had more sense than to take anything liver-flavored, especially from a stranger.

"Did you want to talk to your father first? I think Teddy will go home as a happier, livelier dog. And the procedure is very simple, especially considering the size and condition of his teeth."

Becky answered immediately. "How soon can it be done?" Not that it mattered when, because she had already decided.

"We do surgeries on Tuesdays and Thursday. We should be able to work him into the schedule this coming Tuesday. Is that enough time?"

"Yes, that's fine," Becky snapped before I reacted. "The poor thing doesn't need to suffer any longer." I thought that I don't want to let her choose if they should pull the plug on me. She's too quick.

He nodded as he picked-up Teddy's front paw. "Speaking of suffering, it looks like he hasn't had these nails cut in a long time. They've actually grown around into a circle. How does he even walk without pain? Like I said before, I wish dogs could talk. We can take care of that right now, if you'd like."

"That would be great; maybe he'll get some relief," she continued. Apparently, I was just along for the ride.

Dr. Erickson picked-up the fearless, six-pound mutt and carried him through the swinging door to an unknown, mysterious back room, where pet owners were not allowed to go. Becky and I sat in the examination room, staring at each other and various posters advertising dog pharmaceutical products, wondering if we had overstepped our responsibility of "watching Teddy." With no mixed signals we seemed to agree, so there was no need to speak.

Five minutes later, or was it five hours later, Dr. Erickson reemerged with a squirming little dust mop in his right hand. "Everything went well. No more circles, just ordinary canine nails. He seemed eager to get on the floor to test his new paws, kind of like a person getting new shoes that just hadn't quite fit right. I made an appointment for Teddy next Tuesday for his teeth at 8:00 a.m. Is that okay?"

We smiled as we went to the table to see Teddy, who honestly seemed like a happier dog. We had been concentrating so much on his bad breath that we completely ignored his nails. Teddy was jumping to get into our arms as he extended all twenty-two inches of his body.

"That's fine doctor. Thanks so much. Otherwise, does he honestly seem healthy?"

"Good heart, good coat, eyes, and ears are fine. Once we get those teeth out, he'll be like a new puppy, only older and slower. Will you be ready?"

"We hope so. Have to see if my dad's ready." A topic I had pretty much blocked from my mind. My dad had a hospital full of trained adults to take care of him, but Becky and I were the only ones taking care of this speechless, little beast, but would we be the ones able to cope with a "new puppy?"

Teddy passed the next few days enjoying all this newly found attention, never leaving our sides. We put an old dog bed in our room, but he definitely preferred sharing our king bed, and he must have really felt the security as he snuggled between us, somehow managing to touch us both at the same time. You'd have thought he was Marmaduke.

Tuesday morning the vet's office was ready, and they immediately whisked Teddy to the clinic's mysterious enclave. I don't think Teddy had a clue about what was about to happen, unless he remembered the great relief that swept over him the last time he was there. He trusted everyone. Who would hurt him?

"Teddy should be ready to go home in about three or four hours. Have to let the anesthetic wear off," Dr. Erickson said, leaving us numb, as the "boy-is-this-moving-fast" instructions whirled in our heads.

We decided to have lunch at the Oakcrest, one of our favorite burger and a pitcher bars. So, we were mellow by the time we returned to retrieve Teddy, wondering what condition he was in. Surprise! He charged out and into our kneeling selves like he hadn't just had every tooth in his tiny mouth yanked out.

"He probably feels less pain, but don't give him anything to eat until this evening. Otherwise, I think he'll be just fine. Would you like the teeth as a souvenir?" the doctor asked like it was routine.

"Huh? No. Why?" I responded like someone who had never heard of such a thing, which I hadn't.

'Some people save them. Some have had necklaces, cuff links, or other pieces of jewelry made from them. Sentimental memory."

Becky fielded that question. "That is gross! No, thank you." Honest reaction, no attempt to cover her repulsion.

When we got home, Teddy drank his water bowl dry, then crawled over to his bed, where he slept for the next three hours. He was so motionless that we had to check to see if he was still breathing. Occasionally he would give one of those canine leg spasms, that I had always assumed were caused by dreams of a running dog. Good sign.

Teddy fully recovered and time passed slowly as the three of us waited for word of my dad's hospital release in Wheaton. Teddy seemed to adjust all right to Madison, not fully aware of what was happening to Bud, but for us humans, there existed a constant aura of dread. We would call my dad and sister Lynn about every third day to give them a positive update on Teddy, which was usually in response to the first question out of my father's mouth. Our reports usually made him feel better after being parted from his best friend for so long. Dad had been in the hospital for almost two months, an eternity at his age without the companionship of his current favorite dog.

Finally, Becky got the idea to try to arrange a visit to the hospital for Teddy and his master. "NO DOGS ALLOWED," was God's edict. The longer he was hospitalized the more dread seemed to seep into us. We got the sense that Dad may never return to his house. We continuously called the hospital and talked to anyone who might help us arrange a human/dog visit. Breaking Al Capone out of Alcatraz would have been easier than smuggling a six-pound mutt in my pocket. Finally, Nikki, one of the night nurses and a real dog lover, had talked to Dad and listened to the dilemma. She had a sympathetic ear and pondered a plan for a brief visit after hours. She didn't have to, maybe even risking her job, but that's what nurses do.

So we all made the journey to Wheaton and stayed with my sister, awaiting the night of the big caper. One cold Tuesday night in November, as though we were waiting for a signal to rob a bank, Becky, Teddy, and I, hid in the shadows of hospital door #6 at the Homeside Elderly Care Facility, until the door opened and Nurse Nikki waved us all in. We furtively entered the institution. Sitting in a wheel chair twenty feet in front of us was an old man we hardly recognized. We had seen him before on short visits, but he had lost even more weight and had shadows where his skin drooped.

"Teddy," he called, arms extended.

Not expecting much of a reaction after such a long separation, I wasn't ready for a little dog to escape my clutches, and almost float across the shiny polished floor without missing a single step, even when he jumped up and into the arms of his missing best friend. Teddy cried and kissed every available inch of the man who had given him so much joy, and vice versa.

"I didn't think I would ever see you again, my best friend," Dad managed to say through copious tears. Such love between an eighty-nine-year-old man and a little gray mutt. Through my own tears, I saw Becky crying, and even Nurse Nikki, who could see no harm in her felonious action. Damn the risk! Now what? We couldn't leave the dog nor could we smuggle out my father. Maybe a short visit was not the best idea. Hate them or not, most regulations have a logical purpose.

Nurse Nikki could also sense that this meeting may not end so well. "Let's hide in this back visitors' room. Nobody else should be there this late." Sounded like she may have done this before. We rolled Dad, clinging to Teddy, into a typical lounge furnished with standard vinyl-covered sofa, love seat, table and chair ensemble, the standard TV set, and a couple vending machines. This arrangement abruptly ended when Teddy decided to jump to the floor and pee on the leg of the corner magazine table. He left a large puddle for a little dog with such a small tank. I immediately grabbed a handful on napkins to absorb the mess. In the morning maintenance people would probably assume the wad of urine-soaked paper towels were caused by a patient's incontinence. Teddy immediately returned to Dad's lap but paused with the barrage of dog kisses. Did he expect to return home to the days of walks and watching-out for his best bud and most recent owner, and probably the best?

Nurse Nikki stood guard at the lounge doorway while we chatted and watched Dad check Teddy's gums without teeth. I couldn't help but remember the day I called Dad and he had told me that he wasn't as pretty as he used to be when his two front teeth had fallen out. Did he mentally send a sympathy message to the dog? They had even started to look like each other.

Odd as it may seem, Teddy soon grew restless and wanted to explore other areas of the lounge. Nurse Nikki barely blocked his exit in time, or who knows how far Teddy would have gone? Like an old Keystone Kops movie, that would have been quite the scene with so many panicked individuals in a chaotic chase down hospital corridors to capture a fleeing small dog. I took this as a portent that perhaps we should leave before we got caught and a few people were in trouble.

I swept up the living dust mop and returned him to Dad's lap, as I tried to explain our quick departure. He understood but was sad to see his little buddy leave. He scratched Teddy's neck with a tearful, "See you later, Teddy. Be a good dog for Larry now," as though he knew that he would never see Teddy again, and he was right. As we left the parking lot, Teddy kept looking back at the door we had just gone through, as though wondering if we had forgotten someone, or why else did we all go there?

So, Teddy permanently moved back to Madison for an unpredictable amount of time, but it turned out to be the rest of his life. When we left the next day, the poor dog seemed disheartened that something was permanently missing from his life wondering why Becky and I had made the long car trip back to Madison without Bud. It was too soon after seeing his best friend and we were going far away. It took a while for him to adjust again to his somewhat familiar routines and places, but he always appreciated the special attention and affection he received.

Many people on our walk commented about how cute he was and often bent down to pat the dog as though they did not know that dogs came in such "fun sizes," like a Halloween candy bar. With Teddy's tongue constantly hanging out the side of his mouth since he no longer had teeth to contain them, everyone assumed that he was smiling and must be a happy dog.

Unfortunately, it was difficult to make any more hospital sneak visits. I would have felt too guilty to impose upon Nurse Nikki's initial kindness, and there did not seem to be anyone else with such a generous heart. So, there were no physical visits from Teddy, just hospital talks from me and/or Becky and telephone calls from home about Teddy's health and activities.

Finally, one bitter day in February of 2006, my father passed away before ever returning to his home. I can't say that Teddy experienced some mysterious convulsion or anything supernatural at the time of my father's death, but he was never quite the same dog that had been living with Dad in the old house with the big back yard and several daily walks, and never tiring of his life with his BFF.

Deciding to leave Teddy at home with a former student, who often house/dog sat during our vacation trips, Becky and I spent a week in Wheaton for the funeral and some of the practical business aspects involving Dad's estate. We were surprised that Dad had planned on being cremated, then having his own urn buried on top of my mother's coffin in Wheaton Cemetery. I had no idea that such a procedure was legal or possible. It creeped me out, but they had had a good marriage, so I felt that if there was an after-life, Dad had a good plan.

The funeral was extremely awkward. Becky, sister Lynn and I were the only people attending, and the cemetery had prepared a space for the urn ready to be interred. Dad qualified for a military headstone set at the other end of the grave opposite my mother's tombstone, so they were truly together for eternity. R.I.P.

Teddy lived with us for another two years. He seemed reasonably happy, though his little legs could no longer propel him up to the king bed anymore. Occasionally, he would try to make the high leap, but more than half the time he crashed to the floor. Good thing he was small and never got seriously hurt. His last few months he simply welcomed his dog bed on the floor in order to be near us.

One cold January afternoon I killed Teddy. Not on purpose, of course, but my volatile temper took over my head, and I made an angry *fait accompli* that still haunts me. I don't recall what had caused the generally rotten day that dispelled my sanity, whether I had lost something, argued with someone over a forgotten conflict, or some trite incident that created my toxic attitude.

In an attempt to "forget my sorrows," I thought that going to a matinee movie would help. It was my standard escape. There was a film (I forget which one, but it had a striking British cast) starting at the nearby Hilldale shopping mall cinema, with the first showing in about fifteen minutes at 1:45. It was a short ten-minute drive plus fifteen more minutes for the usual repetitive previews, almost creating a double feature for cinephiles.

I felt it best to let Teddy outside to do his business in the back yard, but I'd only be gone for two hours, so no big worries. Teddy went out, sniffed the frigid air, and immediately returned to the warm house. No "business" done, but I left anyway.

Inexplicably, there were no previews that day, but I was still going to sulk and pursue my favorite escape. If only I had gone home, Teddy would have lived a little longer, maybe years.

Still in a foul mood, I returned from the movie, which I could not recall at all – plot, stars, music, thumbs up or thumbs down, etc. I entered through our garage door to the lower level of our bi-level home. Teddy was waiting seven steps up in the foyer and raced down in joyful greeting, as do most dogs when the master, or almost anyone returns. I immediately led him to the back door and let him outside where he usually made his usual dash to the back fence, but not seeing his neighbor dog on the other side, Teddy barked once in futile greeting, then raced back to the house, anticipating tug toys and treats. As we started up the stairs, my eyes caught a pile of dog poop on the hallway carpet going down the lower-level hallway.

That was the moment I lost my mind. He was such a small dog that I could have picked-up his mess in seconds, but unfortunately, I had reached my theoretical boiling point for the day.

"Teddy, what is this? I let you out right before I left!" I shouted, like he was deaf and not a dog. "That's a bad dog!" Besides my unreasonable angry shouts, I stomped my foot on the floor for emphasis.

Teddy rarely, if ever, had seen me in such an insane state, and at the sound and gestures of my theatrics, he turned and raced up the stairs, away from the unknown demon that was terrorizing him. I heard him lose his footing and trip on the top stair and expected to see a little gray body come tumbling down the steps, but he somehow kept going. Adrenaline? After the required thirty-second cleanup, I continued my stomping routine up the stairs to let him know that I was still angry. I could hear him running down the upstairs hallway to our bedroom, where he clawed his way under the bed for shelter.

I went to the kitchen and open a beer, normal routine for late afternoon. I plopped into my reclining chair and turned on some senseless television. Usually, I waited for Teddy to jump up with me, because his age had diminished his jumping ability, so I sometimes just picked him up. I was already reclined and reading the morning paper. Around the side of the chair, I could see a timid gray figure slowly inching closer to me, wondering if I had been exorcised or was still possessed.

Possessed. I saw him about to try to leap up to the recliner's foot rest.

"Teddy, no! You're a bad dog," I screamed. I hadn't cooled, but I began to think about the idiocy of my irrational behavior.

In mid-air, trying to make a jump which was too difficult at his advancing age, he became startled at my angry shout and lost concentration. He fell short of the footrest and hit his throat on the edge. He crashed onto his back, and I quickly transformed back into a human. I picked him up and held him on my lap, trying to calm him by petting his head and back while profusely apologizing. He was still confused about what was happening and he jumped back to the floor, where he started coughing like he had a bone stuck in his throat. I carried him to his water bowl, which seemed to alleviate some of the hacking, but not for long.

He stumbled back to the living room and settled into his daytime dog bed, where he proceeded to cough, his little head resting on the cushioned edge. I lay on the ground next to him and scratched his head while apologizing in soft tones to let him know that everything was back to normal, like it should be. But it wasn't and never would be.

Becky got home around six and asked me what was happening as she saw the odd tableau. With tearful guilt I hastily explained that I had gotten mad at Teddy and yelled and stomped my foot, causing the terrified dog to race away and that he had stumbled on the stairs and may have hit his throat on the top step or it may have happened when he had tried to jump onto the reclining chair.

She could see and hear that Teddy was struggling. Instead of accusing me of being an idiot and acting like an asylum inmate, she knew that I would give anything not to have had anything happen.

"Let's get him to vet," she wisely took charge. "It's after six, but there's a 24-hour emergency clinic on Gammon Road that's open 24/7."

Just when I felt helpless, Becky extended a spark of hope. Fifteen minutes later we walked through the clinic doors. I carried Teddy, not wanting to put the usual choke chain around his neck. In my mind, at least, I didn't think that Teddy was hacking as much during the short car ride. Maybe it had something to do with Becky's calming presence and Teddy feeling safe if I was holding him. Ironic, I thought, but I figured that he still trusted me and that I wouldn't let anything else happen to him. Maybe the car ride was exciting and kept his mind off the constant suffocating and striving to find his next breath. Maybe it was wishful thinking, but I could have developed scenarios all night as long as Teddy kept breathing.

"What can we do for you?" asked an all-business voice with no empathy from behind the counter.

"I think my dog Teddy fell and hit his throat on a step or on the footrest of a reclining chair. He's been hacking for a couple hours now."

"Has he had anything to drink?"

Becky and I looked at each other in search of an answer. "We honestly don't know."

The desk attendant, who could have passed for an understudy in the play Grease, must have had the feeling that she probably got all the useful information and would be able to repeat to the vet what we had just said. It seems that he must have been close and listening. A Doogie Howser aged "man" came out of the backroom. He was dressed in a white professional coat, and I prayed that he was just there to carry the patient to the real doctor.

"I'm Doctor Hudson, Let's take Teddy to the examination room and see if we can help." Good manners but he did not exude confidence. I would have thought that an emergency clinic would have had its best, most experienced doctor on duty. But maybe it was just the opposite. Last hired, last choice. I could only hope that Doctor Hudson was the first option. I started to follow him, but was stopped.

"I'll take him, Mr. Ehrhorn. Sometimes pets get too excited when their owners are near. We'll be fine." I would have thought the opposite would be true. Shouldn't owners have a reassuring effect on their pets?

I reluctantly surrendered Teddy to this high school prom king and watched them disappear. Teddy did not seem to struggle, but at the hand-off I could see that he was hacking again.

Stunned into silence we took a seat in the cavernous waiting room. Never did understand why they had such high ceilings. Birds, maybe?

"Mr. Ehrhorn, I have a couple survey questions for you," said the prom queen from behind her desk. Too soon for any news, but I still strode hopefully up to the desk. She gave me a clipboard with the required paperwork for me to fill. As requested, I returned it to her after I had hastily given my life's information to an adolescent stranger.

"And how will you be paying for this?" was the first and most important question, which raised my temperature and blood pressure considerably.

"Money," I replied as though I had been hit on the head with a large mallet, wishing she would go away. What about my dog?

Not missing a beat. "I mean would that be cash, check or credit card?" I forgot that my anger was the reason that we were there. Agatha Christie could have written a great novel titled <u>Murder in the Veterinarian's Office</u>, in which I would have been set free due to extenuating circumstances.

Time to be practical. "That depends on the size of the bill."

She feigned a look at her computer screen, as though she had no ball park figure of what today's robbery charges would be, if they were able to save Teddy.

"It should be about 225 dollars for this evening," she responded coolly, as though quoting a price for an expensive dinner.

I had often heard the term "whore-house prices" before, and at that moment I understood the actual meaning. I understood that we had been there twenty minutes, including a ten-minute visit with Doogie.

"Fifty dollars for the office call and one seventy-five for professional services."

"So, does that mean that Teddy is okay now?" I held onto hope. What's money? I just wanted my dog back.

"I don't know. You'll have to discuss that with Doctor Hudson." So we sat for another ten minutes before the "vet" carried back Teddy, still complete with cough.

"I'm sorry Mr. Ehrhorn, but I couldn't really feel anything that would be causing his cough. I thought that a stick or some other foreign object might have been partially ingested, but there was nothing visible. Your best bet from here is to take him to your regular vet in the morning. They'll have better and more advanced equipment, x-rays for example."

"Do you mean that you don't have an x-ray machine and that you could not even take an x-ray now?" I asked as viciously and rudely as possible.

"Well, no. We are just an emergency service -- broken bones, animal fights, odd behaviors. We could hardly set-up a complete hospital or clinic."

Thank God, Becky stepped in because I was about to propose an Agatha Christie sequel – <u>Slaughter In the Veterinarian's Waiting Room</u>, and I would still be exonerated.

"Why did we just get billed for two hundred, twenty-five dollars?" she challenged. The prom royalty was ready to handle this problem, probably normal reaction from other extorted couples.

Dr. Hudson quickly turned into the CEO of a one-star emergency vet clinic.

"Office call is standard. We do have to keep the lights on and pay taxes, just like you. The rest is for my professional services. Even though I could not find anything, I still did my best using my veterinarian skills."

Becky and I looked at each other in astonishment.

"Send us the bill," I shouted as I grabbed Teddy and the three of us raced out the door without paying and before the SWAT team was called. I looked back, almost challenging them to come and try to take Teddy. Several weeks later we did receive a bill, but I wrote "Take us to small claims court you incompetent morons" on the bill, and we never heard another word.

We drove home in silence, except for Teddy's intermittent coughs. Maybe all the activity had dislodged something and he was getting better. I carried Teddy into the kitchen and gently placed him next to his water bowl again. He sniffed it but had no interest in drinking.

Beck and I went into the living room to sulk and hope that the night would pass uneventfully. Teddy came in and tried to jump onto the recliner's footrest like he usually had, but he was hesitant and quit after a few feints. I simply reached down and scooped him up in one hand and settled him on the blanket already on my lap. Why hadn't I done that a few hours ago? Reaching down was such a simple thing to do.

I stroked his side and kept a close eye on his mouth, from which a cough emerged about every ten seconds. Stroking him gently, I prayed that he would make it through the night. Maybe Dr. Erickson could save his little life.

"You're the worst dog I've ever had, Teddy," I said, not realizing that they would be the last words he would ever hear.

We sat and watched the brave little service dog trying to breath. Gradually, with a final labored breath, he went still and despite prayers and denials, there was no further movement. I looked at Becky to tell her, but I could see that she was watching and felt as helpless as I did.

"We tried, Lar. Nothing else we could have done," she cried.

"It shouldn't have happened in the first place," I responded angrily, really at myself.

"It's not really your fault. Every day dogs get hit by cars or are mauled by other larger animals or simply die of old age."

I knew that she felt awful, but inside I took full responsibility, and I would never get over my own angry selfishness.

I pondered my next move. "I'm going to sleep on the sofa bed tonight with Teddy." I just wanted to be alone with my dog.

"Okay," Becky replied with full understanding and sympathy.

So, we all went to bed with Teddy on my left side. I guess I hoped that some miracle would start Teddy breathing during the night and I didn't want to chance missing it. Throughout the night I kept trying to detect breath. By sunrise, there still was no hope.

Dr. Erickson readily agreed to see us the next morning, and the three of us solemnly entered his office with Teddy's body wrapped in his favorite blanket. Other pet owners could not see what we were carrying, but I knew that they all sensed tragedy, as they averted their quick glances.

I put his body on the table of examination room #3, Teddy's usual room, and Teddy's little pink tongue was still hanging out the side of his mouth, just like in life. We started to weep again, and Dr. Erickson asked if he could take away Teddy. First, he asked if we would like some more alone time with Teddy. Becky and I said our farewells to that little dog that had probably given some comfort to who knew how many other people. And he was gone forever.

The next day we were notified that Dr. Erickson, for some reason, wanted to know if we wanted him to perform an autopsy, which wasn't needed, but it was Teddy. He called the next week and he confirmed that Teddy had died of asphyxiation from a crushed trachea. He assured us that many dogs of Teddy's size passed away the same way, because their windpipe was so thin and fragile, especially in an older dog. Could have happened by falling in the back yard or trying to jump into a car. It was just Teddy's time. Of course, he said all that for my sake, knowing that I was probably suffering from irredeemable guilt.

"Teddy had lived a good life and done so much for other people. He was a proud, service dog and his life had been spent helping others, no matter how small he was. People should be able to live as fully as Teddy had," the doctor said.

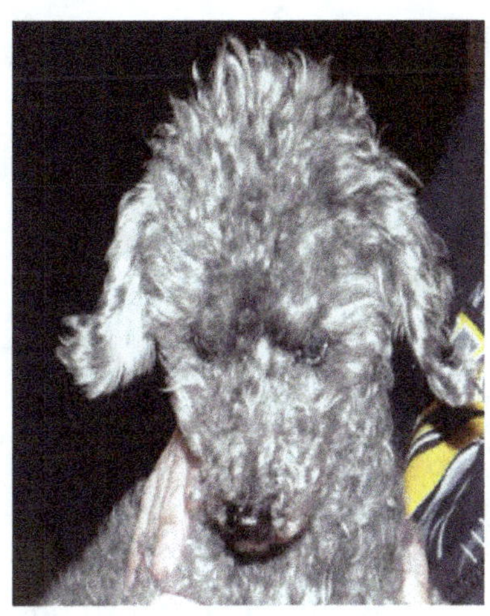

Teddy at home

Teddy ready for school

Chapter 10
I May Be Small But. . .

"Dogs are always good and full of selfless love. They are undiluted vessels of joys who never, ever deserve anything bad that happens to them." Steven Rowley, writer/screenwriter

I was born into a world of darkness with only my mother and littermates for comfort and guidance. I saw a little more of my world each day and eventually was able to see my complete family and my surroundings. We were all small and seemed to center on the mother, who was very protective of all of us and would break up the occasional spat when one pup tried to take another pup's food or chew thing. Most of our early days were spent in a small wooden pen with a hard floor, water, and food bowls for each of us, and only one door in and out, but we were comfortable; there wasn't much to do when you can barely see and have rather limited knowledge or skills.

One day we all went to a wonderful, soft, and cool ground, not at all like the hard surface in our dim room. It felt free, so we all began

161

instinctively to run and jump and nip at each other. There were walls on all sides of us, too big to look over, but with a large open sky. Before long we were all tired and ready to rest. One by one a big woman picked us up, put our faces to her face, nose to snout, and said the same thing to each pup. In my case she said "Scruffy," and put me back in our new bigger room and sleeping place, which was very welcoming.

This happened every day for a while – outside, playtime, picked up to nose level and told "Scruffy," until one day when we were all playing, and the big woman yelled, "Scruffy!" I picked-up my head at the sound and started to run towards her with my littermates following closely. I got to her first and was given a small bit of something soft and chewy that was different and tasted good. No one else got any.

The next day almost the same thing happened, only she yelled, "Dustball," and another pup got a head start and received the same prize that I had gotten. The next day I heard, "Scruffy" again, so I immediately raced to the woman, where I was given another tasty "treat" as she called it. The others got nothing.

This activity became fun, but after a time I wasn't chosen at all. Silver, Queenie, and Rascal were all called. I soon realized that each of us only responded to one word in order to get a treat. I was Scruffy, so I no longer raced at the call of the other words. Finally, I heard "Scruffy," and quickly ran to the woman. Only Rascal followed, too. It was an unusual way to have fun, but that was dog fun.

As we grew, slowly we learned more new words. Someone would hold a treat at nose level, then slowly raise it over our heads so that we would follow it with our eyes and our back ends would automatically drop to the ground as we stared at the offered treat. Then she would say, "Sit," and if we stayed, she gave us the reward. It was easy but boring, and the result was always she same. Soon we were doing things without any rewards/treats.

We spent many days doing such routines, which were not much fun, but some days we were all let out onto the warm grass so that we could run and chase and bark and nip each other's ears – real dog fun. We were all just little guys about the size of a person's foot, but one day we were let out with some big dogs, all scattered around in our play areas. Some would sniff us, surprised to find such similar animal in the same form except for size. But everyone seemed friendly and no one showed any fear except for Dustball, who barked at one of the big dogs, but he soon ran when the big one barked and growled back. Fortunately, some people stood between them, and everything returned to normal, but Dustball never barked at a big dog again.

We learned many new play activities, all attached to a command – stay, sit, down, fetch (which was really fun), and "No!" (which over time became scary, probably because the person always sounded angry for some reason). Often, we could hear many noises from the other side of the walls. No one except the people knew what could make such loud sounds, but they did not seem to worry, so we learned not to either. Although we grew used to the noise, we just assumed that they were part of our world, and that we just had to learn to live with them, sight unseen.

We all slept in one room with a soft ground, instead of the hard ground on which we had spent our early life, and there were water and food in bowls lined up against one wall. Anytime one of us had to pee or more, we held the urge until someone opened a door, picked us up and put us on the grass. Sometimes one pup would pee in our room, and he was taken outside and told "No," which was scary. No one ever hit us or hurt us, but the voice sure made us tremble. Eventually, we all learned to use a small door by the people door that swung open when we pushed it with our noses. It became fun to go outside any time that we wanted.

Days passed and we continued our daily routines, sometimes fun, sometimes boring. Our whole world changed one day when some new people, a man and a woman, came into our room, kneeled, and waited for us to jump on them, which we instinctively did. Eventually, they picked us up, one at a time, and held us high in the air while, they looked at us as they twirled our puppy bodies. It was fun for a while, but grew a bit worrisome about what they were doing.

One morning a woman in a white coat took us to another new room, one at a time, put us on a table, checked our teeth and body parts, while telling us what good dogs we were and playfully rubbing our necks. Suddenly we felt a quick jab in our necks, like we had been bitten by one of those nasty bees we had met in our yard. Then she returned us to the others, and grabbed another pup.

But these new people seemed to have a different purpose, more playful, and no prick at the end. They talked with one another, while we just stood as though awaiting something – more play or another life. Finally, one couple picked-up Rascal and me in two hands and looked into our eyes, searching for something. They had kind eyes.

After a minute of handling and talking, they put me on the ground and walked away with Rascal. He looked scared but didn't bark or cry; he was only a handful of silver fur, nothing to worry about. But I never saw him again and our lives continued, though a bit emptier.

After Rascal left, we all slept in a tighter circle, as though trying to occupy his spot and protecting the rest of us. It was about then that we noticed that mother was also gone, though we could not recall her leaving. We slept and continued day after day, acting as though Rascal and mother were still present, but something was not quite right; there was an emptiness and loneliness. Unfortunately, not only did Rascal not come back, but a few days later Queenie also vanished, leaving three of us to be fearful of having to go through the people doors and vanish forever. We slept in a tighter circle until just Dustball and I were left. What was on the other side of those doors? Who were all these strange people? What did they do with our brothers and sisters? Did they come from the other side of the wall with all the noises?

One day I had my questions answered when it was my time to make the mysterious journey. Two seemingly nice women picked me up and carried me through the doors. Dustball watched me be carried off, our eyes wet from fear and wondering if we would ever see each other and play together again. As the door shut, I gave a farewell bark and he answered the same way.

Instantly I found myself in some kind of crate with an open front until the woman shut its door. I tried to get out, but it wouldn't open.

"Scruffy, it's okay," said the woman. "You'll be fine. Just sit for a minute."

I understood a few words, but her tone had always been gentle even when she said "No," so I settled, crossed my paws, and waited. They sat with other people who had taken care of us and sometimes laughed while they read some papers. I think their name was "Foster," because they used it so many times. Was I now Scruffy Foster? I had learned the people's way of naming each other. For example, the man who cleaned up after us was called "Tubby

Johnson." The woman who checked our bodies and stuck us with an occasional needle was "Hot Duhr." At least, that's what they called each other, though I noticed not always in each other's presence. An odd system of naming, but I thought I could make sense of it. Anyway, they all seemed nice and non-threatening, except when they split-up our dog family

The two women who carried me off in that crate were called Sarah and Mary "Foster," I assumed. They put me in my box in the back seat of the "car," a word I soon learned when they excitedly asked me if I "wanted to go in the car." At first I thought I was going to another home to see my missing litter mates – Silver, Queenie and Rascal. Perhaps that's what dogs' lives were meant to be. But my only fortune happened when Sarah took me out of the crate and put me in the front seat next to them. I still couldn't see anything, but Sarah held me up so that I could look outside. I had never seen so many wondrous things. It's what was making all that noise behind the wall. Everything was moving so fast that I did not have any time to be afraid, just amazed.

Over time I learned so much, especially when we made short car trips and Sarah let me sit on a pillow that she put on her lap. Nothing frightened me much anymore, and I soon learned many new words. Buildings included hospitals, schools, stores or, my favorite, McDonald's. Also, over time I learned two words I would come in contact with too many times –dying and death. Then there were the special days that did not happen too often but were very clearly marked – Christmas (bring a tree inside the house), Halloween (wear silly clothes), and July 4th (The one I hated most because of all the noise). And two simple words I used every day – day and night.

Also, I soon learned to sleep in the car while Sarah and Mary went to many places and returned with bags full of stuff – sometimes things to wear, sometimes with things to eat, including treats for me. It was a good, safe life.

We lived in a big place where we had plenty of room and a big back yard, where they kept teaching me different activities to do, even taking long naps with them, much like we had all started to learn in my first home. Nothing we did was painful, so I became a quick learner. On some days they put me on a leash (a word I did not like at first, but soon accepted), and we walked around the yard. The only problem was that I couldn't run or play during this time or the leash would stop me from going faster. Other times they just let me go without the leash. I don't know what they were teaching me, until one afternoon when I was given a clue about what was expected of me.

The three of us walked out the front door of the house and instead of going right to the car, we walked out the front yard gate and onto a long path (sidewalk). As we walked down this new street, I became even more amazed, like a whole, bigger world. More houses, more yards, more cars, more people! Where would it ever end? I was so excited that I had to stop, lift my leg and pee on a bush. Neither Mary nor Sarah seemed to mind. It was like I had discovered an even better world.

We walked and occasionally someone would let me sniff a hand and then pet me. Sometimes I would see Mary talking to someone who was pushing another person in a chair with wheels, and she would give something to the person in the chair. He/She would come up to me, chair and all. I was a little concerned about the chair being so big that it might roll over me, but it always stopped in time. I was just a little dog, after all. The person in the chair stuck out his hand, which held a treat. I took it and he began to laugh. Then he petted me. I was no longer worried about the big chair, and I greeted others the same way. Seemed an easy way to get treats. Each person had talked to Mary first, so everyone must have been safe. Nice people.

We began to take longer walks and we crossed busy streets and even went into a place that seemed to be created for dogs – large, grassy fields with endless, winding paths and benches holding people who were eating. Eventually, I ate, too, on days when Mary and Sarah brought a basket. All the people seemed friendly and wanted to pet me. They always asked Mary first, who readily agreed. Thank you.

A few times a smaller person would pet me too hard, but I only let out a little cry; I had learned never to bite anyone. Someone else usually scolded the person for me and gently rubbed the little person's hand on my back and say, "gentle." If the park had too many people, Sarah would take me off the path and tell me to "sit," which I did. I was getting better at commands every day.

One day we went to the park with a blanket and the basket of food. So many people and dogs were there that it was hard for all of us to walk. Mary carried me, for which I was happy; I could see so much and not have to worry about being stepped on. Once a big dog, like the ones at my old home, barked and came at me with snapping teeth. It scared me and I instinctively barked back and stood on my back legs. Mary cut that act short, but not before a man yelled, "No," and pulled back on the big dog's head. I tried to think of what I had done to earn a loud "No," but could only think of my bark and standing on my tiny legs, and that was pure instinct. I hadn't thought about what I was doing. Should I have not done that?

After that excitement and more walking, I started to feel like I had to do more than just lift my leg, but I tried to hold it. When there were fewer people and dogs, Mary spread the blanket on the ground and brought out the food for us to eat, I hoped. She even put out a bowl of water for me. Other people passed us and pointed and seemed to say nice things about Mary and Sarah. Maybe they said something about me, too. One person even called me "Dustmop," and I wondered if he knew my brother Dustball.

It was growing dark, but no one seemed to be leaving, except that there were fewer dogs present. I thought it strange that we had spent so much time in the park. I still had to go to the bathroom, and I did. But Mary picked-up my mess in a bag and tossed it in a barrel. It was nice that there was such a thing.

It had been a wonderful day until it turned frightful when night came and it turned dark. Suddenly there were loud sounds coming from the sky, worse than the kind that happened during heavy rains. The sounds were followed by bright lights, also like a storm. Surprisingly, the people appeared happy and made "oooh" and "aaah" sounds. I was scared and tried to hide under our blanket. Then another boom followed. And more and more. Would it ever stop? It was the most scared I had ever been. Finally, Sarah saw me digging in the blanket and picked me up and held me tightly in her arms. These awful explosions continued with people's approval. At last Mary and Sarah picked up our basket and blanket and dog, and we started to follow the people back to the paths. On our way home, I could still hear the bangs, but they were not as loud and I felt safer in Sarah's arms.

As soon as my paws hit the walk outside our house, I raced into my bed and curled up with a cuddly bear that they had given me on my first day. I was still shaking, but exhausted – a full day outside in the park followed by a terrifying nighttime canine assault had exhausted my little body. Never again, I hoped.

Luckily, I did not have to endure such torture again, but there seemed to be a new process to learn. After many walks in the park and to other unknown places, I became used to people and never felt anxious about strangers and bigger dogs. Nobody even gave me treats anymore while meeting me, and I learned to "sit" any time they commanded. "Stay" was difficult at first, because Mary would let me run loose and suddenly yell, "Stay!" if I was too far. The first times I kept running, but soon they had a long rope around me and pulled it when they said, "stay," so eventually I did, even without the rope to stop me.

The new outside training seemed to be useful, especially one morning when we all went to a new building, which I leaned was called a "hospital." Sarah carried me and held me while I tried to understand what we were doing. First, I noticed the strong smell throughout the building and its inhabitants. Sometimes the bad smell was replaced with a smell like one from home, when Mary and Sarah sliced some groceries that we got every week from a farmer's market. They bought bags full of food, which they cut- up and put into bowls, but not for me. Occasionally they would drop a piece on the floor and instead of picking it up and putting it in their bowls, they would, shout, "Five-second rule" followed by "Scruffy," which was the signal that what they had dropped was now mine. Sometimes it was delicious; other times I refused it. Not a game to get excited about

One other odor that filled the hospital was very unpleasant. It was like the smell in the kitchen when Mary or Sarah left something on the counter overnight. The food began to wrinkle and turn colors, like the occasional dead creatures I would find in the back yard. But how could such an odor reach all parts of this hospital? No matter when we went there, that smell roamed the halls to greet and to accompany us.

To have such different smells coming from all the rooms made me wonder if the people ever got outside to smell the fresh air. I visited hospital and places like this one many times over my growing years, and there was always a sense of sadness and doom there. Most of the people were sitting in chairs with wheels, like we had seen in the park. I had learned to approach strangers, but I was still small and watched hopefully for someone friendly to come my way.

Slowly we went from the crowded entryway and down a long hallway, bigger than the one in our house. This hospital seemed like a home for old people. I was surprised when Sarah put me on the floor and attached my leash. She led me into a room, where an older woman was sitting by a table and staring out the window. She looked like she had been sleeping but turned at the sound of us entering and acted surprised. Mary called her "Betty," and I heard my name, too. I felt Mary take off my leash and let me go free. I walked straight to the woman, who reached down for me and I jumped into her hands and she settled me in her lap. She had a great view out her window and a very comfortable chair. She spoke to me in soft tones, and I immediately began to lick her rough face and tasted the water leaking from her eyes. She was smiling and seemed happy to see me. Mary soon grasped me, but the old woman held on tight a little longer. She seemed friendly and had such a nice view of a large garden that I wanted to play in it. Maybe later.

Betty held me for a while and constantly petted and rubbed my ears. She never got up and I felt that maybe she was tired. Like most of the people we had seen, there was an aroma coming from her, only it seemed strong. I think we liked each other. Soon Mary carried me away, attached my leash and we went back to the hall. Many people in the wheeled chairs were being pushed by smiling workers. Mary put me on the floor and everyone reached out their hands, so I licked a few, and Mary guided me to another room.

Again, Mary took off my leash and let me loose on the slippery floor. I instinctively ran to an old man who, like Betty, was staring out his window. Seemed to be what they did for fun, but he saw me and tapped his legs, so I ran and got a good jump despite the slick floor. I was a good jumper, and soon he was holding my head in his hands and talking to me. It was good training for any future encounters. Like Betty, he had a big chair with a garden view. I could have stayed there, too.

Mary said something to the man and I heard "Ralph" and "Scruffy," so I gathered that she was making introductions. "Scruffy, huh?" he said as he continued scratching my back and belly. Ralph, too, smelled like everything else. I began to think that everyone here was older than other people I knew, like Mary and

Sarah, and Hot Duhr and Tubby Johnson and most people we had met on the streets and park.

The day ended after visiting some more rooms, where we saw most people sitting in comfortable chairs but not all with the garden view. Some people were sleeping, so we didn't talk to them. Sleep seemed important to them. Dogs can fall back to sleep fast, but not all people. Everyone we visited felt nice and safe and I seemed to make them happy. Their happiness made me happy.

Once we got home, I was so tired that I turned down Mary's collar invitation to take a walk. Sitting with them and watching movies, which starred mostly people with an occasional dog, I soon was sleeping next to Sarah, and everything was good in my world. I remember being carried by Sarah to the big bed, and she put me in the middle next to Mary. I started to get up and go to my own bed, but Mary pulled me into her and said, "Stay." I was confused, but I was soon asleep, cuddled between two big people who made me feel fortunate and happy.

For many sleeps I was on the big bed with Mary and Sarah. Some days we would all return to the hospital with all the older people – same smells but so different from Sarah and Mary. Usually I saw the same people, but Betty and been replaced with Doris. I don't know where Betty had gone, but I assumed she had felt better and had gone home. Only that still lingering awful odor puzzled me.

One time Mary lifted me onto a big bed, where someone named Helen was resting but not sleeping. She turned her head and smiled, so I assumed everything was okay, except for that powerful sickly smell, but I went to her face and let her know that I was glad to meet her and hoped she would get better soon, like Betty. That's what I felt, but Mary pulled me away from the old lady's face and placed me on top of Helen, a move which seemed to please her as she continued stroking my head and back. Soon I was resting comfortably.

"Helen" and "Scruffy" were the only words I could understand again, so I guess more introductions had been made.

"Scruffy," and "Fluffy" rasped Helen, but I had no idea who Fluffy was.

A short time later, Sarah picked me up after I had looked into Helen's colorless eyes for too long. The sad, old lady said goodbye, but there was a feeling that this visit was different and foreboding, and I wasn't sure how to react. Helen was gone the next time we went to see her, and like Betty, I never saw her again.

So, the cycle seemed to be. I would meet people, who were always glad to see me and pet me, but eventually disappeared. Many of these similar people had a very strong, bitter odor, which I grew to interpret as the last time for me to visit. Even Ralph, who I thought was stronger than the rest, vanished one day. I soon felt like I grew to know what that sickening odor was – decay and death. Even plants at home gave off such a scent. I really hoped not to smell it again.

Just as I thought my life was settled with Mary and Sarah and occasional trips to the dying hospital, everything changed in one day. The women went around the house and picked-up all my favorite possessions–squeakers, partially chewed rawhide chips, balls, tug toys and empty water and food bowls. They put it all in a bag and put it by the front door. I did not know what was happening, but they both walked me out to the back yard, which they rarely did. Maybe both took me to the park, but never just to the back yard. They seemed sad as I walked around the fence and peed in my usual spots. Finally, Sarah called me into the house.

I went to my bed, as usual, but it wasn't there. The uncomfortable feeling I sometimes got at the dying hospital came over me, but I could not smell any awful odor. Mary put on my leash and we all went to the front door. Sarah found another rawhide stick by the front door and saved it for me.

Then we walked through the front door for what felt like the last time. I would normally be excited by this time, but the aura was ominous. When I got in the car, I saw my dog bed in the back seat. As we drove away, I kept looking at the house, wondering what I had done that was wrong. It was clear that they were moving me, but I never understood why. Despite Mary's constant consoling, I couldn't help but feel sad, something I hardly ever felt when I was with them.

I had pretty much consumed the whole rawhide chew that Sarah had given me at the beginning of our trip. We stopped at a much smaller house that I vaguely remembered visiting a couple times. It seemed like a nice place, but although I had a suspicion, I could not imagine why they had taken my bed and bowls and toys. But when you're my size, there's not much you can do on your own, so I followed Mary on the leash to the house. They didn't take my things from the car, so maybe I was going home again.

When the door opened and because Sarah led, I knew it was safe. Suddenly something flew by Sarah's head and broke against the wall behind her. A piercing shriek filled the room. The scream changed to a word that sounded like "Doggie," and it came from a child who was racing towards me. I recognized her from other times we had visited, and I braced myself for her to run over me.

Just before she was about to trample me, one of the new people caught her and lifted her away from my shaking body, which caused another piercing "Doggie" cry as she tried to reach down and kept yelling "Doggie" over and over. The man said something to her and gently placed her on the floor. He held her tightly while she sat on the floor and put out a hand to pet me, and I willingly, but cautiously, approached her waiting hand, hoping that she would pet me, which would have been fine. I could vaguely recall her as being nice and always good for some petting. When we had first met, they had called her Kathy. I wagged my stump because all people seemed to like that and took it as a sign of approval. Kathy even gently hugged me like Mary and Sarah always had done.

When the man (Steve) slowly released Kathy, she sat next to me and began her petting skills. Sometimes the woman (Laurie) would help Kathy and guide her hand while saying "gentle." I was fine with either. I don't think that Kathy ever meant to hurt me, but I was small and she was excitable. Sarah picked-up some broken pieces of whatever had just missed her head, not frightened or angry. In fact, everyone in the room was suddenly very still, despite the previous yelling and destruction.

Sarah removed my collar and everyone went through the house and into the back yard, which was just like Mary and Sarah's. It was mostly grass inside of a fence. In the middle was a round bowl full of water. It looked awfully high, and I did not know how such a small dog like me could ever get that high. Then I found the solution. The birds flew to it, sat on the round edge, and drank. Some birds pooped in the water, so I didn't think I would drink that water anyway. Besides, I brought my own bowl.

These people must have had a big need for water, because besides the tall water bowl that the birds could use, they also had a large bowl, big enough to water horses. I didn't think it was for me, being as small as I was. I tried the water anyway, though it was warm and had a funny taste, not like the cold water that Mary and Sarah had always given me. Soon Kathy flew right by me and jumped into the odd water bowl, laughing all the way. I was soaked like I was getting a bath without the soap. Kathy kept pointing at me and saying, "Doggie" again, until Laurie ran over to see if she was okay. Laurie just stepped into the water; it barely covered her ankles, and carried a happy Kathy to the grass. I guess Laurie assumed that I was okay, because I did not react except to get out and shake myself dry. Everyone laughed and seemed good with my reaction, so I shook off some more. Good thing I was little and the water bowl (I later learned that it was a kiddies' pool) was not just for drinking.

Once things seemed normal again, I decided to explore more of this new world. I wanted to pee on some bushes, but there were small fences in front of the flowers. I could have easily jumped over those low protective fences, but I sensed that they were there to keep things out, including me.

Mary picked me up and rubbed a towel around me, like after my bath at home. Then she put me down and pretended to chase me. Completely free, I ran circles around the yard while they clapped to keep me running. Kathy started running, too, but she soon fell and started crying, so Steve picked her up and carried her into the house, though she didn't seem hurt at all. The rest of us followed, but I would not have minded playing some more. I saw my own water and food bowls in a place in the kitchen and immediately went for some water; it was cold and made me feel better.

In the big room Kathy was still crying, while Steve sat next to her on the couch and held her tightly. I wondered if that was how they got her to finally become quiet. I went to them, jumped on the couch to get close to Kathy, which immediately stopped her crying.

"Doggie," she said while reaching out to pet my back. She started to hug me too tightly, so I immediately smacked her on the nose with my tiny paw. Surprisingly, Kathy's tears had turned into laughs, and everyone sighed in relief, as the big people started to talk more seriously. This house seemed to be constantly changing from chaos to everything's fine.

It was my turn to feel sad when Mary and Sarah both held me and rubbed my belly and back and even kissed me on the head. Then they turned and went through the door and left in the car, as I watched them through the window by the chair. I would see them some times during a short visit, but I felt that I would never go to stay at their house again. Apparently, I had a new home without them. Why? My fault? I'm sorry.

That night was unusual. Steve read to Kathy on the couch, and I was placed next to her while she calmly petted me. We both listened to his reading; he had a soft, soothing voice. Of course, I got the joy of being petted by this new, gentler Kathy. No tears, no shouting, and just soft strokes. Steve's soothing voice and my presence put Kathy to sleep. I was close behind. That man could read.

I woke-up when Laurie took Kathy from Steve and they carried her away. I assumed that they had forgotten me, but, like most dogs, I can fall asleep almost anywhere, almost instantly. The same is true about waking-up.

Steve came back for me and carried me up to their room, where my old dog bed was waiting at the foot of their big bed. My suspicions rose higher that maybe I would be spending more time there. I guess I wasn't returning to my first real home with Mary and Sarah for a while, if ever. My old blanket was present along with my favorite squeaker mouse. There was even a water bowl with a few treats.

Most of that first day passed slowly. I took a few trips outside, but spent most of the time alone with nothing to do except wait for someone to come back to this strange, new home. I had just gotten comfortable when the quiet was shattered by a scream of "Doggie, Doggie." I had heard that word so much that I wondered if I had a new name other than Scruffy. It was Kathy who seemed to be yelling for me, not at me. Steve and Laurie were with her and Laurie released Kathy's hand. She immediately recognized me and launched one of those hurried attacks at me, before Steve slowed her impact.

Kathy pet me again and said, "Doggie."

While Steve took her hand and said, "Gentle, Kathy, gentle," until she was calm and smiling.

After eating and watching television, it was time for another day to end. I had a head start and was napping in another dog bed that they had put in the living room so that I could be part of the family, I guess. A voice cried, "Doggie, bed." She looked at her parents. Kathy started to pick-up my bed while I was still in it, so I guessed that sleep for that night was cancelled. Laurie and Steve were talking quietly away from Kathy, who kept staring at them. She wanted something and trusted her parents to know what it was.

Finally, Laurie said, "Okay," and led Kathy back to her room, as Steve carried me in one hand and my bed in the other. He put my bed next to Kathy's, then left and returned with my water bowl, squeaker and blanket and put them by my bed, but not too close to Kathy's. I didn't mind if Kathy wanted to pet me or play with my squeaker and blanket. I didn't care if she wanted to drink out of my water bowl. At least she didn't smell like death.

Laurie sat on the bed and petted Kathy's head like Mary and Sarah used to do to mine. This was my first night away from them, but although I missed them both, I felt safe in my new home. I closed my eyes, but soon felt Laurie kneeling by me and petting my head and saying, "Good doggie," which I thought was nice since I hadn't really done anything special to earn any praise. Kathy was sleeping soon and so was I.

The next day gave me a routine. Everyone got out of bed and met in the kitchen. Kathy always hurried to me for a pet and a hug, a good way to start a day for anyone. At first, she always came at me hard, but Steve always taught her to "be gentle," as he guided her hand over my back. Eventually, she didn't have to be watched anymore; she had learned to be gentle. Then she would laugh and follow Steve, so I went too, and watched Kathy put on different clothes every day. One great thing about being a dog —always having the same clothes, never any need to change them. We returned to the kitchen, and Laurie let me out the back door so I could relieve myself. That, too, felt good.

When I came I, they were all eating food that smelled delicious. I saw my bowl full of kibble, so I ate some. Then something wonderful attacked my nose. They called it "bacon," and Kathy was sharing hers with me. I quickly grabbed the meat before they changed their minds. Both Laurie and Steve said "No, Doggie!" They had ordered at the same time, but not before I had already eaten it. Then Kathy started to cry and Laurie hugged her tight while Steve patted me on the head. Mixed messages. Were they mad at me or not? They had said, "No, Doggie," so I had assumed that I had done something wrong; after all, it seemed that Doggie was my new name now. Not sure why Kathy was crying, but I sure wanted to thank her for the bacon. I hoped the scolding wasn't my fault.

Laurie brought Kathy to me, and again she stopped crying and hugged me as her parents watched. Kathy had learned not to feed me bacon, but as she grew older, we became best pals and she sometimes dropped little pieces on the floor while I was always watching and hoping. If either parent noticed what was happening, they never said.

After eating in the morning (breakfast), Steve and Kathy left the house. I did not know where they went, and later Laurie would leave and return with Kathy. I was happy when Kathy was around, not only for the amazing greeting she gave me, but because following Laurie around the house all day was boring. Sometimes I sat with her on the couch while she watched television, an activity that Mary and Sarah had often done, too. But Laurie's shows also appeared boring, totally lacking in any animal activity, and I could not keep my eyes open. The naps were good to prepare me for Kathy's return. I saw one show that I had enjoyed before. The contestant spun a big colorful circle and then one woman kept turning letters and the people playing would guess at words, and then they would yell and scream like they were being mauled by a rabid St. Bernard, but they seemed to be having fun. It was a game for all people and pets. One time at Mary's, she had watched Animal Planet, which showed alligators grabbing dogs out of yards, and vanishing with them. It really scared me and I worried if my new house had any alligators. Kathy would protect me.

At least when Kathy came home, we could run in the yard. Now when Kathy fell, I ran right to her and she stopped crying. Her parents never knew. Usually, Kathy and I would run in the yard, but there were days when things didn't seem quite right. As much as I liked to run, Kathy kept running and wouldn't stop. I don't know how she kept going for so long; she would even flap her arms like a bird. When I got near her, there was an odd smell coming from her breath. Not like the dying breath; I would certainly recognize that. When I got worried, I would run to the back door and bark as loud as I could until Steve or Laurie came out and ran to Kathy and carried her into house where they would put her on the couch. I would follow to see how she was. Kathy seemed calmer with her parents, and they even patted me on the head and said, "Good dog."

When I felt that the time was right, I would jump on the couch and nestle in Kathy's shoulder, which earned me a hug.

One day they stopped calling me "Doggie," and my new name became "Patty." I don't know why, but Kathy seemed to have chosen it and always called me Patty. She kept saying, "Patty, Patty," so I guess she liked the sound of it, and I really didn't care. What's in a dog's name? She was always nice and happy around me and kept sneaking me bacon. I wished that I could have done more for her.

Days passed routinely until one day Laurie picked me up and put on my leash (odd change of order to our day), and we left in the car. I stood on the front seat and was able to see all new people, cars and other dogs. Some were the same that we saw on our walks, only I was so high that they all seemed different. Short trip and Laurie stopped the car in front of a large building, like the hospital. I hoped that it wouldn't smell of decay again, but on the outside, I could see many kids playing and laughing and chasing each other, and they had good smells like flowers and bacon. It wasn't death; it was young life. My little body twitched as I was eager to jump out of the car and join this chaotic but fun game. I realized why Laurie had leashed me. Not that I'd run away, but I would race to join the fun.

Unlike my usual waiting in the car while Laurie went into the stores, this time she opened the door with my leash in her hand, and let me jump out but not to play.

"Come on, Patty; let's go see Kathy." I heard my new name and Kathy, so I guessed everything would be good and safe.

She led me through a big double door that made loud crashes whenever anyone opened it and let it close. It was like the hospital with long hallways, rooms, slippery tiled floors but no one was in the hall to greet us or wanting to pet me. Instead an ear-shattering ring echoed from the walls and the halls filled with chattering, fast-walking children. Immediately I was in Laurie's hand as she didn't want to see a little dog get trampled by a herd of youth. Some of the kids walked up to Laurie and asked if they could pet me. Soon I had little fingers scratching my neck and rubbing my head and touching my nose. Everyone was nice and some even waited for a turn. I felt special.

Eventually, after all the kids had cleared the hallway, we got to a big room, where some boys, looking guilty, sat in chairs along a wall. Another woman, Lisa, talked to Laurie, who set me down on top of a large counter. Lisa didn't look like a doctor, but it seemed like I had been here before.

They talked and I looked around. Lisa talked with her hands so much that I wondered if she thought that Laurie was a dog or at least spoke dog. One time she yelled at some of the chattering kids and they instantly became quiet. Another woman (Ms. Rockow) appeared from a door behind the counter, which made the kids get stiff and nervous. She spoke softly with Laurie for a minute then barked a name and pointed to her open door. One kid hung his head and reluctantly went. She came up to me and for some reason I immediately cringed. I had seen her in action. Instead, she scratched my neck. Looked like my pleasant personality had saved me from her wrath. I couldn't figure why those kids sitting in chairs seemed so afraid of her. She and Laurie talked for a while, then the woman left and made sure that she slammed the door to her office loud enough to scare me.

Lisa left through the door and Laurie followed with me on a leash. We entered another long, narrow room that had many things to sit on, including a bed like mine, only different. Something unusual was about to happen. The light went darker, and I began to feel uneasy.

The door opened and another woman entered. She said something to us, then to someone behind her and a group of kids came in. Some sat on the couch, while others sat on some funny round chairs without legs, but all of them were smiling at me and said, "Hi, dog." Not another name change, I hoped. Then, one by one, led by the woman (Misses, which I assumed was her name), came to me and held their little hands out for me to smell, which was weird but I could not smell any threat from any of them; in fact, most smelled of innocence, a scent that dogs can quickly detect.

Laurie put me on the dog bed and said, "Stay," even though I wasn't tired.

Soon Misses said a name and one little boy sat next to me. Then he opened a book, like Kathy had at home, and began to read to me. Seeming unsure, he stopped a few times, then petted me until he could finish. Misses said his name again, and he patted my head and gave me a small treat he had hidden in his pocket. What was that for? Nice kid, I guess.

The next boy did the same, except he seemed afraid of me. Misses gave him a book and he refused to take it and turned his head. I licked his arm, which made him flinch a little, and Misses put the boy's hand on my back and helped him pet me. She opened the book again and when he flinched, she said "No" and kept moving his hand across my back. He was scared; I could feel it on my back.

Finally, he tried to read to me, but he didn't get too far before he got stuck and kept saying, "B b b Big . . .' He started to cry, so I got as close to him as I could and started to lick his pants. He giggled, pet me on the head with Misses' help, and he started again. This time he only read a few words and did not get far before he had another block. I didn't mind. He seemed nice and was really trying. Misses took his hand and led him back to the couch, still teary-eyed, but okay. He was a tough kid; I didn't know what his problem was but I could not imagine a little boy had to live like that his whole life. Wish I could have helped him. Misses talked gently to him and rubbed his head. Universal gesture. Then she gave him a treat. He had certainly earned it. Much to my surprise, instead of eating it he brought it to me, held it out, and I took it with a slight tail wag; he replaced his tears with giggles.

So the day went. When one group left, another took its place. Always the same routine – smell everyone's hand, listen to each student read a book from Misses, give the dog a treat, repeat. I was full of treats by day's end, but I was ready to go home. I was wrong. The door opened and I could hear a voice call, "Patty," and there was Kathy.

Laurie called Kathy to her, while I awaited another bunch of hard pats, back scratches, and unwanted treats. Kathy went first and we read as usual. The other kids watched closely, leaning from her how to read to a dog. After being read to by a few more kids, Misses turned on the lights and Laurie led me to the car, with many farewells following us. I guess there was no time left for playing.

It had been a great day, but not my last. I learned that place was called a school, and when Laurie asked me if I wanted to go to school, I grew excited and headed towards the car.

More of the same with occasional surprises. Sometimes at school I went outside with Laurie holding my leash, and we watched the kids run up and down the field, kicking a ball. I really wanted to get off my leash and show them how fast I was, but I guess they had rules, and one time I got to play kick the ball only with Kathy, who was not as fast as the other kids.

Many days I did not want to leave the reading room. In fact, one day after everyone had read, Laurie and Misses held me as the kids came up one at a time and brushed some paint on my nails. I thought it was silly, but it didn't hurt, and all the girls and a few boys looked like they had painted their nails, too. Wonder if Laurie and Misses had to hold them. They all laughed (kids seemed to do that more than adults), so I paraded around the school and house and yard showing off my painted paws, but soon the colors all wore off, and nobody ever did it again.

Slowly I sensed that Kathy was getting older and bigger until she was almost as tall as Laurie. I was able to recognize birthdays (cake, funny hats, presents, ice cream for me) and Kathy seemed to have many of them. She seemed to change, too, but kept most of herself. She would still sneak me bacon and we slept in the same bed, but she seemed to be taking more of the bed every night. She rarely got mad or threw things any more. She had changed, but we didn't. Kathy had thrown a special "doggie bed" at the foot of the bed, my own place to curl up and sleep. She was thoughtful about her Patty having comfort. Laurie and Steve came in every night, just as they had when I had first come to their house, and wrapped the blanket tightly around Kathy, scratched my ears good night, and I think sometimes they even whispered, "Thank you, Patty," to me. No, thank you. It seemed like something serious was about to happen, but most nights we just slept, and I felt safe.

Then something major did change. Laurie and Steve sat on the couch with Kathy and started to show her papers and pictures, even some of me. Kathy seemed to get agitated, like the first day I had moved there. There were times when she ran to her room and cried. I followed but did not know what to do except to lie next to her and cuddle, which helped a little. But this tension continued night after night. One night Kathy held me on her lap and scratched my back while she kept saying, "Patty, Patty, good dog." It seemed that Kathy was protecting me from something that was causing the sadness that surrounded all of us.

One night the old Kathy reappeared. She had another fit and ran to her bedroom, this time slamming the door, which she had not done for a long time. I was shocked and scratched at her door. Soon it opened and she let me in, but slammed shut again. We lay on her bed and both fell asleep together for the last time.

The next morning, I still felt uncomfortable, like everyone knew a secret except me. They all gave me special attention, and Laurie caught Kathy sneaking me bacon, but she didn't say anything. Steve took Kathy to school, but there seemed to be some extended, sad farewells, accompanied by Kathy's tears and an extra cuddle from Steve, before they were finally gone. Laurie was misty-eyed as she watched them leave, then returned to the kitchen to talk to someone on the phone. She proceeded to do her normal morning house cleaning, but she did more than the normal. She even gathered my toys, chews, and the blanket that Kathy had put on the bed especially for me. I sat on the couch as though everything was normal, but people can't always deceive a dog – to many superior senses at work.

I had just about fallen asleep when I realized that this was another case of something important happening that involved me. Laurie walked out of Kathy's room, carrying my bed and piled it by the door with my toys and blanket. Was I leaving for good? What had I done wrong? I tried to take good care of Kathy and was friendly to all those other kids at school. And I thought everyone liked me. So, what was happening? I was so worried that I went to scratch the back door, a sign to Laurie that I really had to pee. Out I went, and I peed on every bush I could, but my little tank was soon empty. Although I felt relieved, that black cloud of worry still followed me. Why would my bed and toys be put by the front door? I lay outside in the warmth, while I relived all my good times in that house. I did not want to leave it. Besides, who could take my place?

Eventually Laurie opened the door and called me. Eager and hopeful that everything was back to normal, I raced into the house, sliding on the kitchen floor. There were two women standing by the front door. One was kneeling with her hand extended, usually an invitation to smell her or to take a treat. I slowly walked closer to her and she said, "Scruffy," which triggered a memory and when the other woman said the same, I forgot all my sorrows and jumped into their arms, my tongue flying to their faces and painting their arms. Names – Mary and Sarah. Same smells and voices, they just looked older than when they had left me here. They played – Mary pushed me into Sarah and she pushed me back, until I got tired of that game and started to run around the house with joy, while the three women laughed. I went to my water bowl for a drink, but it was gone. Quickly, Laurie got another bowl and filled it. Thanks, but where's my bowl?

I wanted to show Mary and Sarah all the words I had learned, but that is no easy trick for a canine. I was still me, only smarter. We all went into the big room and I sat on the couch between Mary and Sarah, jumping from one lap to the other while they rubbed my back and belly. It was wonderful. I would feel awful if I had to leave Kathy, but if I had to go, I was hoping that at least I could go back with Mary and Sarah. Did they know that I was now called Patty and not Scruffy? Would I get my old name back? Such is the life of a dog.

The three people talked and wrote on some papers, while I just absorbed the happy feelings from them all. We all got up at the same time and walked to the front door. Mary carried me and Sarah carried a bag full of my stuff, including my bed. Laurie picked me up, scratched my neck and rubbed her nose against mine. Weird, she rarely did that. I think she may have been crying. Wouldn't I ever see Laurie again, either? As life turned out, I never did see her or Steve or Kathy again. I had spent a large part of my life with them, and then in one day it was over. I wished I had had the ability to thank them all for what they had given me, especially Kathy.

We got into another car, different from the old one that had carried us to Kathy's house. Change. Everything was dumped in the back seat, and I rode on Mary's lap, while Sarah drove. New car, older people, I wondered if they still lived in the same house. I knew my way around that place. I liked that house, our walks down that street, a nearby park. Maybe life would be okay without Kathy, but I had never felt so much a part of a person as I had of her.

We drove but my view from the window was wasted, just too tiring for my attention. All those anxious moments had just drained any desire to play, even with Mary and Sarah, so I fell asleep on Mary's lap. Everything was good and I still felt safe.

I don't know how long I had slept, but it felt like it was time to get up and go outside to pee. Mary must have felt the same way, because Sarah parked the car and Mary lifted me outside and slipped a collar with an attached leash over my head. I guess we were at their new house, because after a lengthy stop to let me water a bush, Mary led me up the sidewalk and stairs. I hoped that it was as good as my last one. If Mary and Sarah were there, everything would be fine. Instead of going in, Sarah pounded on the door while Mary and I stood by. Whose house was this? Soon a woman answered the door and welcomed us. Mary held my leash but put me on the floor. The first thing I sensed, almost before being completely in the house, was that unpleasant smell, like from that home for old people that I used to visit. It was a house full of decay and death. Not like Kathy's school, which had been so full of life. I hoped that we weren't going to stay long or that Mary and Sarah had not moved there.

The woman (Jane) led Mary and me down a long hallway, while Sarah went back outside. The hallway was dark and gloomy, and the smells grew stronger. Some of the odors were strong like those that Laurie would make some mornings when she cleaned her house. Soon we entered a room with a large bed. In the bed was an old, broken woman who was sitting up with the help of some big pillows behind her back. I say "broken" because she had several tubes going into her arms and some machine next to her bed had a clock-like box that was constantly lit and changing. I remembered them from the hospital, but there they usually meant that death would soon arrive. I felt bad for the old woman, who was called Nana.

"Teddy," she garbled and Mary put me on the bed. Nana petted me gently on the head. She seemed nice, just decaying, so I ran up the length of the bed and gave the old woman a few smacks, which, like always, caused a grin and something like a giggle. Jane quickly grabbed me, but not an angry grab, more like a notice to be-gentle grab, like a testing period, which was something I had been used to. So, I backed off with the kisses, but the old lady kept petting me while saying, "Teddy, Teddy."

The people talked and I nudged closer to Nana. I soon got used to the unpleasant odor, but she also had a more pleasant, friendly scent that balanced the bed. I was awoken when Sarah came in with my bed from Kathy's house and put it on the big bed. What did this mean? A bed on a bed. One small dog. Mary put me in my bed, and it was like I was lying on the floor. No major change in sleeping habits that I could not grow accustomed to, but I sensed major life changes.

Before they left, Sarah took me outside to the yard and waited for me to empty myself, which made quite the mess, because there were no rules yet about where to go in this new place. Soon Sarah just opened the door to let me in, expecting me to know where to go. I went in and was invited to lead, but Sarah could sense that I was unsure, maybe even a little afraid, so Sarah took the lead. I followed her down the hallway and back into Nana's room.

On the floor at the foot of the bed were my food and water bowls. Next to them was a small staircase leading up to the top, where Nana and my dog bed awaited me. Because I had people watching, I assumed they wanted to see if I could climb the stairs. None of them had any idea. Not too difficult but the steps were not quite normally spaced. Mary patted her hand on my bed. With my four short legs I was able to make it and dropped into my bed for a satisfied audience.

Nana was sleeping, so I decided not to lick her face. Maybe tomorrow. I got the feeling that this was my new home, but it might be okay with a little more training. I, too, was growing older, and had grown awfully tired when I played with Kathy and her friends. She seemed to have acquired more energy than when I had first arrived. I went to sleep. I thought about Kathy as I slept, and my dreams were of Mary and Sarah scratching my neck and belly, and even kissing the top of my head. I slept until the next day.

I woke- up to a big hand lifting me and carrying me to the backyard, where he put me on the grass and went back into the house. Not sure what to do, I peed on the same bush as last night. Now what? The man who had brought me there did not return, so I guess I was on my own. I sniffed all around the back yard, recognizing some scents from Mary and Sarah's and Kathy's yards. Sometimes Laurie had cut off some flowers, put them in a big glass, and brought them inside. They were all pleasant smelling, not at all like the ones of decay from the hospital.

"Teddy. Teddy," came the voice of a gentle woman from the back door. It was Jane, who had greeted us last night. Seemed like a nice lady, so I didn't hesitate to go to her, lest everyone forgot me and I was forced to spend the day alone in the big backyard.

Jane and a man were standing at a counter in the kitchen, but it was too high for me to see if they had food or just a place to lean. Soon the man put a bowl of cold water and a bowl of kibble on the floor next to it. He said, "Teddy," when he put the bowls down. I didn't see anyone else, so I wasn't sure if I was Teddy or Patty or Scruffy. I would probably answer to all. I did not see Nana.

Jane and Andy ate at a table, while I had a long drink of water and tried the kibble, which was much like the food at Kathy's, with a slight difference in taste. Not bad, just with a different crunch. Best of all, when Andy was finished eating, he just put his plate on the floor and said, "Teddy." I went to the plate that was full of new smells, including bacon. I didn't see any kibble, but I decided to lick the plate clean. Wonderful – slimy, tasty, and almost a whole new world. I tried to get everything off the plate, but my tongue was too strong, and the plate moved around the floor. At one point I put my paw on the plate in order to hold it still and get every taste. When I finished my task, Andy patted my head and said, "Good, dog, Teddy." I was the only dog, and apparently, I was the new Teddy, but I didn't know why I was good. Anyway, I would gladly do that task again.

Jane opened the back door and waited for me to follow. So, I just went outside again and waited for her to tell me what to do, but she just closed the door and left me alone again. More time to find things, I guess. More mysteries, mostly pleasant. That quickly changed when I had my nose to the ground and looked up to check on a foreign scent. There was another animal in the yard. It was about my size but it had the biggest ears sticking straight up. His nose twitched when we made eye contact. In his paws were leaves from those nice smelling plants. He had cut down a whole plant, like Laurie used to bring into her house, and was eating the leaves with some long teeth.

"Get out of here!" yelled an angry Andy from the back door, and then he was running at us, swinging his arms. Had he forgotten about me? The other animal dropped his leaves and Andy chased it, but he got away behind some other bushes. I was scared, and Andy brought me back to the house. After he talked to Jane, I didn't feel that they were mad at me, but that back yard business sure made me thirsty again.

"Damn rabbits," barked Andy.

I quickly assumed that the tone of voice and words referred to that animal with the big ears I had just seen. They seemed to think of it as bad and an unwelcome visitor. I wondered if that was why they had brought me to this house – to scare away damn rabbits. I could do it with Andy's help, but I wasn't as fast as I used to be, nor would I know what to do with it if I caught him.

Just when I had settled on my job as a chaser of damn rabbits, Jane called for me to follow her. She held a tray of food, and the household smells grew stronger as we got nearer to Nana's room. Jane went in and Nana was propped up in bed again. Jane put down the tray of food on a table by the bed, then patted my bed atop the steps. I was more concerned about those enticing smells coming from Nana's tray, but I figured I could see better, so up I went.

"Teddy, Teddy, come here," she called softly but with a rough voice. I ran up to her to give her a quick kiss but Jane pulled held me back a little, then picked up that tray full of food and set it over Nana's lap. Looked like the food that we had eaten with Andy. I sat staring with my little tongue hanging out.

Nana began to eat and I became jealous and wondered if she would share with me the way that Andy had. She even had bacon, one of my favorites thanks to Kathy sneaking or spilling some down to the floor for me to clean up. I never did learn if Laurie and Steve ever caught on, but I think they let Kathy get away with some things, sometimes. Nana kept eating, and then her teeth fell out. I had never seen such a sight. Jane quickly grabbed them and put them in a glass of water by Nana's bed. Nana did not get mad; she just drew me nearer and petted me while calling me "Teddy." Like Kathy, she could feel the need to feed her new little friend.

That was pretty much our morning procedure, except Nana's teeth didn't fall out every day. I did see them again, however. One night I was very thirsty after sharing some salty treats with Jane and Andy while watching tv. They had put a water bowl at the foot of Nana's bed, but I couldn't see the steps very clearly at night. Luckily, I remembered that glass of water where Jane had put Nana's teeth, and I could easily reach that. So I climbed past Nana, who growled when she slept, and I was able to get to the glass and have a few sips. It tasted awful, but it was all I needed. I decided to wait for light the next time that I needed a nighttime drink.

Sleep time passed every night with very little happening. Morning was always two meals – one from Andy and bits from Nana. When I went outside in the morning, I saw goddamn rabbits a few more times and chased them away. I spent much of the day with Nana in her bed, where she often spent long times sleeping, which was fine, because I started to really love those naps.

Major days went at their usual pace except in winter, when snow really made it difficult for a guy my size. Our day would start with those wonderful smells arriving to our cozy beds. I thought I was in heaven, like the story we dogs all knew about Rainbow Bridge. Jane took me outside and put me in a space that they had cleared of snow for me in the back yard. As soon as I was done doing my business, I went racing back to Nana, who was my favorite person in this house. She always greeted me in the morning with that toothless smile and say "Teddy, Teddy," which made me curl closer to her. We were a lazy team growing old together.

One day our room changed when Andy brought in a tree to the living room and a small one to Nana's room. I remembered this from Kathy. At first, I thought the trees were for my benefit so that I didn't have to pee in the snow, but I quickly learned that I was wrong. It was Christmas and everyone was in a good and loving mood. Andy and Jane would add small lights on the tree; it was beautiful. Don't know why they didn't have Christmas more often, unless it had something to do with the snow.

One morning Jane and Andy came into our room with a couple boxes wrapped in colorful, happy papers and gave them to Nana one by one. She smiled as she ripped off the paper and opened the boxes. I could tell that she was very sick but cheerful about the presents. Finally, Nana had one last box, which she gave to me. What? I sat staring until Andy tore off some paper and pushed it closer to me. I may have been a dog, but I was a fast learner. Everyone seemed to tear off the paper first, so I held it with my paws and started to remove the remaining paper with my tiny teeth, like Nana had done, only without her teeth. After the paper was off and Jane had taken away the scraps I had created, there was an odd stick, one that made me want to chew on it, not like the ones I found in the back yard. I started gnawing on its edges and saw Nana watching me. She seemed so pleased with what I was doing with this new stick that she had given me, that I wasn't sure who made the other happier. After a while, my little jaws began to ache from chewing on the stick, so I went to sleep by Nana's side. I guessed Christmas was over because the big tree in the front room soon vanished, along with Nana's own tree. Anyway, I really liked Christmas, no matter where I was living as long as I had nice people around me.

Sleep after sleep passed, but I was content. Everything was quiet, except when Andy and Jane came to feed Nana and do other stuff that did not smell good. Sometimes they even washed her whole body while she was in bed, but she seemed to like it and afterwards we took a long nap. Nana could not feed herself anymore, and I wished that I could help somehow. I was down to just one breakfast a day, but I really didn't miss Nana's extra bits that she had sometimes given me, but she still petted me and said, "Teddy, Teddy," though her voice got softer and hoarser almost every day.

There were few visitors who were all nice to me and patted me on the head and called me a "good dog." Some people even took me to the back yard so that I could relieve myself and hunt for those damnrabbits. Sometimes they even walked me on my leash, but they hardly knew that I was there. I thought it odd, but there were always two people who walked me, and they had serious talks on our walks, No fun. As soon as I was released from the leash, I shot down the hall, almost flying up to Nana's bed. When Nana wasn't sleeping, she always waited for my kisses, though she did not giggle much anymore. But she was always happy to see me, her best friend.

Time passed and Nana and I slept most of each day. The house was very quiet and the stale bitter smells from Nana's room grew stronger. People were kind to me, but staying with Nana so much made me constantly exhausted, so I rarely socialized. It was such a change from my life with Kathy, where I was always ready for signs that my help was needed. I guess Nana and I shared the same energy, if any existed between us.

There were a few days when Nana spoke weakly on the phone, but she still talked a long time, and I could still sleep. A few people that I had met came to see Nana, and they didn't stay long but always brought things for her – candy, which I could not have for some reason, good-smelling plants, and pictures. They all seemed like nice people, but sometimes I could hear them talking quietly outside Nana's door, and they all seemed angry about something.

One day Jane came into the room to talk to Nana, who just kept sleeping. Jane grabbed the phone, punched it with her fingers, and began to yell frantically. Nana did not react, and I just lay touching her. Then a loud crash and running through the hallway and Nana's door burst open. The first man through the door saw me on the bed and tossed me to the floor. I yelped and cried when I hit the floor that hard, and I crawled out of everyone's way trying to understand what I had done wrong to be treated so meanly. I would never hurt Nana.

Eventually, several men put Nana on a cart and left with her. I was hurting, something I rarely felt, but I was really worried about Nana. Where were they taking her? Why? Was she okay or just tired? When I finally limped to the front room, Jane picked me up and held me on her lap, while Andy sat on a chair and looked sad. No one spoke but they all stared at the tv, as though looking for answers. Jane took me outside to pee, then carried me to Nana's and my bed, kissed me on the head and vanished. What was I supposed to do? What was my purpose now?

Life continued, but without Nana it seemed that something important was missing. Jane changed the decaying plants in Nana's room and replaced them with healthy ones. Otherwise, I kept the same routine – outside bathroom, breakfast, scare goddamn rabbits, eat, sleep on Nana's big bed, be with Jane and Andy, eat, pee, go to bed. Repeat.

I was shocked when one day those people who pushed me off the bed returned with a special surprise – Nana. They rolled her into the house sitting on one of those chairs with wheels and lifted her into her bed. It was exciting, but at first Jane kept me away from Nana. She looked thin and wilted like a dying plant, but she still remembered me and said, "Teddy, Teddy" when Jane finally released me to give Nana kisses. She seemed different, and soon she closed her eyes to sleep, while still patting me on the head. Jane left us alone.

The next day we tried to return to our routine, except June no longer brought up her breakfast on a tray; instead, Jane put spoonsful of food into Nana's mouth, but I no longer begged or wanted to share Nana's treats. I don't think Nana even had her teeth.

Still, the time passed and Nana seemed to grow weaker, though she still called me Teddy and petted me with one hand. Every day I could smell the awful odor from the hospital, and it seemed to envelope her body more each day. My nose was sensitive, but I felt that Nana needed me. No one from outside came to see her any more, and only Andy, Jane and I kept her company, but still she slept more and more, sometimes smiling in her dreams

One night I heard her say, "Teddy," but I had a feeling that she meant another Teddy. So, it went. Each night she breathed less and less, until one night I felt her feeble hand drop onto my back, so I got up and climbed onto her chest and put my snout to chin. The smell of decay was so heavy, and the breathing was so quiet, until she crossed over into death. I would stay there until morning.

Jane was first to check on Nana, and I immediately got out of her way. Jane kept talking to Nana and shook her. Jane had been here before.

"Andy! Andy!" she shouted much more loudly than usual. Andy rushed into the room, Jane said something to him, and they immediately held each other and began to cry for a long time. I collapsed next to Nana and waited for them to tell me what to do. I knew that this was a sad morning and not the usual routine.

"Come, Teddy," Andy said as he tapped his leg, the cue for me to follow. I took one last look at Nana, licked her hand, and followed Andy. It was the last time I ever saw Nana. Hard to believe. My Nana. I spent the rest of the day out of the way in the back yard or on the couch in the front room. I wasn't in the mood to chase any damnrabbits, even if one had gotten into the house. That afternoon people came to the house and took away Nana, but I did not move. Now what?

The last time this happened, Kathy had gone away the same way – not carried out but she had just vanished without a word. That night I slept in my bed on Nana's bed. There was too much room, yet it seemed empty, so I climbed onto Nana's big pillow. It still had the same smells of decay and death, but I also found the good Nana smells – flowers, breakfast overwhelming the bed, and her not so pleasant breath, but I would never forget Nana, I spent the night where she should have been alive but still in my mind.

Several empty days passed, and mostly I spent them outside or on the couch. I stayed clear of Nana's room because Andy and Jane kept removing Nana's things from her room and putting them in boxes stacked by the front door. I would occasionally go to them for a sniff of Nana.

One day the doorbell rang, which I had learned meant that someone was at the front door, so I ran to it and barked loudly, in case Jane and Andy had not heard it. I assumed that was part of my job.

"Hush, Teddy!" said Jane as she opened the door. I did not know how to react to the surprise – Mary and Sarah both entered and immediately knelt for me to rush them and deliver kisses. It was a natural reaction that made everyone laugh and smile. Those two could always do that to me. Sarah spoke to Jane who answered with one word, "Teddy."

"Teddy, Teddy," they said and I wondered if they would call me "Patty" instead.

Mary and Sarah said how sorry they were about Nana's passing. Then Jane said something that puzzled me. "At least she'll be with the Teddy again, the love of her life." Was I going to die, too? Another thing to worry about.

We all gathered and sat in the front room to talk; I just listened. I recognized a few words – Nana, friend, happy, husband, but could not connect so many random thoughts. The one thing I did see was Andy carrying my bed and a bag with my things in it. I went and smelled the bag, but unlike Nana's bag, it smelled like me. Did this mean that I was leaving again? I did not stay as long as I had stayed at Kathy's, but everywhere was precious to me.

Sarah, Mary, and I soon left in their car, after many sad hugs and neck scratches, and head-to-head contact with tears. I really had liked Jane and Andy, but their home would never be the same without Nana. Then it was off for a long trip. Those damnrabbits were lucky; I had a feeling that I would never get back there. I slept in my bed on the back seat with an occasional awakening by the outside noises and bright lights.

We did stop at one place with those lights shining down on all those cars that were parked, but the place seemed busy. Sarah took care of the car while Mary walked me on a leash to a place where I could pee on some bushes. I could smell that several other dogs had also peed on those same bushes. Odd. Is there a special bush called a "pee bush"?

When we got back to the car, Sarah was gone, so I waited in my bed. Guess she didn't want to go on the special pee bush. Soon she came back carrying a big bag of food with wonderful smells, which I recognized immediately as MacDonald's. She climbed in and immediately gave some of the food to Mary. Then she took out more food and pulled it apart with her fingers. Sometimes Steve had brought home similar food in the same bags; Kathy had loved it.

Other times Steve would cook the same food outside on a grill, but Kathy preferred the bag stuff. Sarah put some on a paper and placed it in my bed. I almost ate it before it hit my bed. That food was glorious, like when Kathy shared some of hers with me. When I had finished all of it, Mary passed me a bowl of cool water, which was also delicious. I was so lucky to have people to take care of me. What did dogs that needed water do if they had none? This was way better than eating kibble. Could this trip get any better? Where were we going anyway? Satisfied and safe, I went back to sleep in my bed, not on Mary's lap, though I think I could have if I had jumped into the front seat.

When we finally stopped, I was rested and hoped for more of that food in a bag. Instead, we were in front of a house with its front lights shining, even though it was day time. Mary scooped me up and we all went to the front door. An older man opened the door, waved us in, and they all exchanged greetings. The old man, Bud, sat on a couch and Mary took me in her hands. I immediately jumped from them, ran across the couch, and came to a stop next to Bud to greet him with kisses, like I did with every willing person I met.

"Teddy, Teddy, no," barked Sarah. "Sit," and I did right next to Bud. He didn't seem to mind. In fact, he liked it and giggled like Nana always had.

"Teddy?" Bud asked, looking at me like maybe I had the wrong name. Seemed like every place I went, I got a new name.

"Yes," said Sarah, and then said more words.

"No," said Bud, "Teddy is good." I didn't know if he meant that I was a good dog, because he had just met me, or if he thought that my name was good. This house seemed nice, except for a slight scent of the decay that had followed me my whole life. Like at Nana's house when I had first arrived there. I had hoped that I would get used to the foul odor or that it would disappear. I didn't care for the outcome the last time at Nana's.

Suddenly I felt a collar put around my neck. It was cloth, not metal, and it didn't choke me when I pulled, but I still did not like it, especially if we were just in the house and not going anywhere. But when you're my size, there wasn't much to be done. The problem was gone when Bud attached a leash and we all went out a back door to his yard. It looked as nice as Kathy's yard. It was very large with lots of grass, big trees and bushes. I could hardly wait for someone to remove my collar and leash so that I could run as far as I wanted. As soon as Bud put me down, I started to race towards the back bushes but was abruptly stopped when I got to the leash's end. I tried again with the same result. Did this mean that I had this wonderful yard but could not play in it? Not even to chase damnrabbits? Not fair, almost criminal. Of course, I was not sure if this was my new home, but I had learned to sense a new house and owner, no matter how much time between jobs.

After talking to Mary and Sarah a while, Bud still held the leash and let me lead everyone around the yard, with the women following. I would walk a few steps and stop to sniff the area. Nothing special, but Bud waited patiently for me to do my dog routine. When we got to the back bushes, I realized that there was a fence on the other side of the bushes. I could smell that those damnrabbits had been there, even though there was a fence to stop them. There was an opening between the fence bottom and the ground that was big enough for a damnrabbit to go under, but not for me. They could come and go as they pleased, but I was a prisoner. This was a bad start, and I wondered if I was to live here with Bud.

Slowly we returned to the back door after walking around the entire yard. It was full of good and not so good smells, most of them wonderful. When we got back in the house, the people sat around a table and talked and signed papers. Done this before, too. Bud had put down a fresh water bowl and a bowl of kibble. Good sign? Bad sign? Mary returned from the car with my bed and a bag full of my stuff. Then she picked me up with one hand and looked at me nose to nose. It was a sad sign of parting but love.

"Be good," she said as tears came from her eyes. Then she passed me to Sarah, who repeated the farewell with even more tears. Sarah passed me to Bud and left me. Although we had done this before, it was as if they knew we would never see each other again. They were right. They were always in my heart and mind, but never again in person.

Bud and I sat on the couch. He rubbed my neck and scratched my back while constantly talking to me His was a soothing voice. It didn't matter if I could understand everything he was saying. I was enjoying this old man and felt safe. What more could a little dog want?

Soon the side door opened and a woman came in, carrying bags full of delicious smelling food, like the kind I had shared with Mary and Sarah. Not sure of my purpose yet in this new home, I jumped off the couch and ran to the new woman to check if I could help her as she put the bags on a table, then she knelt to see me, smiled and picked me up to ruffle my fur.

"Hi, Dad," she said, both words in my mind, because Kathy had always greeted Steve the same way. Her name was Lynn, and she often came to see Bud, usually carrying at least one bag of food, all from heavenly smelling places. Other days some nice people drove up to the house and brought food for Bud, but this food was not as good as Lynn's. In fact, after the kind people had left, Bud would put most of their food on the floor and offered it to me. I sniffed it and realized why Bud would not eat all of it either. Occasionally I ate some, but there was no real pleasure in it. Bud always had kibble ready.

"Teddy," Bud responded to something Lynn had said. I assumed that Teddy was my real name now, which was fine. Bud was sitting at the table and taking food out of the bags while Lynn put a little plate under the food that Bud was pulling apart with his fingers. Then she started to eat her own food (Italian beef), and I just sat on the floor and gave my best sad and hungry dog act, a skill all dogs are born with. Eventually, Bud took the plate that Lynn had prepared and put it on the floor for me. I had difficulty understanding, but I ran to the plate and almost in one swallow, cleaned the plate of the tasty meat that we all had. What a first meal!

Other days I got excited when I saw Lynn's car in the driveway, but she had no food. Instead, she took Bud away, and they were gone for a long time. They would return with several bags, as had Sarah and Mary every week. They put all cans and boxes on the kitchen shelves, and there was usually a treat box for me, too.

Bud would feed me kibble every night. Most times I ate only a piece or two, because it hurt too much. One time I even swallowed one of my little teeth. My mouth became so uncomfortable that I stopped eating kibble and hoped that Lynn would bring me some of that delicious food in a bag. I grew weak and could hardly walk with Bud any more. Not knowing why I would not eat and seeing that I was acting feeble and I simply was not as lively as I had first been, Lynn brought some new food for me. She opened an envelope and poured the contents into a bowl. I sniffed it and nothing smelled bad. There was a layer of some liquid on top that I could simply lick off the meat. The actual meat was little chunks, like a soft kibble, and I could chew and swallow it without pain. I was so hungry that I licked the bowl clean. My teeth still hurt and had the smell of decay that I had easily learned to recognize and ignore somewhat.

Still, my teeth were constantly aching, and I wished that I had had the power of speech so that I could tell them that I wanted the pain to stop. Bud would sometimes give me hard treats, but I never ate them. Many teeth came lose and I would swallow some of them. Other than the food, which was edible now, thanks to Lynn, life with Bud was good. We would walk around the yard on a leash, and I stopped trying to get loose. Except one time when we were near the back bushes and I saw one. Toothless or not, I barked and made a lunge for it, but my leash held me back.

"Damn rabbit," said Bud so I knew that Steve had the right name. Rarely saw another one during my time there, but I wouldn't have tried anyway. Those walks around the yard were the basic activity of the day, no matter if there was rain or snow. Bad weather had made us take longer to get ready for our trips around the yard than for the actual walk. Bud always had special shoes and a heavy coat; he even bought me a coat. It was a good fit, but there were days when I wondered why it took him so long to put it on me.

When we weren't walking, we would sit in a room by the back yard, and he would watch something on television, while I looked out of his glass door to the yard. Bud would sleep with his feet up and I would squeeze my little body next to him. It was like I was with Nana, except I had to share one chair with Bud. Sometimes he would make popcorn, which my dwindling teeth could still chew and enjoy. Other people came and went, but other than Lynn, I rarely saw anyone twice.

Until one day when my life had a major change. There was a loud knocking at the side door, and Bud and I were napping in the back room. I thought that I had better check whatever it was, because that was about my only job in that household. I raced down the hall and reached the door just as it opened. Nobody but Lynn ever came in and she never knocked. I kept barking with my most ferocious yaps, which was not like the big dogs' threats. Still, I did my best and even jumped at the intruder, but he was too big and not afraid. I bounced off him like he was a wall. I was getting tired from all this barking and jumping at the same time, when I heard Bud's voice behind me, "Teddy!" Then this new man bent down and stuck out his hand so that I could smell it. Behind him was a woman, who also bent down to pet me, and she seemed nice and not too afraid. I could always trust a woman for some reason. Bud's hand scooped me up and we went to sit on our usual place on the couch. They talked while I listened and soon I knew their names – Larry and Becky, and eventually I learned that they were family, which explained their bold entrance into my house. At this time whoever would have guessed that we would become so close. I decided to test these people, so I jumped out of Bud's arms and up next to Larry, who immediately held me with one hand and petted me with the other. I was trying to reach Becky to give her kisses, but apparently she did not like dog kisses. She may have liked dogs, just not their kisses. In fact, she called me "sewer breath," and Larry agreed, but I could still kiss him.

We were interrupted by someone else entering through the side door without knocking. It was Lynn and she had her hands full of food in a bag. The heck with meeting new people; Lynn was here with gourmet food. Larry and Becky must have really liked that delicious food too, because they went directly to Lynn and gave her long hugs and grabbed some of those bags. Lynn must have been a good cook, because we all had a great lunch.

Larry and Becky came to visit Bud's house sometimes, but not every day like Lynn. They would do things in Bud's house. One time they even brought a bunch of fences and made a small enclosure in the back so that Bud could just open the back door and I could go outside without a leash, run, and do my business. I don't know why they just didn't put a big fence around the whole back yard so that I could run all day long. I guess that I wouldn't be able to when there was snow, because I was too short. I don't think Bud was too fond of the snow either, so the small yard was just fine for a small dog.

Another time they visited because Bud and I could hear a strange noise in the back room. It sounded like some other animal, but I really wasn't sure, nor did my barking make it stop. Anyway, Larry and Becky stayed until they had fixed the problem; I don't know how, but the noise left. During those few days I grew close to Larry, because he never went to sleep until everyone in the house was gone.

I cuddled next to him and even climbed on his chest, nose to nose, like I had with Nana the night she left us. Becky kept saying "sewer breath" and pushed me away but Larry always cuddled with me.

One night, after Becky and Larry had gone to their home, Bud got out of bed and fell in the hallway. I was afraid but went to him lying on the floor. He seemed happy to see me but I could tell that he, too, was scared. I couldn't help him and there was no one else to help, so I just sat by him and barked at times, to which he reacted by talking and petting me. Eventually with much struggle he was sitting on the floor and seemed better, but he kept falling when he tried to stand. He must have realized that I was too small to physically help, so he tried crawling back to his bed, where he was able to pull himself up high enough to roll onto the bed. Exhausted, he lay there for a while until he finally reached and pushed something next to his pillow and collapsed.

A short time later I could hear someone in our kitchen. I knew that wasn't right, so I ran down the hallway and barked to either scare the strangers away or to cry for help. Some large men in the hallway were running towards me. They looked at me, called me a "good dog," lifted my scared little body and set me down behind them. They kept going towards Bud's room and I followed with my barks to help them more. I could see the first man checking Bud like I had seen in the old people's hospital and at Nana's. They were trying to help him, not hurt him. The two men left, putting me on the couch on their way out. I would have followed but they had closed the door

Soon the door reopened and I felt better when I saw Lynn. She could fix Bud; she always did. Behind her other people followed and carried a big bed with wheels. I had seen those rolling beds before, and they were never a good sign. Lynn sat on the couch with me and petted me while I was shaking and watching for Bud. Despite her attention, I really did not feel happy and did not wag my tail. She talked calmly and we watched Bud being rolled out. I almost felt sick I was so scared, even with Lynn there. I remembered how almost the same thing had happened to Nana, but she had come home to die.

After all the people had left with Bud, Lynn stayed while she talked on the phone. I could not tell who she was talking to or if Bud would soon be back. She took me to the back door and let me outside, which I greatly appreciated after all the excitement.

Lynn was crying when she let me back in, but I did not know how to help her. There were times in my life when I wished that I had been born bigger. Still, Lynn seemed to feel better when she was trying to make me feel better. Must be some kind of trick. She and I slept in a room where visitors slept. We both had a hard time sleeping, and I worried about Bud and thought back to the hospital and Nana. I wanted things back to normal. Lynn did the best she could to take care of me during the day – walks on a leash, even out of the yard, car rides and even trying to play with a ball, but I was just tired and worn; I suspected my older age was slowing me. That routine did not last long, and many sleeps later she took me on a long car ride.

She had put pillows on the front seat so that I could see far. I could not remember seeing any of this countryside. At first there were many cars, but they were replaced with fields and other animals, including cows, which I had seen in books at Kathy's school and house. I slept and woke up when we finally stopped in a parking lot. Lynn picked me up and carried me to someone. At first, I thought it was Bud, and eagerly jumped into his arms but I realized that it was Larry, who looked just like Bud, only not as old. Disappointed, but a good second choice, Larry hugged Lynn, being carefully not to squeeze the little dog. He took me to his car and put me on Becky's waiting lap; she still didn't want any kisses. Another surprise – Lynn gave Larry and Becky a bag full of my bed, toys and treats. Crying, she patted me on the head and I gave her a quick kiss. Lynn said some words like "good dog," and walked back to her car. What was happening? Did this mean another end and another home?

They seemed like good people, even if Becky did not let me kiss her and called me "sewer breath," a name I recognized but did not understand. She played with my nails, which had been hurting for a long time but I had adjusted. I felt lonely without Bud and feared that I would not see him anymore. With Becky and Larry at least I felt safe.

When we got to their house, I was exhausted but glad to be in another home with safe people who I knew. They put my bed next to theirs, because their bed was as high as Nana's, without steps and since I couldn't jump too high anymore and I didn't think anyone would pick me up every night, I learned to sleep alone on the floor next to them. I bet most dogs never slept as good as me. It was a short trip to the kitchen for water, food, and treats. The next morning, I found that they also had a big yard and they let me wander anywhere I wanted, up to the fence. Trading Bud for my new freedom hardly seemed fair, but it could have been worse.

One day Larry and Becky took me in their car, and I hoped that it wouldn't be for another long drive to another new home like the last time. It wasn't, and we arrived at a building next to a pizza place; I loved those smells. Unfortunately, we didn't get pizza and they carried me into the building and into a small room and placed me on a counter. I had seen places like this, and soon a large man entered and greeted us calmly. When he approached me, he put out his hand to sniff, and I could smell all kinds of animals, including cats and dogs and a few unrecognizable, but I did not feel afraid. He even gave me a small treat, which I tried to chew but it hurt a little, so I just dropped it.

He immediately picked up my lips and checked my remaining teeth. Then he picked up my paws, shook his head and said something to Larry. A friendly woman came in the room, and she carried me to a bigger room, where another man checked my paws, shook his head too (must have been a code), and picked up some kind of a cutter. While the woman held me tight, the man proceeded carefully to cut my nails. He was very good because he never hurt me, like those people by Bud's house had. Maybe it was the kindness of the woman who held me, and they were quickly done and put me on the floor. The pain was all gone. I could live with these people.

The woman took me back to the first room, where Larry and Becky were waiting. Between my nails not causing pain and their presence, I wagged my tail hard and even peed a little on the woman. Sorry, just so happy. Once I was on the table again, the big man started to check me over, while Larry listened and nodded. Then we went home and I realized that my adventure for the day was over.

I felt better running in my new yard, and I even thought I saw a damnrabbit, so I barked and ran fast at him, but he got away through a small space under the fence. It felt good to run without pain again Damnrabbit was lucky this time, but there's always tomorrow. Becky took away my kibble and poured some soft meat onto a plate for me. It was good and a new taste. That night Larry picked me up and let me sleep on the big bed with them. Maybe he thought my paws still hurt, but I just liked being there. I stretched as far as I could by their feet so that I could be touching them both at the same time. It was wonderful.

One day we all went back to the place that made my nails feel normal again. I wanted to call it a hospital, but just for animals? Now that my paws were good, what was the plan? We went right back to the same room, where the same woman was waiting for me. Larry held me on the table while she checked me, for what purpose I did not know.

Larry and Becky ruffled my head and belly, said goodbye and left. Was I getting another home? Why? I grew afraid and started to shake and whine. The woman Cheryl held me and tried to soothe me while another woman came in; she was hiding something. Cheryl held me tight with my head facing the wall, so that I could not see the other woman. Soon I felt a sharp poke in my skin. I had had that experience before. It didn't really hurt much, just a surprise.

This time Cheryl carried me to the larger room where they had cut my nails. She placed me on the table and petted me, which really felt good because I was getting so tired that I could hardly keep my eyes open. Soon I was sleeping, seeing some awesome (a favorite Kathy word) sights, such as fields of green and countless friendly dogs running and playing. No one was tired or thirsty or hungry or sick. It was a great place to be, but I wondered where I was. I remembered one of my innate memories of a place called Rainbow Bridge, but I wasn't sure how to get there yet.

When I awoke, I was on a soft blanket in a cage. Other dogs were near, and they were really barking, but I was just too tired to join them, so I went back to sleep, hoping to find the last place I had visited.

Cheryl was lifting me again and she carried me back to the small room and set me on the smaller table. My legs weren't there, and I began to fall, but Cheryl was waiting as if she had expected me to fall. So she set me on my side again and petted me with one hand and scratched my head with her other hand. Sometimes she would grab a leg and bend it so that I knew that I still had legs; they just didn't work as well.

It was about this time that I realized an odd taste in my mouth and that my tongue was hanging out one side and touching the table.

That wasn't right, but there was something else out of place. It was my teeth. They weren't just out of place; they were gone. But with their absence the discomfort and the pain, were also gone. I tried to give my best good-dog smile, but my tongue kept falling out.

Eventually Cheryl put me on my legs and I didn't fall down any more. Then she brought me the best thing I could ask for – a cold bowl of water. I started to lap it up like I had never had it. Even my non-functional tongue was working at full speed. She let me drink until she thought that I had had enough, I think. She put me on the floor and led me back to the smaller room and let me explore it without falling. The big man came in and put me back on the table. He shined a light in my eyes, and then lifted my lips. Even though my tongue slid from side to side, he smiled. I wasn't sure, but I think I often heard people call me "cute."

Suddenly there was a knock at the door and in came Larry and Becky. If I hadn't been so unsure of where I was or of what had happened, I would have cried. Instincts took over and I jumped toward Larry, who picked me up, and I covered him with dog kisses from a dog minus full control of his tongue. Even Becky leaned in and I gave her one too. Wow!

The people talked, but I was waiting to get outside --- too much water too fast. Soon I was on my leash and lifting my leg on the wall by the pizza place. Still, we didn't go in, just home. That was okay. I didn't want to stay or eat pizza. I just wanted to sleep.

I was dog-tired for several days. While I usually looked forward to walks and playing in the back yard, now I was content to sleep on the cozy blanket that Becky had put in the sun for me. I was glad that no damnrabbits came, because I did not have the strength to even bark, let alone chase. I did notice that my missing teeth no longer caused pain, and I even slept better. There were only empty gums, but I cannot say that I missed those teeth. I still ate the same food, but it was more fun to eat now. They had even bought some soft treats that a toothless dog could enjoy. At night I sat on the couch between Larry and Becky. They had put some stairs for me to climb to their bed, like the ones at Nana's, and I found a new permanently shared bed. Guess they felt that I couldn't jump very high anymore, and they were right.

After a while I began to feel like my old self. I still couldn't jump or run much, but maybe I had just grown old. Then came the day I did not expect. The three of us got into the car for an all- day trip, only stopping with lots of other cars to go to the bathroom and to get some good food, which they shared with me. And it was so much easier to chew without using my teeth; the gums did their work without complaint.

Finally, we arrived at a house that looked vaguely familiar. I wasn't sure until I saw Lynn greeting us all. Was Bud here too? Is he not sick anymore? We all went in the house, and I immediately jumped up on the couch waiting for Bud, but when he didn't come, I went right back to sleep while they all talked in the kitchen. That night we all got into Lynn's car, which was odd. I sat on Larry's lap, which was warm and safe, although I did worry about this strange activity.

After a short drive Lynn parked in a dark place. We all got out and Larry walked me on the leash so that I could pee on the building, always a pleasure. We just stood and stared at a door. Finally, a woman appeared and waved us in. Larry picked me up and took off the leash. We went into the building, which smelled like a hospital. I sure was getting used to that awful odor. Once inside Larry held me off the floor, and I looked down the hall.

"Teddy," came an old broken voice. It was Bud, and I forgot all my aches and raced down the slippery hallway like I had in Kathy's school. I skidded a little but ran straight to his waiting arms and kissed every place I could find, both of us crying. I think even Becky and Larry and Lynn were crying. They must have been as surprised as I was. Who knew that Bud would be here?

Soon Becky was pushing us in Bud's wheelchair while I continued my assault on his face. All this excitement made me want to pee again despite my short visit outside. Guess I was getting old, because Bud used to go to the bathroom at night, too. Not wanting to pee on Bud, I jumped down from his lap and relieved myself on the nearest table leg. As long as I was on the floor and everyone seemed occupied, I decided to explore. I found a doorway but the woman in white blocked it. She might not have wanted Bud to escape, either. I went to his chair and he picked me up like old times.

I sat on Bud's lap and he cuddled me the way he used to do. The people talked and I sat quietly, enjoying the company. I assumed that we would be taking Bud back to his house with the back yard and our leash walks. Suddenly I felt Bud's fingers in my mouth, where my teeth used to be. He said something to me, but he didn't sound mad like he didn't want me anymore. I thought of how Nana and Bud both had put their teeth in a glass of water by their beds. Would I get one too? I wanted to leave with Bud now, so I jumped down to see if that woman would block my way again. I walked around the room and found no other exit. For me alone, maybe, but not for all those people and a wheelchair

Larry lifted me and put me back on Bud's lap. We all went back to the hallway where I first saw Bud, and I was happy that we were all going home. But I felt a drop on my head, and looked up and saw tears falling from his eyes, tears of sadness. He held me tight and talked to me like he wasn't going with us. Like we would never see each other again. I thought that to be true the last time, but this time I think he felt it, too. So did I. And sadly, we were both right. I barked a farewell at Bud and he waved a tearful goodbye "See you at Rainbow Bridge," I thought.

The next day we made the long trip back to Madison. Life felt different, even emptier and eternally sad, despite all the efforts of Larry and Becky. I guess they couldn't know what it was like to never again see someone who had meant so much. Larry took me for long walks on my leash. Many people stopped and talked to us, but I never really cared. Becky and Larry treated me special, and I made room for them to take the spot that Bud had occupied.

One day Larry and Becky left for several days, but I didn't know why. I sensed some sadness when they packed their clothes. A nice girl named Carly stayed with me and let me sleep on the big bed with her. She took me for long walks and drives, but I still missed Bud and was beginning to miss Larry and Becky, too. They had never left me for this long. It took me ever so long before I accepted that Bud was gone forever, like Nana. Maybe they went to the same place. I wasn't sure if people had a nice place like Rainbow Bridge to go after they left us, but I chose to believe that they did.

Once they got back, every day was much the same —time in the yard while I watched Becky dig in her dirt like a dog, so I wanted to help, but she didn't seem to want my assistance. She even put-up small walls around where she dug, I assumed so that I could not get over them. Two more Christmases passed, but they did not take me to get a tree, like they used to do.

One day Larry took me in the back yard to do my business. I went out but felt no need to do anything, so I did my usual run around the yard, but not as fast, to the back fence, where I gave my usual growl to the neighbor dog, then returned to the house. He had put some treats on the floor, which was a sign that I was going to be alone for a while. I landed on the couch, ate my treats, and slept. A loud noise outside scared me awake, but that was all. Except that now that I was awake, all I could think about was my need to poop. I usually did that earlier, but Larry brought me in before I really needed to go, and things got worse and more uncomfortable. I went downstairs by the back door and hoped that it would magically open for me. When they both left me, I could not judge how long I would be alone. Once, it was dark before they came home, but they brought me some delicious food in a bag. What I remember about that day beside the food was that I had messed in the house and they did not get mad at me. They even felt bad that they had left me for so long and cleaned my mess without yelling at me.

Although it wasn't dark yet, I hoped they wouldn't be mad if I pooped on the floor. Boy, was I wrong! Larry went downstairs to let me out, but soon turned around and stomped his feet as he pointed at my mess and used his "bad-dog" voice. I would have cleaned it if I had been able. He had never yelled at me like this. No one had. To make it worse, he even stomped his foot at me, like he was going to get me. I was really scared and started to run up the stairs. I was going so fast that I slipped and landed on my neck. It hurt but I kept running from Larry. I took a few more steps and coughed and coughed, and I had a hard time breathing.

I went by my water bowl, and soon Larry came, pounding his feet hard on the steps and I was still afraid. Instinctively I went to the bedroom and crawled under the bed, a place where I usually felt safe and sometimes slept. I heard him get something from the kitchen and then the sound of his chair moving, usually a good sign – I could sit on his lap and he would sometimes give me popcorn, not that I wanted any now.

I crawled out from my safe space and slowly went to the front room to see if Larry was any better. I stared at him. He seemed calm but I had never seen him that mad, so I carefully walked to the front of his chair. He usually had the shelf where he rests his feet lowered so that I could make the short jump from the shelf to his lap. This time the shelf was too high, but Larry was so mad that he must have forgotten to lower it for me. I used to be able to make that high jump, and I wanted to see if he was the old Larry or the angry Larry.

I concentrated on the jump, like when I was younger. My eyes on the shelf, I leapt with every effort of my tiny legs. I was almost there, going to make it, when Larry yelled, "No, Teddy, no! Bad dog!" all words and tone I understood. I became scared again, lost my concentration, and felt my throat hit the shelf. I fell onto my back. Everything hurt and I hacked some more.

Suddenly the old Larry was back, and he picked me up, gently brought me to my water bowl, where I was able to take a few laps. Then he did something he had never done. He stretched out next to me on the floor with our noses almost touching and scratching my head while using soft and kind tones to comfort me. Things seemed back to normal except for my coughs, which I hoped would soon disappear.

Becky got home and Larry told her, I assume, why we were both on the floor in the kitchen. It didn't take long before we were all in the car. Larry held me while Becky drove fast. I seemed to be able to breathe easier, but I still had a cough. We arrived at another building that had the smell of hospital all over it. We went to a big desk (don't forget, everything was big to me), and a nice girl behind the desk talked to them. Soon, another man came out and took me alone to another room. Why couldn't Larry and Becky help me? I became afraid again, and I started to hack harder.

Once the strange man had me alone and on a table, he started to shine a light in my eyes and down my throat. Lucky those teeth were missing. He felt my throat like he was choking me, so I understandably coughed for him. A few more feels and listens of my chest, and he was done, because soon I was back in the other room, where Larry and Becky seemed to be talking with the nice woman. Larry seemed angry again (don't get him mad!), I wanted to warn them. He quickly swept me off the front desk and we hurried out the door and into the car. We drove all the way home in silence with only the sound of my coughing.

When we got home, Larry again put me by my water bowl, but I really did not care for my food or water. They went to the front room and I slowly followed Larry to his chair. He put a warm blanket on his lap, then lifted and settled me, like we usually did. I snuggled comfortably in his being, except that I had a harder time breathing, but he wasn't mad anymore and seemed to be glassy eyed. Becky sat on the couch and watched us, and she was crying. It was okay now; he wasn't mad anymore and I still felt safe.

"Teddy, Teddy," Larry kept saying as he stroked my side and rubbed my head. "You're the worst dog I ever had." My senses were dimming, and I struggled for breath .Yet, I had a serene sense of what was happening, but I still felt safe and secure. Light grew dimmer and I

could only hear Larry whispering my name. Somehow my memories took me back to my beginnings with my pup mates – Silver, Queenie, Rascal, Dustball, and as I was known then, Scruffy. I couldn't help but wonder where they had all gone and when I would see them again. After my canine family, I envisioned the first people who had helped me – Hot Duhr and Tubby Johnson. They were good people, too.

"Teddy, Teddy," softer but soothing.

So many people who I was so happy to have met – Sarah and Mary, who first took me home with them and to the park with the scary fireworks. They took me to live with Steve and Laurie and their ever wonderful daughter Kathy. I always knew she was different from anyone else I had ever met, even kids at her school, but she taught me so much about love and patience.

"Teddy, Teddy," softer yet, but soothing.

Crossing my near dream state were Steve and Laurie and poor Nana, who I never knew in any other state than sick. She was old and ill but full of love, always lying in her bed with me by her side. It was my pleasure.

And, of course, there was dear old Bud, who may have been my favorite if dogs were allowed to choose. I thought of Larry and Becky who had done everything they could for me after Bud was gone. I just wished I had had a little more time to thank them all for how much they had done to make my life so precious. It seems that after I had visited my past, the fading lights were completely gone, but not for long. Everything slowly became brighter, like when I was first born and waiting for something to happen. I was no longer on Larry's lap, but that other place that I had briefly visited – a pasture with so many happy and healthy dogs playing and chasing and running. There were even some damnrabbits frolicking amongst the dogs without causing any trouble. Perhaps the oddest sight was a dog standing on top of a cow.

Then I heard a voice again calling, "Teddy, Teddy," but it was two voices and they were loud and clear. I looked up at Rainbow Bridge, and there were Bud and Nana, both healthy and smiling and waving to me.

I lost my tooth

Always have my license

Chapter 11
From Katrina to Snowfall

"It's not what we have in life that matters, but who we have in our
lives that matter."
Emily Dickinson, American poet

Four years passed slowly before we took another dog into our lives. The time the dog-less break was nice, because we did not have to get a dog/house sitter every time we wanted to vacation or just go for a weekend. My usual caretakers had left home and gone to college, and they had spoiled us, so it was difficult finding someone new who was reliable for long periods of time, but we did take more vacations and tried to enjoy our new independence.

No matter where we went, and we had touched all seven continents, our dogs were always with us. One time we were sitting on a pastoral hillside in Scotland, when from nowhere appeared a border collie. "Macduff, Macduff" we would both say. Buenos Aries was full of dog walkers who often had four or five dogs on leashes and who were walked all at once, which reminded us of how difficult it was to walk one dog at times, and all the breeds triggered memories. Even in Sofia, we came out of a small store and there was a dog chained to a bike, waiting for its master. Whenever you go someplace without your dog, especially for long periods of time, your dogs are still with you.

After extensive searching and still feeling that something was missing from our lives, we found many rescue-dogs on-line, and took our chance on a dog that resembled Toto, who would be on display Saturday at our Pet Heaven Store on the east side. We decided to checkout this cute guy, if his picture was any sign.

When we first saw the dog, his name was Binky. He was sleeping in the top portable kennel, stacked four high and six across, like a showcase of canines. All the dogs were waiting to be adopted from their travelling canine crew. Every Saturday, Shelter from the Storm Rescue Service transported twenty-four cages from its humane shelter in Madison to the local pet store chain, hoping that someone would adopt at least one stray dog and take it to its forever home.

Unlike most of the other dogs, who were busy barking, yipping, and pawing their cage doors to get anyone's attention, Binky was lying on his side with his face mostly fur- covered in case anyone might show some interest. I didn't think that this was his first visit to be adopted. He was either bored from unsuccessfully have done this side show too often, or he really did not care. He had shelter, food, water, and an hour a day of outdoor exercise with other strays like him, and socializing was apparently not a routine he embraced with an unsure future that may lead to further disappointment but nothing to fuss about. Who knew his history?

I was never sure why anyone would ever name a dog Binky, a word usually associated with a baby's pacifier. Certainly, this terrier looked nothing like an infant's mouthpiece. His ragged face looked like a cross between an eighty-year-old grandfather in bad need of a good grooming and a broken-down prizefighter. A tooth was missing from the right side of his mouth, exhibiting mottled gums and a bit of pink tongue hanging out unencumbered, not unlike Teddy's gap. His black nose appeared normal, like a black marble imbedded in a small ball of straw. His eyes were not visible behind the mop of fur hanging like a store awning over his forehead. When he turned his head, one pointed ear stood erect, and the other folded nearly in half.

I had found Binky's picture on the internet, and that photo shot from above, showed him standing on a floor, not looking like a Westminster champion or even a participant, but when I looked closely, I would detect an upright posture that showed some spunk and an unclear background of a dog who had survived some stressful times. His eyes looked alert and wary.

Never having heard of a Silky Terrier, I checked the American Kennel Club standards. A brief history related that Binky was half Yorkie and half Australian shepherd. The British brought their Yorkies to Australia to breed them with Australian shepherds in order to "improve their coats." Whether improved coats meant more weatherproof to resist the damp, rainy Yorkshire climate or cosmetically more colorful, was unclear. Binky's coat, once groomed, presented a mélange of colors –black, white, grey, silver, and brown, which, combined and highlighted by the sun, created waves of blue. It was a beautiful symphony of colors, like a Jackson Pollack creation, only with some order. At the end of World War II, GI's brought the unique breed home to the states, where they proliferated to a qualifying number in order to be officially recognized as an official dog by the American Kennel Club. I really don' think that the dogs cared, at least not outwardly.

I had come to Pet Heaven purposely to see this strange, little dog that children would undoubtedly run after and call him "Toto." I had buried four dogs in my adult life, and thought that for the first time I would get a rescue dog. People often make comments about adopting a child because the world has so many that need good homes. Seemed to apply to pets, too.

My wife took it upon herself to open the cage and remove Binky for further inspection. She was quickly stopped by an attendant who made clear that it was best if they removed the dogs from the cages. I thought it odd but was later told that the dogs, especially unknown rescue dogs, might snap at a stranger, and the shelter did not want to be responsible for a wounded customer. Not a great start in building a trusting relationship, I thought, but I realized that a dog kept in a cage might be fearful of being grasped by a total stranger, even me. I soon learned that old Snaggletooth was quite skillful when defending himself.

Once Binky was safely on the floor and had a choke chain around his neck, we were startled by the dog's werewolf appearance. Only slightly over a foot tall, his coat dragged on the floor, not like a neatly groomed show dog, but more like a dread-locked Bob Marley, whose greasy coils swept the floor on our short tour around the store. He walked quickly, hoping to explore more area than the confines of his little prison. Who knows how many hours a dog was free of its cage? I wasn't sure if there were laws that limited his solitary confinement. I wondered how he'd fare with our vast, fenced-in yard.

Becky and I walked around the store and tried to ignore curious shoppers who wondered why we would take a mop for a walk around the store. At first sight, Binky immediately lunged towards a wide, double-glass doors exit. It was as if he had planned the escape, which may have already failed several times, but maybe this time his luck would change. I couldn't imagine where he would have gone on such a busy Saturday, but I suspect that he was thinking, 'Anywhere, but here.'

I started to pick him up with one arm, but he surprised me with a quick snap of his jaws, but even with a missing tooth, I suspected that he meant business. Without problem Becky picked him up and was greeted with a few dog kisses and a snuggle into her shoulder. As time passed, I developed a feeling that Binky definitely disliked men. Becky set the dog back on the floor, hoping nobody had noticed our recent incident. Soon we were greeted by a woman named Maureen, according to a volunteer tag on the red Bucky Badger polo shirt.

"Can I help you?" she asked politely, not noticing the rabid dog at our feet. Again, I had a feeling that Binky had been through this before, but then was rejected and put back in his cage. I had a sense of why.

"I was wondering about this dog," was all I had to say before a quick look and she replied with "Sure, that's Binky. Here's a copy of his statistics and background."

Before I started to read his "statistics," like he was a potential scholarship candidate for a Big Ten football team, I had one question that really bothered me.

"Who would ever call a dog 'Binky'?"

She stared at me as though considering me unfit for adopting the dog if I had to ask such a stupid question.

'Okay, Dummy,' she thought, but instead saw a potential customer to take another dog off their hands and replied, "All rescue dogs have to have a name. We can't just assign numbers--too impersonal and hard to keep track of. So, everyone working at the shelter gets to assign one name. Mrs. Stewart's grandson always asked for his binky, so she decided to give the name to Binky here. Isn't that cute?"

With no barf bag in sight, I thought, 'Sure, cute as having diarrhea at a wedding. I guess I should have been grateful that the kid's favorite word wasn't mama or poop. No matter, this little guy was no Binky, Maybe Harvey, just something more canine.

I quickly scanned his stat sheet while Binky and Becky kept close eyes on me, trying to gauge my inclination.

Breed:	Silky Terrier
Age:	8 years, 2 months
Weight:	11 pounds
Size:	small
Altered:	yes
Danger:	no
Color:	mixed brown, black, silver, blue

The basics were followed by two pages of veterinarian information, including vaccines, general check-up dates of vet appointments, chip installation and number.

"Sorry, buddy, but maybe you're better off," I kidded him about the altered condition. Apparently, no sense of humor. Nowhere did I see an explanation for his missing tooth or his one floppy ear. I read once that God irons cach puppy's ears to stand erect, but some intelligent dogs would flee immediately after the one ear had been opened and ironed so that they could explore their new world of sights and smells, and not even God could catch them to finish the job. Legend said that a dog with one erect and one floppy ear was a sign of an intelligent dog. Could Binky be one of those super-intelligent creatures? Nah, I decided as I looked at the living rope mop bundled in my wife's arms.

"Excuse me, Maureen," I addressed the volunteer, "I have one more question."

"Ask away."

"I scanned most of the dog's paperwork here, but I never saw any indication as to where he came from; do you know?"

She thought carefully before answering, "All of our dogs are rescued primarily from three states—Texas, Louisiana, and Tennessee. These three sates tend to have a lot of flooding, which causes hardship not only for the homeowners, but tremendous stress for their animals, everything from gerbils to cattle. Judging from the timing that Binky arrived in Wisconsin and the time that he's been with us, I would guess that Binky might have been a survivor of Hurricane Katrina."

That bit of information knocked me back a little; I never would have expected a Katrina dog would be held in my wife's arms. Was it coincidence or fate? We had seen news videos of people on rooftops, some holding dogs, waiting to be rescued, but never expected to have one in our home.

Becky and the dog kept staring at me, waiting for a verdict. Thirty seconds ago, I thought how cool and noble it would be to rescue a Katrina dog. Now I realized that the dog was either very good at surviving or was abandoned because no one wanted him. That never-knowing detail was definitely part of deciding to choose a rescue dog.

Binky yawned and his tongue rolled out as he squirmed to get closer to Becky. In turn, she hugged him tighter and ruffled the top of his head, as all four eyes increased the intensity of their vigil. It looked like they might already be bonding on some level. This was like being forced to decide on if I thought the plug should be pulled on a dying, hundred-year-old aunt. I swear that the dog was conspiring with my wife and that he just possibly could think on a higher level than I could. He was a survivor for a reason.

"Okay, we'll take him," I proclaimed, which made Becky smile large and Binky yawn again. Little brat!

We had planned on bringing two dogs home so that they could keep each other company, double our fun, and save two lives. I hadn't seen any dog other than Binky, but there was one that caught my attention – a special needs dog named Paul, a black mutt who took cute pictures. He was vastly overweight and had a thyroid condition, which meant a strict diet and large vet bills. We weren't poor and who else would be willing or able to adopt him? Rescuing a Katrina dog would be a good deed, but saving a sick dog would almost be considered as saintly in the animal kingdom.

I asked Maureen if we could see Paul, also, to see if he and Binky were already friends who would get along just fine and be willing to share a home

"Sure," she said. "Julie, could you bring Paul out of his cage so these nice people could see him?"

To me she said, "You know that he has special needs and may require more attention than Binky. I hope he's not the jealous type."

Julie brought the black chunk of fat and handed him to me. Paul was closer to being a bowling ball than a sleeping dog. Still, if we could help him lead a good life, maybe even with the help of Binky, it would be worth the extra time and money. Paul and Binky sniffed each other, but no kisses. I think they knew each other but nothing special. Hard to predict the future.

"Do you think we could handle them both?" I asked Becky with slight prejudice in my tone. She apparently did not oppose it and replied, "Sure, why not?"

"Okay, we'll take them both," I told Maureen and she smiled and dug through her folder for Paul's papers. She pulled one out, and it had a red tab sticking out. I assumed it was a special needs marker.

"Carol," she called over her shoulder, "were you fostering Paul this last week?"

A rather large woman ('thyroid' I thought) ambled over to see if there was a problem.

"Yes, I've had him for three weeks now. Other than his health problems, he's a sweet little guy," she said with a little pinch on Paul's nose.

Maureen hesitantly asked her, "Did you take him for his vet check-up that was scheduled for Wednesday?"

Carol's brain was apparently taxed as she pretended to spin through her mental Rolodex, trying to find Wednesday. Light bulb time!

"You know, thinking back, I had to change my hair appointment to Wednesday because Mary Kay was taking a long weekend so she could go see her granddaughter in Minocqua. I guess I completely forgot about the vet. But I'm sure he's okay." Maureen cut her off before she could give some lame excuse for her careless error.

"You know we can't let a dog go for adoption without the proper health check. We could lose our license. I'm sorry folks, but you can't have Paul this week."

And just like that, because of someone's futile beauty shop appointment, two dogs' lives were changed forever. Maybe the dogs would never have tolerated each other, but maybe they both could have had more fulfilling lives.

I looked at Binky, whose tongue was again hanging-out.

"Perhaps you'd like us to hold him for you until next week, or look at one of our other dogs." This woman knew how to sell dogs, but apparently not how to select one for everyone's lifestyle and desires.

I scratched the top of Binky's head and those soulful eyes looked happy.

"No, we'll see how just one dog at a time works. We can always get another. Who knows, we may feel the need for a more active dog."

Boy, was that the wrong to say if Binky was even listening.

On the way home Becky held Binky on her lap. She was daring enough to roll down the window and let him stick-out his head. I was afraid that he might try to jump to freedom, but she held him by his back legs and he seemed to have no desire to escape. No matter where he had come from, his nose was going like an outboard motor. A dog's nose is 15,000 times more sensitive than a human's, and it looked like Binky was making the most of it. At times he would be afraid by a truck or bus's air brakes or some hot rod's specialized non-muffler, but Becky scratched his back and held him tightly until he seemed to relax again. With all that he had experienced, which was still unclear, he might have learned and adapted quickly. All I could think was that I have to get rid of that name Binky.

We pulled into our garage, and the dog did not know what to do. He had probably been passed around so much lately before getting to his new home that everything must have seemed extremely foreign, causing additional stress. Beck carried him to the back door of the house and released him into the back yard. NASA could not have developed a faster booster rocket. Binky just ran to one place and looked through the picket fence, then raced off to someplace else. Our yard was beautiful. Becky had planted so many flowers according to height and color so that we would have an enjoyable garden all summer. There were snapdragons, marigolds, lilies, roses, heather, etc., arranged along accessible winding paths. I had contributed most anything that was not living – ponds, small waterfalls, statuary, including bears, rabbits, and the mandatory flamingoes. It was a team effort, and one of Becky's nieces had even asked to have her wedding there. That was Binky's new back yard, and he seemed confused that he could not find any exit, but he kept running until he stopped from exhaustion. During all that exercise, we had not moved but stood and smiled at his antics. He still seemed confused but not afraid. Surely, he must have had access to some wildlife in his past.

I went to him and carefully picked him up, not forgetting his reaction at Pet Heaven, and carried him up those twelve strange outdoor stairs. When I took him inside and set him on the floor, he immediately went to a big bowl filled with cold water. Could dogs smell water? I thought he was going to finish the whole bowl. He seemed to decline the adjoining bowl of kibble and began to explore the rest of the house. Drooling on every inch he covered. He sniffed around the living room while we discreetly followed. Other than the freedom to smell, he didn't seem to want anything.

Becky and I sat on the couch waiting for the return of Binky. He saw us on the couch and went back to his unsure/afraid mode, perhaps a memory from his past. Instinctively, Becky patted the cushion and Binky joined her without hesitation. Another memory? Perhaps he came from a nice family that allowed him on the furniture. Casually, not sure of the dog's reaction, I pulled a liv-a-snap treat from my pocket. Without hesitation he took it and jumped off the couch until he found a private place under our desk, where he began to scratch fervently on the carpet, as though hoping to find a place to hide his little treasure.

Becky was puzzled and worried that our new dog was going to ruin our rug. She didn't hesitate and grabbed him from under the desk and scolded, "No! No!" without slapping his butt. Luckily, Binky did not bite her. When she put him down, instead of going back to retrieve his treat, he headed back to the door and stood there, waiting for it to open. Was this a sign that he wanted to go out and do his business or that he wanted to escape that dreaded "No" word? I opened the door and watched him quickly maneuver the twelve stairs down to the back yard. Once on the ground, instead of racing around the yard again, he casually walked back and forth, down the garden paths, and as though examining what he had raced past the last time. He even paused to lift his leg and water some marigolds. Not sure what Iowa Becky the gardener was going to do to stop more assaults, which would probably occur several times every day. I sensed a hefty bill for some small fencing.

Because it was getting dark, we turned on the outside floodlights, but Binky did not seem to notice. Too much for the nose to examine. Becky and I watched him work his way around the yard, like a professional dog surveyor. He never showed fear or the need to escape, and his new owners sensed that he was going to be a good dog.

I threw one of my old flannel shirts for Binky to use as a warm rug on the outside deck, along with a bowl of water. Every nice evening, we had a happy hour, and Becky and I drank a beer or two on the deck. That first night we enjoyed the unintentional performance of Binky, which literally made us smile. We took a Katrina survivor into our house and he seemed satisfied, even though he had only been with us for a few hours. I sensed that he already felt safe. I wondered if thyroid Paul had found such contentment.

Hating to end our tranquility, I bent over our deck railing and called, "Binky! Binky!" No reaction from the shadows, so Becky gave it a try. "Binky, Binky," and a dog appeared from under a hydrangea bush. Becky clapped her hands and the dog looked up at us, then raced up the stairs and saw that we were just sitting and drinking. He assumed that the water bowl was for him and before offering a thank you, he drank and snuggled on the old shirt and watched over the now dark yard, like a border collie watching his flock.

"Son of a bitch! I called him first and I'm assuming he heard me, but didn't really care. Did we get a dog for you or me?"

She thought, trying to be diplomatic, "First, of course he is a son of a bitch, but your tone did not sound friendly. Second, he's a family dog, not mine or yours."

"Okay, but tomorrow he gets a new name. I am no longer going to shout 'Binky' all over the neighborhood."

"Okay, but I kinda' like his name. Your dog, your name. Our dog, his name stays Binky."

That was her way of affirming my ownership, though nothing official was signed. No lawyers were involved, yet.

Once inside, we sat on the couch again with Binky at our side for about two seconds when he seemed to remember something important. Perhaps an appointment or food? He jumped down and made a b-line to the desk and retrieved his hidden treat. I had assumed that he had forgotten it, but he had no pause to retrieve what had been given to him. Not sure what to do with it, he tried to chew it on the left side of his mouth. Never did find out how he lost his tooth but he seemed able to cope with its absence.

After such a busy day, it was time for the ultimate trial. I went into our bedroom and retrieved a new tartan-patterned dog bed, which I put on the floor by the couch. I could sense that it was a foreign object to him. Apparently, he had never had his own bed in Louisiana or wherever. I fantasized that he had come from a rich, stereotypical southern plantation, and that Binky, (real name probably Beauregard) had his own room, complete with his own queen mattress. Well, he'd have to learn to rough it now.

The dog was almost asleep on the couch. He likely had a taxing few days – flooding, hurricane, loneliness, and fear while trying to survive, probably without help, and a long ride in a cage to a completely foreign place – Wisconsin.

"What if we left him here on the couch?" whispered Becky. "Would he be scared when he woke-up?"

My computer-brain weighed our options. "He's exhausted and should sleep for the next two days. Let's leave the light on for him and see how it plays out."

She kissed me quick, smiled, and replied, "Okay, Mr. Motel 6, we'll leave the light on."

Quietly we moved away and put a throw pillow on the dog bed, just in case. Maybe Beauregard was used to pillows and would soon learn what the dog bed was for. He was snoring when we left him alone on the couch.

"Good night, Binky," and I followed my wife.

We were both sleeping hard, dreaming of places other than Madison, Wisconsin. Suddenly we felt a thud on our bed and something was between our legs. We looked down, and from the overhead light in the hallway, we saw a brown mass of tangled fur, snoring right where he had landed. I was about to push him down, when Becky sensed my intent and grabbed my arm.

"Shhh. Let him be. He's tired and unsure of his future. That dog has probably suffered more hardships the past week in dog years than we've had in our lives. You left the light on for him. Let him sleep. He's not that big. You're the bed hog."

I smiled and realized that she was right again, kissed her and rolled back onto my side. Maybe Binky had lived the life of Beauregard. Otherwise, how would he know to come to our room and jump on the bed? Not a real high jump, but it still required some strong legs. Maybe he had been working-out. Probably had his private gym at the plantation. I went to sleep picturing Binky walking on his own treadmill.

Morning came and, as usual, Becky was up first. She liked her morning coffee and newspaper and especially her alone time. I usually got up an hour later, but I was anxious to see if Binky had been good or if he had ruined our entire house. Surprisingly, there was no carnage. In fact, he was already outside sniffing. He had added fertilizer to our lawn, which was my responsibility to cleanup. Iowa Becky was not an organic farmer. Our first major challenge was scheduled for two days later when we would take Binky to a highly recommended groomer at Lori's Pet-a-gree. We'd had two dogs that had required grooming. Not sure of this dog's background, but I hoped that Binky had been spoiled in that Louisiana mansion and was used to being bathed and groomed on a regular basis. I thought of <u>The Wizard of Oz</u> and how the Cowardly Lion had been transformed. Maybe Binky would be lucky. Whoever booked the appointment was not sensitive to my needs, and asked for the dog's name. I figured that I was paying the bill and she did not need the dog's name, but she was insistent. We hadn't chosen a name yet, but she didn't seem to care. I suppose if I had asked to see a heart specialist and refused to give my name, the receptionist might get a little snooty.

After an awkward moment of silence, I said, "Binky," hoping that I wasn't on speakerphone.

"Binky?" she yelled back in disbelief.

"He's a rescue dog from Louisiana and that's the name they gave him, so let's go with that."

"Okay. You could change his name right now if you just want to make it Duke or Rover, and change it later."

Tempting, but humiliating. "No, just leave it."

And so, Becky, Larry and Binky were off to the Salon Fido.

We had to leave him and pick him up in three hours. Sounded like another burger and beer day at the Oakcrest Tavern. I doubt that the dog would like his grooming appointment, but I assumed that being cleaner and lighter and able to see would be worth the suffering. C'mon Binky, toughen up!

I was wishing we hadn't drunk a whole pitcher of Spotted Cow (Becky's favorite beer, not mine, but it was her turn to choose.) Feeling light-headed we returned to Lori's, eager for a full report. We sat and patiently waited a couple of long minutes. If he hadn't rushed at us, we wouldn't have known who that dog was. I had a flash back to when we had picked-up Teddy at the Barking Lot in Wheaton and they had brought out he wrong dog. The major difference from this case is that we honestly were not sure if this was the same dog that we had brought in.

As he joyously continued to slobber all over us, we were dumbfounded at the changes. It was like the story of how Michelangelo sculpted <u>David</u> – cut away all the stone until only the statue of <u>David</u> remained. The groomer must have sheared the blob of matted fur until only a dog was left. Completely gone was the floor-dragging fringe. Present was a cute dog face that truly did resemble Toto. Big brown eyes, one pert ear and one folded ear, and a beautiful coat of light brown, white and black thin fur that magically gave Binky mystical blends of gray and blue. I could see where the name "silky terrier" originated. Damn – he was a good-looking dog. Handsome enough to be a show dog, but we've already been down that road, and once burned . . .

That evening we were sitting on the deck with our happy hour beer, which we didn't need after our lunch at the Oakcrest, but we wanted to honor the arrival of our new dog. Becky didn't talk much, but I could see the wheels in her head were working hard. She had something important on her mind.

"I found the dog's new name," she announced smugly. I had a feeling that it would be more fun if I didn't ask what it was. She was eager to tell me.

"Who's your favorite author?"

"Hemingway." She knew that, so I guess I was supposed to contemplate a more thoughtful answer. "But that's an awkward name for a dog. At least Macbeth, Macduff, and Dickens sound good and made sense."

She gave me that piercing look, followed by Iowa sarcasm, "How did I marry such a dolt? First name?" as though speaking to a seventeen-year-old third-grader.

"Ernest," she barked. I tried to return the "dummy" look, but, of course, fell short.

Patience gone. "Ernie, dummy! Call him 'Ernie!'" Iowa Becky wins again.

"I guess he kind of looks like an Ernie," I replied trying not to sound over-enthused. But it was true that he did look like an Ernie.

"Ernie!" I yelled at the yard-roaming dog, but got no acknowledgement.

"Ernie," came the feminine, trusting voice, followed by a scampering dog up the steps, where he was rewarded with a treat. How long had this been planned?

"Come here, Ernie," I called as Becky slipped me a treat. He hesitated, cautiously approached, and I ruffled his neck and gave him the treat.

Thus, Binky died and Ernie was born.

Ernie was quick to adapt to his new name and life. He was content to spend all day in the back yard, no longer trying to escape. His biggest entertainment was chasing squirrels that quickly learned that this dog meant business, and made it up our trees or over the fencing. It seemed that he did recognize these bushy-tailed, tree-climbing rodents and simply enjoyed the freedom to scare them, no harm intended.

However, our yard also had an ample supply of chipmunks, rare appearances by mice and voles, and, of course, as Iowa Becky the gardener liked to refer to them, "goddamn rabbits." Ernie seemed like an honest hunter-want-to-be, but never killed any living creature. Although, one time he swiped at a fleeing chipmunk and sent it tumbling, but Ernie never closed on it for the death blow. Just enjoyed the hunt. Maybe he was aware of his name and felt the need to enjoy hunting to support the legacy of manhood presented by Hemingway, but I doubt that he was that well-read. Ironically, he seemed to enjoy all the back yard wildlife, even the birds that he would watch hypnotically. Because of his resemblance to Toto and other animated dogs, I started to think that maybe we could have named him after Disney, but I did not want to call my dog "Walt." Maybe after naturalist John Muir, but if I had started yelling, "Here, John," half the neighborhood might have responded.

I never felt that I had to entertain this dog. He always seemed grateful to be there with us. One night Becky and I were sitting on the couch with Ernie, watching something mindless on the tv. For no reason that we could ascertain, Ernie jumped down, went over to his dog bed, circled once and plopped down. He seemed to be studying us with great interest.

"What do you think he's thinking?" asked Beck.

"Probably about how good-looking I am," I replied smugly.

Punch on my shoulder. "No, really. With his hair cut, he's better looking than you."

Ouch! I pretended to read Ernie's mind. "Probably his days before coming to Wisconsin. Other than Katrina, he probably thinks back to his good old times."

"Yeah, I suppose youthful memories never leave you. From the way he acts here, I'd say he had a decent life as a puppy, but I'm glad he's here now."

I kissed the top of her head "Me too."

For the first week or so, we let Ernie jump in our bed. He didn't take much space as he slept between us. His only requirement was that he had to be touching one or both of us like Teddy had. Probably made him feel more like part of a family and safe.

Mornings soon formed a routine when Becky always got up early and let Ernie outside. During the warm seasons we often kept our patio door partially open all day, except on rainy days when we had a hard time getting Ernie to go outside to do his business. The rain terrified Ernie, and thunder and lightning really made him cower, but luckily we were home most of the stormy seasons, and Ernie seemed to act like a piece of gum stuck to the bottom of our shoes, as he followed either one of us anywhere we went.

His normal meal was a half can of soft dog food. He gobbled that like he had been starving. Don't know what they fed him in the South, but in the North, he added a few pounds to his trim figure in just a few months. Of course, he always had kibble next to his water bowl. He sometimes crunched a few bits, but was not overly fond of any of the many kibble flavors on the market. I wondered if dogs could really taste any difference between salmon flavored and beef-liver flavored kibble. I would think that a dog would always think that kibble was kibble, no matter how they packaged it. Becky suggested that we add a little water to it, but I told her that was silly. After all, he was "just a dog." Occasionally I would take a few table scraps and bury them in his kibble. By morning he had eaten all the meat scraps and our floor was covered with kibble. He seemed to be a smart dog except when he wasn't.

Ernie began to settle into a comfortable daily life, including sleeping as much as possible. Sometimes I caught him lying on his side with his little legs pumping like he was racing for Olympic gold. An intermittent cry would often accompany his movement. Whether it was a good or bad cry, we could never tell. Becky seemed to believe that he was reliving something awful and she usually woke him with a shoulder shake. He would slowly open his eyes, look around the room, and put his head back down, but he appeared too uneasy to return to sleep directly until we both pet him, which made him seem to relax.

During the day he would often rest on the living room couch, love seat, or dog bed. It took a full year before he stopped jumping on our bed at night. Then, for some inexplicable reason, he began to sleep by himself in the living room. Becky said that she almost always found him on the love seat, which was bigger than his dog bed and had a special plush Animal Planet blanket that my sister had given him.

Six months passed before we introduced Ernie to the person who would play a major role in his life – our trusted veterinarian, Dr. Erickson. We had been with the good vet for thirty years, or two hundred and ten dog years. Unlike the groomer's, we could be in the same room when the vet gave him a physical examination. Ernie was visibly trembling while I held him on the examination table. Of course, Dr. Erickson did his magic and seemed to put Ernie at ease after he had let Ernie sniff his hand and given him a little liver treat. I would not have sold out so easily or eaten anything that tasted of liver, but Ernie had no problem crunching it down like a steam roller through crushed gravel.

Dr. Erickson felt the dog's body without problem. Just to be sure, he kept feeding Ernie scraps of liver treat. I bet no other dog would touch those treats. He shone a light in Dicken's eyes and ears, and ended by lifting his gums and checking his teeth.

"Looks good to me. Nothing wrong I can detect. Should live at least another ten years."

"What about his missing tooth?" I immediately asked, wondering if it might cause any future problem.

"I don't know what happened, but I'd say Ernie broke it on something or someone, and a concerned dentist extracted the rest. I couldn't feel any piece of broken root. I can sense a good dog in there, but if he's a rescue, thanks for giving him a forever home, and please be patient, no pun intended."

All was good with our dog, but I don't think he was fond of other dogs. We would meet other dog walkers and partners. Ernie would stop and cautiously extend his snout within inches of another dog's nose, but then bark and snap at the strange dog. Fortunately, he never made contact, and we would walk in the street when he crossed paths on the sidewalk with another dog. Everyone in the neighborhood got to know that Ernie seemed to be a nice dog, just sensitive.

Becky and I were both guilty of spoiling Ernie, but after talking to a neighbor who had just bought a new puppy and had taken her to training classes, I wondered if Ernie could be taught to be more social. Who knew what had happened to a rescue dog? Maybe he had made some canine or human friends, but also some angry ones that had acted like bullies.

A local Pet Heaven store, like the one from where we had purchased Ernie, held classes for socialization and training for adult dogs. We enrolled Ernie in six o'clock classes on Wednesdays for six weeks. They also held advanced classes, but one step at a time. Becky and I agreed to attend alternate weeks.

At our first lesson, Ernie was excited to see all the dogs, smell the familiar odors, and, of course, he sniffed all the rawhides, treats, and toys that were displayed at a dog's nose level. Shrewd marketers! He acted like a toddler in his first toy store. The classes were held in an enclosed pen in the middle of big box store. There were five of us at the first lesson, ranging from a red setter to a miniature poodle, not unlike Teddy.

The instructor's name was Ron, and he immediately let it be known that this cage and class were his domain. My guess is that he was a student at a local two-year college, where he was just accumulating credits in order to pass and substitute for the challenging freshman-required courses at the University of Wisconsin. Either that or he had flunked out of beauty college, and/or bartending classes. I don't know who he was trying to impress, but he came off as the biggest, pompous ass I had ever seen in a position of "authority."

"My name is Ron and I'll be the instructor for this class. First, I'd like to make it clear that these lessons are directed at the dog owners as much as at the dogs. That means you." Long pause, followed by a firm stare at each of us. Two people looked taken aback at such a firm taskmaster. They flinched. I was tempted to put two fingers down my throat to simulate vomiting, but I held back, afraid that Ron might give us detention. Instead, he gave us each a clicker, guaranteeing that by the end of the course, we would all be able to get our dogs to react to clicks – one for stay, two for heel, three for . . .. We were all lost and confused by the fourth click.

Ernie and his master just wanted to leave, the dog because he was confused about what we were doing with these strange dogs. When the poodle came near him, Ernie played his usual "you're-intruding-on-my-space" mode and snapped at the dog's nose. Bigger dogs showed no fear, but the smaller ones ran back to their owners. Great start! Class bully!

The first class was uncomfortable. Ron talked but no one listened. He gave us each a clicker and "homework" on how to practice with its use. Was a clicker supposed to be like a passing bell in school? When Ron talked to Ernie one on one, the dog just turned his head, ignoring him. Perhaps something in Ernie's past had permanently ruined him, but Ron could not reach his "special needs" student.

Becky took Ernie the second week and came home with the same disappointing result. All Ernie wanted to do was socialize but he didn't know how. She also had a few select names for Ron. Iowa Becky had transformed into Rodney Dangerfield. So that happened and after all our training of walking the store aisles and attempts to get Ernie to stay when he heard two clicks, the poor dog showed no desire to cooperate with Ron and his clicker education. I still believe that given I.Q. tests, Ernie was smarter than Ron. After six weeks of futility on last night of class, each dog was singled-out and owners were given a "Graduation," certificate. Ernie was the only one to get a "Certificate of Participation," and a coupon to repeat the same class at half price. Becky and I agreed that Ernie would probably do no better a second time under Ron's instruction. Home schooling was becoming quite the trend.

That night after the last class, Becky sarcastically commented, "Do you realize that we probably have the only dog-school drop-out?" The song from the musical <u>Grease</u> came to mind. A bit unfair, I thought, Ernie flunked out, not dropped –out.

I chuckled and then addressed the problem, who was sitting on the couch wearing a huge grin with drool running out of his toothless corner, as though laughing at something.

I grabbed his head, made direct eye contact, and told him, "Ernie, you're the worst dog I ever had." He gave a glint of acknowledgement, and continued his wise smile and uncontrollable drooling. Thus ended the formal training of Ernie, the silky terrier.

Life flowed by without major interruption, until an early arrival of a foreign entity to Ernie – snow. It was Wisconsin, and by Thanksgiving we'd had six inches of the powder. Ernie had no idea what was happening. I assumed that his southern background had never exposed him to it. Poor thing probably hadn't even learned to ski yet. At first, he just stood on the snowless back porch and looked, trying to decide if he could bite it or if he needed to. He became more confused when more snow had floated under the protection of our upper deck and landed on his nose. He tried to lick it but to no avail. Tongue too short.

I went a few feet into the yard and called him to me. He hesitated, not knowing if it was strong enough to hold him, even though it held me. I walked farther into the yard, stooped, and called him again. He must have finally trusted me and raced to my side, where I ruffled his head and called him a good dog, which caused him to start his dog laugh. I stomped my foot at him, our sign that I was ready to play. Off he dashed, recreating the wide circles he had run when we had first brought him home.

This time he was surprised when he rounded a corner and his four little legs slid out from under him. He tumbled and rolled, but when he regained his feet, he took off again without missing a step. Ernie was a little sluggish learning to slow down to avoid falling, just like people learning to drive again after the winter's first snowfall. But I didn't think he minded, because he kept repeating the playful activity until he ran out of gas and went to the door. I think he had fun for his first time in snow.

Once in the house Ernie went right to his water bowl, then to his dog bed and conked out even before eating. Soon he was snoring. Wisconsin winters were going to be a real challenge for a southern-bred dog.

"Whew, wet dog smell!" Becky pronounced to anyone who was listening, especially the perpetrator, who was far away in dreamland. We made pasty for supper that night; it was a classic Wisconsin meat pie full of ground beef, and even the smell of the cooking beef did not move Ernie's interest.

Playing in the snow all day became routine to Ernie. After all, how many snowflakes could one dog catch in a day, and then what would he do with them? Ernie didn't care; it was just a never-ending cycle of fun. Some days we had to bring him in because the wind chill factor was zero or below. He didn't have much concept of cold, even while wearing his red dog coat with his name embroidered on it from Land's End, and there were times when he couldn't stop shivering, and he really appreciated getting under his Animal Planet blanket. Either I Becky or I would rub and massage his little shaking body until he stopped.

By Christmas we had more than a foot of the white stuff to clear. I even had to shovel a four-foot by four-foot space in our back yard, so that our four-legged shorty could do his business. One neighbor questioningly said to me, "Did I see you shoveling your lawn today?"

"Dog," was my only reply, humiliating all-around.

Beside snow, Christmas meant another arrival – our son Larry was home from college for two weeks. The two "siblings" seemed to get along well from the beginning. The kid from the county fair ten years ago had become a 6'4" and 220-pound man. Instead of fearing the stranger, Ernie sought warmth and shelter from this friendly giant, even sleeping in Larry's old downstairs bedroom on some freezing nights. Ernie still got walked every day, especially because the neighborhood was good about keeping the sidewalks clear. Sometimes Larry walked the dog, but those walks seemed much shorter.

After one major snowfall and before the plows cleared the streets, only a skilled walker, me, walked in the driver's side deep tread of an SUV while the dog walked in the passenger side tread, right down the middle of the street. It was the only time that I didn't pick-up his droppings, figuring that by spring no one else would know. Some days it was just too cold to walk, freezing or below zero. Ernie didn't seem to like travelling far around the neighborhood, tolerating the frigid weather, probably knowing that we would soon get back to a warm house.

One night I let Ernie out the back door to give him a few final minutes of going to the bathroom and sniffing time. I don't know what he was able to smell in the snow and cold, but Iowa Becky claimed to see an occasional vole pop up its head. That night the Green Bay Packers game was on, and it was considered sacrilegious to miss any of it, at least for Becky and our son. I was always genetically a Bears' fan. When I went to bring Ernie back in, he was usually waiting by the back door and would race into the warmth. That evening he was not waiting. I called and walked a few feet into the yard, but there was no sign of him. Had he gotten out or hurt? He was a southern-raised dog, and did not have any idea of how to cope with it. Slight panic, so I called Larry for help. Without hesitation he stepped into the foot of snow and trudged around the back yard, calling for the dog while he searched under the long dead yard plants, bushes and lawn ornaments, the flashlight bobbing all over the yard.

"Dad, look at this."

He shone the light on the gate, which was slightly ajar. The deep snow had prevented the gate from fully closing and not allowing the hook to reach the eye, leaving a bottom and side gap big enough to welcome Ernie's curiosity.

"Sorry, Dad, after our walk this afternoon I had a hard time shutting it because of all the snow, and I really didn't think Ernie could fit through the gap. We were both so cold and eager to get back inside. I should have come back and shoveled the snow away from the gate. Sorry. We can find him."

He sounded as apologetic as possible, so I couldn't show my intense anger, which said, "How could such a moron get into college?"

"I'll walk and you drive around. It's not quite freezing tonight, so maybe we can find him before it gets too cold," I directed.

We set a time record for donning our winter gear – jackets, boots, scarves, gloves, and caps. I automatically walked left because it was the path we usually walked. Larry turned right with his car window down, and we yelled and flashed our lights all over the neighborhood. I was surprised that nobody called the cops to report a couple of strangers (who could tell who was under all that winter clothing?). Thankfully, it was not a twenty-degree-below night yet, and the current twelve above would probably not be fatal if we could find him soon. We were already uncomfortable and I could not imagine what Ernie must have been feeling.

We tried for over an hour, then went back to the house. Maybe he had found his way back. No such luck. At 11:00 p.m. we realized that it was too late to recruit any helpers. I called the police, whose only suggestion was to call the animal shelter. He explained that with all the careless winter driving, most officers were busy responding to car accidents. But they always kept an eye open for any distressed animals.

All three of us agreed to give one more hour of search time. My thoughts bounced around my mind like a pinball machine gone mad. Maybe someone found him and took him into a warm house. I would certainly bring in a freezing dog or cat. Maybe he slipped, rolled down a hill and couldn't get back up. Maybe, God forbid, he got hit by a car or city bus. Maybe he was still searching for a way home. I had seen many news clips of dogs that were left behind at some far away camp site but found their way home journeying over hundreds of miles. But not through Wisconsin winters. I could only hope that he had found shelter by a store with a heat exhaust vent, where a homeless person might find some warm shelter. Poor little guy – he had to wonder what he had done to deserve such a fate.

As agreed, we returned home around midnight and tried to get some sleep. I couldn't, so I thought I'd give it one more hour of drive-around time. No clues. Any obvious paw prints from our house had been buried. No witnesses to ask. All gone. Even Ernie.

I was dozing on the sofa when the phone rang. It took me a full five seconds to realize that Ernie couldn't use a phone. There was always hope. Smart dog; he had survived Hurricane Katrina.

"Hello, this is Officer Marx at the west district police office. I am trying to reach a Larry Ehrhorn."

"That's me!" I shouted like a contestant on <u>The Price Is Right</u>.

"We don't usually call so late, but being a dog lover myself, my instincts told me to bend an unwritten rule. From the panicked sound of your voice, I think I made the right decision."

"Yes, yes, what is it?" How long could it take this guy to get to the point, ignoring my panic and not allowing him to speak? Alive or dead?

"We found a little terrier named Ernie. We picked him up as a stray around ten o'clock at the University Avenue Quick Mart. The night manager said that he looked like he was waiting for a ride home or at least for someone to open the store door so that he could get inside for some warmth. He had seen the dog try to slip inside the door twice, but it's a cold, late night and there weren't many customers. Finally, Tom, the night manager, just let the dog into the store, and then he called us." I thought I heard Ernie bark, but I'm sure the officer would have said something. Wishful thinking.

"It's a good thing that you had him chipped. We have a special chip reader in our office, which gave us all the information we needed – dog's name, owner's name, address, and phone number."

I had completely forgotten that almost all dog rescue services now add an identification chip imbedded between the dog's shoulder blades. All I had to do was supply the information on-line that corresponded to that chip number, pay a twenty-dollar lifetime fee, and it may save a dog's life. It did mine. Sure, looked like that system worked.

In my excitement and relief, I almost forget to ask about Ernie's condition.

"Is he all right? No frozen pads or anything?"

"No, he seems fine. We played with him a little in our office here, but he didn't seem too eager to play ball with a couple cops. We get that all the time. He seemed to get along better with Karen than the three men on duty. Anyway, Karen drove him over to the Dane County Humane Society, who always has a vet on-call. They'll check him for frostbite to his paws and ears, and general health. You can get him tomorrow morning. They open at nine. Do you know where they are?"

"Yes, thank you for bending the rule and calling me," I answered more calmly.

"Speaking of bending the rules, you might want to thank Tom, the night manager at the Quick Mart. If he hadn't broken the 'no dogs allowed' rule, he said that from the way that Ernie was shivering, he doubted that the dog would have survived the night. Say hi to Ernie for me."

We had never been to the Humane Society, but we anonymously sent them a hundred dollars every year. Looked like money well spent. That night we all fell asleep at the same time. The next morning, we decided that the whole family would go to retrieve Ernie from his helpful prison. Becky had started to make breakfast, but I was in a more celebratory mood.

"Let's all go to the Coppertop for breakfast. The Humane Society won't open for another hour and a half."

Coppertop always served good breakfast, but no one was famished, just anxious. Half hour drive from the west side to the east side, and we were there before they opened their doors. Finally, a woman unlocked the door, made eye contact, and waved us in.

Not surprisingly, we were the only people in the waiting room. Must not have been any other delinquent dogs that picked a cold night to explore the neighborhood. As angry as I was in the inside, I thought I'd cry when they brought Ernie through the doorway. He gave a yelp and raced to us, slipping on the tiled floor. He got up and stumbled to me and began delivering kisses, which was not always his typical reaction to show joy; he really must have been glad to turn back the clock and be where he should be. We all joined in the happy reception and were almost out the door, when a commanding voice stopped me.

"Mr. Ehrhorn," the voice of authority. Probably some fee, which was fine since they had saved my dog.

I approached the counter, while Becky held Ernie as he had started to scramble to our car that he could see through the glass door. The woman handed me four small pieces of paper that were small enough to be parking tickets, but unless Iowa Becky had been careless, they couldn't be. Maybe a neighbor had reported a slow-moving car surveying the neighborhood, late on a cold night, but police didn't give tickets for that. They really didn't think that I was responsible for a recent rash of burglaries to parked cars, did they? Or worse, that I was some perverted window peeker? Damn dog.

I closely analyzed each slip:

1. Animal at large—$25.00
2. Lack of city license—$25.00

3. Lack of rabies tag—$25.00
4. Impoundment fee—$50.00

Panicked, I began to plead my case. "But he had a rabies tag on his leash, and nobody buys a city license."

She shook her head implying, 'We can't do anything about that,' but she gave me an honest explanation. "First, you can't say that no one buys a city license. We currently have more than 12,000 licensed dogs in the city of Madison. Second, he had no leash, which legally made him a stray and his tag would have been attached to it. I would say that the fifty dollars for saving him and boarding him overnight was well worth it, wouldn't you?"

I was dumbfounded because she was absolutely right. Was she a distant relative of Iowa Becky? Of course, she was right, and last night I would have paid much more to have my dog back by my side, safe and sound.

"Yes, thank you. Of course, you're right," and the Ehrhorns took the family dog home again. Ernie seemed to be glad to be home, at least that's how I interpreted him. He went straight to his water bowl and even ate some kibble. I plopped down on my recliner and got ready for some real sleep. Ernie suddenly felt the need to be close to someone he knew. Ernie jumped up and lay his head on my chest, and I pet his coat and scratched his neck. It was time for the talk.

"You know, Ernie, you're the worst dog I've ever had. My other dogs gave me problems at times, like racial prejudice, epileptic seizures, losing dog shows, complete teeth loss, but none of them ever ran away and became a convicted criminal. More than a hundred dollars in fines, and you don't seem too worried about it. You're also the only dog to flunk out of school. What am I supposed to do with such a loser?"

I could hear him breathing heavily and rhythmically. Ernie was in a deep sleep, and probably never heard a word of our heart-to-heart. But at least he was where he should be.

Ernie never left our house on his own again. Daily he was happy taking two walks on his leash, complete with rabies tag, and still investigating his back yard. No show dog, no companion dog, no working dog stricken with seizures. Just a great dog that seemed to appreciate being saved from a hurricane and being sent to

Wisconsin. Who knows what his existence before us had been like, but at least he had led a fulfilling life.

His demise started when he was about fifteen, an old age for a dog. It began with a seemingly small incident. As all dog are wont to do, he always had to sniff everything. When he was on his leash, I didn't have to worry about squirrels or other creatures to chase. I wasn't watching him too closely when he barked and stuck his head into a barberry bush, scaring a chipmunk from its hiding place. Too late, I pulled him back, but a barb had cut his eye. I carried him three blocks home. After trying to wash and soothe the eye with a damp cloth, we could see that he was in pain.

We rushed him to Dr. Erickson, who confirmed that Ernie's cornea had been scratched and that he continuously wanted to scratch it, which would irritate the eye more and not allow it to heal. The good doctor began by applying a couple drops of something, which caused Ernie to violently repulse, like pouring iodine onto a large cut. I was still trying to hold him tight but I had never seen anything this out of control, including Macduff's epileptic seizures. Dr. Erickson kept stroking the top of the dog's head while speaking in soft, soothing tones, but those drops must have hurt like hell.

Left with no choice, the good vet felt that he had to put a surgical cone around Ernie's neck so that he would not be able to further damage his eye. Talk about torture. We all felt horrible, especially Ernie, who had no idea what was happening or why. After receiving instructions on how to apply the same agonizing drops three times a day, we took him home. I carried him up any stairs because he could not get his paws on steps that he could not see; he could barely see anything. Once on the kitchen floor he could maneuver about, but not fully.

The first place he went was to his water bowl, but even with our help, it took him a long time to put his cone flat on the floor to try to drink. He still was not able to get his short snout close enough to the water. Becky and I quickly filled a large Tupperware bowl with cold water and exchanged bowls. His tongue was finally able to lap up some water, and I thought that he might empty the entire bowl. We put his kibble on another inverted bowl, but he had no desire to eat. Becky cooked some ground beef, but the poor dog was still in another world. Finally, he went to the living room and collapsed on his side in his bed. Although he had slowed down over the years, I never thought I would see him that weak and submissive.

The condition did not improve. We were not able to get drops in his eye three times a day, and we had to take him to Dr. Erickson's office, so that they could administer at least part of the dosage in the eye. This 24/7 routine lasted four days, until Ernie was able to go cone-free. We received a stern warning to watch him closely and be sure that he did not try to scratch his eye, which was more challenging than teaching a dog to sing opera.

He became more at ease without the collar, so maybe the drops did help heal. He seemed happier but still exhibited none of the old spirit. We would walk with his leash, which was progress. While walking on all fours, he could not scratch his wound. At night he would all sleep in our bed so that if he had moved much, one of us would have been able to stop him from scratching.

It was the beginning of the end. He rarely ate, even people food, and we had to carry him up and down stairs to go outside. We could see that he was losing weight, along with his character. We took him to the vet, who ran blood tests and asked questions about his quality of life. The tests told us that his systems were slowly shutting down, one by one. I did not want to let go yet, so we took him home. No matter how much we pet and cuddled him, there was little positive response. We kept waiting for some part of Ernie to return to us. The major clue that he had gone could be seen when we asked him if he wanted to take a walk, and instead of making a beeline for the door, he just plopped down on his bed with an I-really-don't-want-to-do-this attitude.

A week later we all made the final journey to Dr. Erickson's office. Becky drove while I held Ernie on my lap. Whenever I scratched his head or rubbed his belly, he seemed to move his tail and pick-up his head, while my tears began to fall on him. He just didn't know that this was our last ride together.

Once in the examination room (they didn't even bother with the routine weight check), Dr. Erickson asked us if we were ready and assured us that we had done everything possible to give Ernie a full, good life. I thought it ironic that he would ask us if we were ready, not Ernie. Probably best that Ernie could not understand.

Becky and I looked at each other and said that we were ready. Dr. Erickson went to another room, returning with a silver tray holding two filled syringes, one much bigger than the other. He put a blanket on the examination table. Becky took my place at the table and rubbed Ernie's neck while the doctor explained that the first shot was just to numb the area and to relax him for the administration of the second, final shot. I watched but felt guilty for not rubbing his chest while he was being "put to sleep." His eyes were looking directly at me, not so much wondering why Becky, not me, was rubbing his neck, as he was telling me that it was okay and thank you. At least that's how I chose to see it.

Then Dr. Erickson injected the larger needle into Ernie's rear leg. He must have felt something because he moved slightly as though to say, "That hurt," his last message to me. The doctor asked if I wanted to hold him at his end. I said, "Sure," and Becky brought him to me in his blanket.

She placed him on my lap and I scratched his head while he took his final breath.

"See you at Rainbow Bridge, buddy. You were the best of my worst dogs," I mumbled.

"That's right," affirmed Dr. Erickson, who really understood what I meant.

I felt wretched that the last reaction I saw of Ernie was one of pain as that last needle fulfilled its purpose.

And then Ernie was dead.

Ernie's first day home

Ernie likes Madison

Chapter 12
The Best Worst Dog

"The one best place to bury a dog is in the heart of his master."
Ben Hur Lampman, American editor and writer

I was just there. I could feel other movements near me, touching me, climbing on me. I could see nothing, but instinctively felt the need to suckle. The major smell was that of the large being, which came to be known as "mother dog." I never felt any need to do anything, except to move, to suckle mother and to sleep, while getting used to constant movement around me.

Soon I was able to see and to hear, which expanded my space. Over time I met others like me and we formed a bond, because we all smelled like mother. Time passed slowly and we all became able to stand and explore our small area. Even as a puppy, I felt heat and none of us could do anything to escape the unpleasantness. Mother would pant heavily while we fed, and I began to develop another emotion. Beside innate discomfort and hunger, I felt sadness for mother's suffering in the intense heat. Still, alone she continued to feed us and lick us in attempts to make us feel cleaner and safer.

A pressure in all our bellies made us want to relieve the discomfort, which we did naturally, but it caused us all to smell and to search for a clean space. One day a man came to our place and sprayed water. One sibling got such a strong spray that it yelped and rolled, trying to escape. A human hand slapped it on its tail end, which made the pup yip again as it tried to hide behind mother.

Our small world rapidly seemed to change. We had all grown bigger and had even less space to move. The man with the water came every so often and sprayed us, which not only helped with the smell, but also the heat. Other than the frightening tone he used when he said anything or when he delivered a sharp rap on our cage, he let us know that he was there and that the water he supplied was a small blessing from him.

Another change happened when mother stopped feeding us and we all had to learn to eat some small hard food and to drink from an often dried-out water bowl. Life was too much to learn all at once for us pups, but we soon realized that we had no other choices. We would often climb over each other to eat and drink. One pup snapped and bit another when it tried to get to a bowl that was almost empty anyway. At times our water bowl was empty and we had to wait for the man with the hose to fill it, which he partially did when he moved down the line and cleaned the stuff sticking to our floor. Our food bowl was often empty too, but someone always seemed to put some hard food in our dish at the last minute before we became too weak to get to the bowl to try to eat.

Our final test came the day that one of the men took mother. We didn't know why or for how long. He just opened the door to our place, swept a few puppies to the side, grabbed her by the neck and carried her away. She yelped as though in pain or in anticipation of what was about to happen and bit the man's hand. He hit her on the tail side, yelled, dropped her to the ground and kicked her. Some other man (Bob) stopped him from kicking her again while she cried on the ground. After pushing away the bad man (Billy), Bob bent down and petted mother while the kicker stomped off in anger.

Carefully and gently, Bob lifted mother and carried her away. Her head was hanging loosely over his arm, and she looked back at us. Her tongue out, she was still able to wag her tail twice and tried to look pleased that she could see us and let us know that she was okay and still alive. It was as if it wasn't the first time she had experienced this farewell departure. It was also the last time we saw mother.

We all huddled and hoped that mother would return. The heat and excitement caused us all to want to eat and drink more, but most of us just closed our eyes in defeat and wished for the cooler night to come. With not much to compare it to, each day was the worst day of our lives, until the next day.

The same two men came back the next morning. They took one pup that had cried throughout most of the night despite our presence, until she finally fell silent. Billy took away her lifeless body and we never saw her again, either. Then they began to move us, one by one, and put us into another place to stay, but there was only one pup per cage. Although it was less crowded, there was no relief from the sharp wire floor or anything to lean on except the wire squares. It took a while to get used to it, but again there were no options.

If I had tried standing for too long, my paws and legs began to ache and my pads would bleed. I lay on my side to take away any direct pressure on my paws. It was to be my own place to stay, without any comfort or mother or siblings. A bowl of food and a bowl of water were on one side of the cage, and that was all for my daily life as a puppy.

From my cage I could see some of my siblings. Like me, each pup was in its own cage and seemed sad and soulless. We would occasionally bark to each other, but the mean Billy would yell and hit the cages with a big board he always carried with him. That would always scare the pups into silence. I felt helpless, like when they took mother.

I could only see my puppy siblings (I wish I had more personal names for them, but there was never enough time or closeness to do so), and we all felt sad. We had never expected to be apart this early in our lives. There were countless pups that I could see in cages stacked as high as a human and as far as I could see. There were all kinds and sizes, many of them barking and they were given warnings, which did not always silence them, but the bigger dogs seemed bolder and stronger, unless directly threatened.

Every few days Billy would pass by our cages with a hose and squirt a heavy stream of water at the floor, which would push our body waste through the wire floors to several lower cages until it reached the bottom cages, finally to reach the outside ground, where it would sit for days and cause more smell and unpleasantness. What could we do but live day by day?

There was one woman who would visit and say soft things, while reaching through the doors and scratching our necks. Her name was Linda, and for some reason another pup bit her finger. Billy yelled at Linda and we rarely saw much of her any more, either. Too bad.

When the nice Bob was spraying our cages, he would add some water to our bowls, sometimes full, sometimes not, and sometimes just a little more to our food bowls, which made the wet kibble easier to eat, but it was still bad. Nobody ever gave us new food, just threw a scoopful on top of the old, so our energy decreased as the days dragged by.

Along with the hot days, there were little flying things that kept going to our eyes seeking moisture. They were impossible to get rid of, and I spent most of my days scratching my eyes and body.

My appetite left me until I lost the desire to eat and waited for Billy or Bob to take me away. I didn't know where they took sick pups, but they never returned. I wasn't sure if they went to a better place. Maybe Rainbow Bridge, which I seemed to know for some reason.

One day there came a short relief. After being sprayed by Billy, several people came to our cages and opened our doors to carry us to the back of a truck, which we had all watched during our time since birth. We were tossed into the back, which was covered with slippery cloths, but at least it didn't cut into our paws.

We were all sizes and shapes but didn't care. We were out of our cages and maybe going someplace where we could enjoy better lives. A new man climbed into the back of the truck with us and closed the lower part of the back, but we still got hot air blowing over us, which made us feel cooler. All the dogs, some weren't pups anymore, looked at each other, not knowing what to do. We rode and rested comfortably, curious about one another. There was a large water bowl towards the front, and I assumed that it was for all of us. My weak legs carried me to the bowl and I began to drink. I was enjoying the cool, fresh water when another pup began to drink next to me. I could smell something familiar and turned my head. We looked at each other as if we should be familiar. At the same time, we both realized that we had shared the same mother and place to *live before we were parted. Hesitantly, we began to quietly cry and returned to our drinking.*

We continued to walk together to find others like us, or our mother, but we saw no one and just sat alone in a corner, leaning against each other. We had lived a long period of suffering, and how long could it last? Surely there was a purpose for dogs. Feeling that I had to give a name to my only brother, I called him Bob, after the one man who sometimes tended us well and was nicer than Billy. Brother Bob seemed all right, considering our lives. His eyes did not seem as bad as mine, and to me it felt good to not have to scratch mine since we had left our cages. Bob was skinny and was missing patches of fur. My coat was not completely missing parts but seemed thin. My bottom was also sticky from the water-like waste that came out. I wondered what Bob thought of his brother now. He looked so much better than I did, lucky Bob – good for you.

We could sense when we had finally stopped, not only from the lack of motion, but the moving breeze was gone and the extreme heat was back. I wondered how long we would have to sit still and suffer, so I was surprised when the back flaps on the truck soon opened and three men began to call us to the back of the truck. We naturally obeyed, not just from fear but also in hopes of some more breathable air.

Each man scooped up a pup in each hand and disappeared, then repeated. As the group thinned, we all scooted forward to get some breeze. Bob and I went together but were soon separated by two men. Odd, but Bob was also taken away by the man named Bob. Soon the air from our being carried around cooled us a little, but my leaking eyes began to itch horribly and my little legs were not free to scratch them. The sun never helped anything in our world.

Soon we were roughly lowered to the cool ground that was solid and did not cut into our pads. There was a load of pups and instinctively we all tried to find someone we might know. Some tall walls blocked the sun, and the air felt much cooler. I stopped to lick my paws and scratch my eyes. After aimless wandering, I found Bob and nudged him hello; he nudged back. We decided the same thing at once. There was a large water bowl and we had to try to get to it. A pup was sitting in the bowl, dipping her head and she seemed almost happy. She looked like us, but did not have the smell of mother or us. I decided to name her Linda, like the nice girl who sometimes came to check on us before Billy yelled at her.

Suddenly Billy pushed through the gate, picked Linda out of the water bowl, slapped her bottom hard enough to make her yip, and flung the pup aside. She just lay there for a while before weakly trying to rise to all fours. Bob and I went to her and nudged her. She answered by picking up her head and looking at us with seeping eyes, but not like mine, which were almost completely stuck closed. Instead, her tears rolled down her face.

Bob and I left Linda to rest, while we tried to find a spot that was softer and cooler against a wall. Again, I wondered if this was Rainbow Bridge. Compared to where we had come from, this place was so much better, but not exactly perfect. Enjoy it while we can.

One hint that we hadn't reached Rainbow Bridge was all the people standing around, staring down at us. There were small walls around us, too tall for pups to jump over even if they had the strength, but short enough for people to see over and point at us. Nobody ever pointed to me or to Bob. Sometimes a person would step over a wall and walk around to see all of us closely. At times a person would pick up a pup, hold it above his head, and check it completely before putting it back.

Other times Billy or human Bob would pick up a pup and walk around the ring, showing it while its puppy legs kicked the air to escape. The people would yell at Billy, who would respond by pointing at that person, then bring the pup to him, who would briefly hold it up to check all sides. Usually, the person would give it back to Billy, but sometimes she would take away the puppy. Don't know where they went, but I hoped it was to a better place, even Rainbow Bridge.

The afternoon seemed endless, but Bob and I found a cool spot, so we just tried to stay cool and rest. We had water and hard food and shade, and we began to appreciate our current surroundings. A few times some people paused to look down at us, then walked away. My eyes were almost completely sealed shut, so I could not tell if they would have been good to dogs or not. One time a woman picked-up Bob, checked him and quickly returned him to my side. I did not know whether to be sad that Bob was back with me, or that Bob had not escaped our intolerable lives.

Finally, the people were gone and so were many of our canine family. Billy, Bob, and Linda began to pick us up in pairs and return us to the truck that had brought us. Because there were fewer pups, we all had more space and water and were able to enjoy the relief of the cooler air. Billy tossed in canine Linda, who was barely moving, so Bob and I went to her to let her know that we were still there with her.

Linda hardly moved and seemed almost lifeless. Still, we lay against her until we sensed her puppiness cross over to Rainbow Bridge, and she was no longer suffering. Bob and I spent the rest of the long trip back to our "home," cuddling against her. The truck had been moving a long time and when we finally stopped, we were again moved from the truck. When Linda didn't move, Billy took her separately to a building corner where a large pit had been dug. He threw her little body into the pit, like he would throw away one of his cigarettes.

Because Linda had been taken separately from us, human Bob carried me and canine Bob in one trip back to our cages next to each other. Except they weren't our old cages but other cages, which really didn't matter, because they were all small and smelly like we hadn't ever left. At least these new cages had bowls of water and food, and were only mildly dirty from the other dogs' waste. Still, the wire floors cut into our pads, so we were better lying on our sides.

At least I could see Bob in the cage in front of me, though we rarely barked to each other, exhausted and fearful of how Billy might react. One night we were sleeping and an awful smell came on the breeze to us. I turned my head and could see a small fire at the corner of the building where Billy had taken poor Linda. Billy seemed to just stand by, smoking his cigarette and watching the flames. He did not show any feelings, so I tried to forget the painful scene and went back to sleep. Unfortunately, I was unable to completely forget that picture because every day I would see a person, usually Billy, take a dead pup, walk to the pit and toss it into the pit. Sometimes Linda or Bob would take the lifeless pup and gently place it into the pit. Linda would often weep.

What could I do other than try to survive each day to avoid the pit? And why bother? I just grew weaker and tried to live. I remembered the first time I had seen Linda, lying in a water bowl, and almost playing before Billy had ruined what little joy she had experienced. Perhaps I could try to curl into my water bowl, though it was only partially filled. With some squirming I managed to fit entirely into the bowl, which offered some cooling comfort and relief to my pads.

Although uncomfortable it was better. I decided to take a risk and, not seeing any people near, I barked to Bob. Listless, he did not move. I barked again and again. Slowly he turned his head and saw me. His head twitched in surprise to see that it was me, and I tried to show him what I had done by squirming in my water bowl.

Bob seemed to understand and tried to force himself into his water dish. My efforts seemed to make me cooler, and I awaited his response. He looked back at me and barked, which I took as a thank you, so I barked once, felt briefly happy, and returned to my contorted position.

I was awoken by a hard spray of water, which dislodged my body from the bowl. Consequently, I hardly got any fresh water. I had already soaked up most of my drinking water in my fur, so it would probably be a long time before I got any more, especially with Billy in charge. His only goal was to finish his job as fast as possible without looking at his lazy results. Thankfully, I wasn't thirsty yet and decided to just lie still and not increase my thirst. The sun and heat had almost gone and maybe I would be able to make it through the night.

Making the night was fairly simple because all I had to do was involuntarily play dead, but the next day was agonizing. Constant heat, weakness, little water, and my eyes were still almost completely stuck shut, so looking and hoping for more water was not even possible. Worst of all, as the day slowly passed, I began to seriously lose my desire to survive. More days like this? I could still see Bob in front of me, also motionless and soulless. I was willing to join Linda at Rainbow Bridge. I had resigned myself to cross over in my sleep that night. I would never understand the purpose of dogs in the world. I was just meant to never learn it.

I gave a final bark goodbye to Bob, but he never responded. Maybe he had decided to join me on our final journey. I hoped, because it seemed that Bob was destined to be a sad, useless pup like me. I took a hazy final look at whatever was near me and closed my eyes even more tightly for the last time. No sorrow, just an ending and hope that it would be my last sleep. My mind would clear and all would be better soon, I hoped against hope.

Not having any sense of time except day and night, my fading life was suddenly shattered by loud noises. Not that I cared any more, but instinctively I managed to open slits through my pasty-encrusted eyes to see the outside. The noise kept blasting me, but I knew that you couldn't see sounds. I still strained to see outside my cage. Blurry, I could partially make-out a long line of cars and trucks with flashing lights on them driving fast up the driveway. They all stopped next to our cages. The sounds were so loud that they made my ears hurt. I sensed that the sounds came from the unusual cars and trucks, which had never happened in our world. I just wanted to go to Rainbow Bridge, but I knew that I hadn't reached it yet, and that I was still suffering in the only home that I had known.

Then I saw Billy, his arms behind his back, being led by some bigger man who pushed Billy into the back of a car. The strangers were all dressed the same with stars on their shirts. Then two other men took Bob, and a third person took Linda to another van. At least the noise had stopped, but the lights kept flashing. I just kept my head down because I was too weak to hold it up any longer. Besides, I didn't know what to do.

Soon the cars with Billy, Bob, and Linda drove away fast. Who was going to take care of us now? My water bowl had been empty for so long and I couldn't imagine anyone else who would fill it or take care of me or Bob or the remaining pups with life still in them. Then there was vague movement outside, but I wasn't sure if that was a good or bad sign.

Surprisingly my cage door suddenly opened wide and a strange hand lifted me out of my prison and carried me to another cage, but the new one was much bigger and had solid floors covered in soft cloths like the one in the big truck that Bob had driven when we had been taken to the other place where we had met Linda. Best of all was a big water bowl at one end. The woman who had taken me from my old cage gently placed me near the bowl, and dipped her fingers into the bowl and brought some water to my mouth. I opened my mouth as wide as I could and began to suckle, like I had with mother. The wetness was reviving and I wanted more. She put my head near the top of the bowl and I was able to drink again. When I felt my will to live trickle down my throat, I drank for a long time and actually was able to stand on all fours. She petted my head.

Soon another pup was brought in and set by the water bowl. I hadn't seen him before, but I could tell that he had been suffering like I had. Instinctively I would have tried to fight for my water bowl, but there seemed to be plenty and I was too exhausted to fight for anything, including my life. We sniffed each other, then lay down on the soft surface, but not touching each other. What was happening to us? Perhaps this was a first step to reaching Rainbow Bridge. No problem because that's what I had planned in the first place.

After a while of rest, I noticed another bowl with kibble, but I felt too weak to make an effort. I would be content with water and a soft place to sleep. It was still hot outside, but the lack of sun and the large cage made the air feel cooler, even if I had to share my space.

Suddenly the cage was off the ground and moving. Whoever was moving us went slow enough so that and nothing spilled and no bodies were hurt. Our cage was put on the edge of a truck and someone pushed us in deeper. Soon, other cages containing many haggard puppies were brought to the truck, some stacked on top of others, some on the truck floor. It was set-up like the awful place we had just left, but here were solid, padded floors, and no waste leaking through to any other cages. And no Billy. The air was cooler, like something we had never experienced. In fact, after a while the air was as cool as the sun had been hot. My pup mate and I huddled for warmth and comfort.

When it looked like the truck was full of cages, the back door was shut and we were driving away. Hopefully, we would never see such a place again. In the truck there was always a light on so that we could see and feel safe. I thought of my brother Bob and wondered if he had lived long enough to be on our truck. I gave as loud a bark as I could and waited or a reply. No other dogs were barking in Bob's voice. But then there was a familiar lone answering bark, and I dreamed of playing in the grass with Bob and Linda, but realized that Linda was no longer with us and that I would have to take one step at a time. I barked back and settled in for the night, curious about what I'd see the next time we could be outside. It wasn't long ago that I had hoped to wake-up at Rainbow Bridge, but that was not to be yet.

I was almost sleeping when some loud roars and sounds awoke us all, and I opened my eyes hopefully to see what had made us all cower. The truck stopped, back door flew up and people began to remove our cages. We were released into a large area surrounded by walls and covered with grass. Once on the grass, we all relieved ourselves in some form, and we just stretched our tired legs, which were still cramped and weak from our previous cages. We were all being watched closely, as if any of us had the strength or desire to run away. There were so many pups that it was difficult to find any special one, like Bob, so we stayed near our cage mates. The fresh air felt good and made most of us feel more alive. We also all felt relief that we weren't back at our old place.

It was day time, but after the cool air of our trip so far, we did not feel the suffocating sun. I could see through one gate and became afraid of so many vehicles riding so closely together and making so much noise on the roads. They all sounded angry, which explained what awoke us all, but nothing appeared to be too threatening. Soon we were picked-up and brought back to our new cages. At least they were big and cool, had water and some new bowls of that food we had eaten all our short lives – kibble. I gave one last bark and thought I heard Bob in the back of the truck. Sad that I had missed seeing him, I still felt good that we were probably on the same truck, and that we should see one another again.

With water, food, and cool air we were all willing to hang-on to hope and simply rest. I tried to befriend all my imprisoned canines, though I realized I had no idea of their kind, just size. All their paws seemed to be cut from their former wire floors, and they seemed to take advantage of the chance to rest their paws off those wires. One pup was so skinny that I suspected that he had already planned to make his trip to Rainbow Bridge. When he relieved himself, there was watery poop, but the new people cleaned it up quickly. Another dog had eyes like mine, leaking and sticky, but open enough to partially see. Unsure of our future I did not give any of them names, not that I knew any beyond our three former watchers--Bob, Billy, and Linda. I would have to start listening closer, bit I sincerely doubted that we would see each other again, once the truck had stopped at our unknown destination. It was the life of unwanted puppies.

Losing all sense of time without being able to see out of the truck and telling light from dark, we finally stopped and felt rested enough to try to look more. The back door shot up and we could see the morning sun, but we were no longer feeling hopeless that it was the beginning of another torturous day--lying in the sun and heat with nothing to do except suffer. Some people must have cared, because at least we were all rested, not thirsty or hungry and less in pain. Soon the cages in back began to be moved to another truck just like ours. As the cages began to disappear from the rear, we could see more of the outside. I looked and tried to find Bob. Then I let out a loud bark. The reply came swiftly from a cage that was already loaded onto the other truck. For a moment Bob stepped on his cage mates, made eye contact with me, and we began to bark, "Hello, brother" to each other, but then another man quickly slammed the rear door to Bob's new truck. The driver climbed into the front of Bob's truck and drove away. I watched for as long as I could. My sticky eyes became wetter, and despite our new lives, I felt sad. At least I knew that Bob had survived and even looked healthier. Maybe when I saw him again at Rainbow Bridge, we could talk more.

Again, our truck moved and we went back to drinking water and lying in the cool air, even without half of our gang of pups. The next time the truck stopped was to be our final destiny. How much farther could we be taken? Our cages were quickly moved to a large, grassy space, like the one we had seen the last time we had taken a long ride in a truck, but the new air was not as hot as at our "puppy mill," a term I had learned from people talking at every stop that we had made on this trip, and they often said it in disgust.

The sun was partly hidden behind a wall. Our first task was to go to relieve ourselves ("potty") the people kept saying. Silly word. Once we had taken care of that, which was a big relief, we were just free to walk around the yard, where plenty of water and food were waiting for us.

Several new people walked around and talked to us, some even picking us up for closer examination, like the last time. The woman who held me, rubbed my back without hurting, and checked my eyes. She shook her head in disgust and carried me inside. Had I done something wrong? It was a large room with smaller tables, each holding a pup with people checking the dog. I was immediately lowered into a tub of water up past my legs, where I stayed while she poured water over me. Instinctively I tried to drink the good water, because who knew how long it would be there.

Even though the water was not cold for drinking, it felt good as it passed over my coat. Soon she rubbed something that seemed to grow on my fur, but when she poured more water on the back, the whole gooey mess seemed to wash down into the now dirty water. And it felt great!

She (Vikki) kept doing it over and over until my back end became clean of all the dirt and body waste that had built-up there. It, too, felt wonderful! She lifted my ears and put something in them as she moved her big finger around in it. She stood me on my back legs and washed my front. I felt as though I was losing my fur; all of my coat was being made clean and my body began to feel different. Vikki took a cloth and carefully washed my head, working her way to my eyes, which hurt as soon as she touched them.

She must have been able to feel my pain, because she stopped washing my eyes and lifted me to one of the smaller tables, where she wiped me dry with a cloth and used something that blew hot air on me, but not an unwelcome hot air this time. She covered my whole body with another cloth, and, despite the heat, I felt like a new dog, the best I could ever remember being.

Unfortunately, the glorious feeling did not last long. Another man held me tightly and held my mouth shut. Vikki came over with something hidden in her hands. Then she opened my eyes and dropped liquid in them that caused me horrible agony. It was the worst pain that I had ever experienced. I don't mean discomfort; my eyes were burning and I could not escape the man's tight grip. In such a short time I went from feeling the best ever to the worst ever. Where was I and what was next? Vikki put something in my mouth. It was hard but I liked chewing on it. At the same time, she rubbed my head and talked softly.

Once the pain lessened, I could start to see the room, people, and pups. Every table had one pup with one person who was doing something with the young dog. I saw others who were being held tightly while another person did something to its eyes, getting the same reaction – stop that! Are you friendly or not? Each dog got something to eat, like I had, and the pain eventually seemed to disappear. We all seemed dead tired and only wanted to sleep,

Every time a dog was taken elsewhere, another one took its place. I was on the table for a while, and the flow of the dogs going in and out was constant. I had the feeling that all of these people were trying to help all of us dogs. Other than the eyes burning, everything they did to us was good. There wasn't any shouting or hitting, and we all had water and food. Who were these people?

Just as I got used to the treatment, Vikki carried me away. She kept rubbing me against her face and saying things I hadn't heard before, "Good dog" and "You're safe now." We went outside, where she put me on the grass. I sniffed for a while, and peed on the wall. As soon as I had finished, she picked me up and carried me inside. We walked between two rows of high-stacked cages. Each cage held dogs; some had two or three bigger dogs; a few cages held only one very large dog. I had not known that some dogs grew to such immense sizes. At the end of the row were stacked more people high cages, some holding several smaller dogs, like me. I assumed that I would be staying with them. That was good. Who knows, maybe Bob would be there, but I did not see any dog that looked like Bob.

Surprisingly, Vikki opened one of the big cages like the ones for larger single dogs and placed me alone inside. There was food and water and a soft blanket and a big hard piece of food like the one she had given me after hurting my eyes. I lay down by the door and I could see several stacked cages, each one holding a pup. I waited for another dog to join me but soon fell asleep. I guessed the cage was all mine for a while.

I was awoken when a man opened my cage, took me outside, and put me on the grass again. There were several pups wandering and sniffing. Sometimes one would get mean and for no apparent reason try to attack another dog or even a person. Someone always stopped the assault in time and carried the dog back inside, to be replaced by another dog that was grateful and happy to be there. I assumed that I was supposed to pee again but I really did not need to, though it was nice to have a choice to do so when and where.

I sniffed a few butts, which was not too unpleasant anymore, and began to rest again without dread or fear. Eventually people came out and carried us back to our cages. No burning heat or sharp wires. We all had more space to look out at all the activity. It was a similar routine as the farm but without the agony. When I got back, there was fresh water, the same food, and that crunchy thing (treats I later learned) waiting for us. I decided to chew on that treat while I stared out my cage door. My eyes did not seem as sticky, and I enjoyed not having to see all those sad pups in small cages with nothing but heat and an occasional threat from Billy.

I was still weak and was grateful to just rest. However, Vikki soon took me out of the cage to a table, where a man (Peter) was quick to hold me tight and point my head up while Vikki was fast to put some more drops in my eyes. This time I tried to bite a hand, but I was too small to do any damage. I hurt and cried, so Pete picked me up above his head, while they both talked to me softly, and Vikki gave me a new kind of treat, something soft and chewy. It blocked my mind from most of the pain, and soon it was almost gone. For many days Vikki and Pete put me on a table and thoroughly examined my mouth, tail, and body. Every day they put more burning drops in my eyes. It always hurt, but I soon learned I couldn't fight it and tried to think about the soft treat I would get at the end. Occasionally, I might feel a sharp poke in my rear end or neck, but I always got a treat, so I didn't mind too much. Besides, I had learned to trust these people now, and I felt that anything they did to me was for my own good

Every day we were all taken outside, not just to go "potty" but also to just walk, run, jump, and sit in the cool grass. Perhaps this is what dogs were meant to do. I began to feel healthier and enjoyed watching the pups at play, and maybe soon I would feel able to join them. Some days strange dogs, both large and small, would come up to me and nudge me with their noses, a friendly gesture, but I just wasn't ready to be social. After all, I had never learned to do what they were doing. Did I just walk into a group and jump on them, like the ones I watched?

The people sat on seats (benches) around the yard and watched us. Nothing bad ever happened, but someone would help if a pup seemed to cause a problem. That pup was immediately brought inside, its playtime over. Otherwise, the people would just sit and talk to us, maybe even give us a treat. Nobody was mean and I felt stronger as time passed and all threats were gone.

As days and nights passed, my eyes grew better and I rarely got burning drops any more. Vikki often put me in warm water and carefully washed my face. Not only did my sight get better, but also my eyes were no longer sticky, and I was able to open them all the way. Nor were there any of those tiny bugs to bother me any longer. With improvement came another surprise. I got two new cage mates. They sniffed me at first, as I sniffed them, and everything was good. At night we would sleep in a group touching each other. Without thinking or meaning to, we all helped each other feel safe. We were all let outside during the day just to wander within our confines. Sometimes I would see some new pups that also had bad eyes or bloody paws, and I could watch them acting the way I had when I first got to this new place. Because I was feeling better and growing bigger, I would often nudge one of them with my snout, as though to signal them that all here was good and safe.

Vikki and Pete still took care of me, though Pete no longer had to hold my snout tightly closed. I never tried to bite Pete again, and I felt bad that I had once. After a pleasant bath and dry, Vikki used something that she moved up and down my back, causing much of my fur to fall off. Then she washed me again and I really began to feel good and wiling to lead another life.

Some days people walked between our big cages, occasionally stooping to get a better look at us. When I saw them coming, I would go to the cage door, hoping that someone might want to take me to a new home. Just instinct, I guess. Slowly more dogs left our home, but because they did not return, I was never sure where they had gone or what had happened to them. They probably went to another new home, certainly not back to the old farm.

While I got bigger and comfortable to my life in a place that people called the "New Orleans Humane Society," I often heard workers talk into something they constantly referred to as a "phone." I wasn't sure what all their words meant, but I learned more and more. The humane society seemed to be a place that took care of dogs (bless them!). I did learn that all the dogs that left and never came back, might mean that they went to new homes. I could not believe that a new home would be better than this, especially after our past lives. But perhaps there was more than this. A few people even took me outside, talked to me, and threw a ball, which meant nothing to me. When I didn't do anything, they left me. Other dogs seemed to know the right things to do and permanently left us.

Finally, the day that took me to my next life arrived. I was happy with the one I had, and despite all my wishing and anticipation for a new home and a fuller life, fear returned as the haunting unknown came back for me. A young woman and two men asked to take me out to the yard. It felt like the farm's Linda, Bob, and Billy, only this time the men both seemed crude, but the woman (Suzi) seemed nice. I sensed that Suzi wanted a dog.

She rubbed my neck and talked to me, while the men went to a corner and smoked, something I often saw Billy from the farm do, but as long as he wasn't doing me any harm, I really didn't care. This new Billy just didn't seem friendly at all, and I began to think that I didn't want to go home with them.

Suzi picked me up and we went into an office, did some paperwork, and left. I never saw any of my humane society cage inmates or friends again. Despite all the petting and ear scratching from Suzi, I felt afraid from the moment we left the humane society in a small truck. The two men were called Frank and Leroy. Frank appeared to have some attachment to Suzi and Leroy just seemed there. As I grew to know him, he seemed nicer than Frank, who never pet me or spoke nice.

We rode a long way to get to a small house (they called it a "cabin"), surrounded by big trees. Suzi carried me in and put me down on the "kitchen" floor and set down a bowl of water for me. Before she had put it on the floor, I had peed on the corner of a table. "Slam!" went Frank's hand on the table, along with some angry words. Suzi picked me up and rushed me outside. I guessed the problem was that she had forgotten to let me pee before taking me into the cabin. I was still fairly little and that long drive had been hard on me. They must have had a no-pee-in-the-house rule. I had already learned my first lesson.

I pretended to finish what I had started. When Suzi saw that I had finished, she cradled me and took me back into the house. Leroy was on the floor cleaning my mess. Frank was standing by the table, smoking and drinking from a bottle (beer) like I had seen mean Billy do on the farm. He yelled at Suzi, and she took me into a bigger room, where we sat on a couch facing something that had moving pictures, almost like they were real. I started to relax a bit as we sat there watching what they called a tv, which, as I was to learn, was the whole purpose of having a cabin. All these people seemed to do after it got dark outside was to sit and watch tv. It wasn't exciting, but I learned to enjoy it because it seemed to calm Frank when he was watching and drinking from those bottles of beer, which was better than scaring me.

The cabin was small, but then I had never seen a cabin. It was certainly bigger than our cages at the mill, but not nearly as big as the humane society. I had the feeling that most people lived in a place like this and called it home. I could only see one big bed in a room for Suzi and Frank. Another room was for Leroy. The kitchen was small with a table, chairs, and some other big items, which they would frequent for beer and food. Then there was a place for the people to wash and to relieve themselves. Guess they were too good to go outside on the cool grass. I did not see or expect a bed for me, but I assumed I would sleep with Suzi in her big bed.

At sleep time I followed Suzi to her large bed, where she lifted me to the top. It didn't take long before Frank came after us, yelling, "No! No! No!" and took a swipe at me. Suzi saved me and cried while she yelled at Frank. Eventually she took me back to the couch and we sat next to Leroy. Her bedroom door made a loud crash when Frank slammed it and she jumped. I was scared and worried for Suzi when she went back to the bedroom. Again, Frank slammed the door. I could still hear Suzi crying and yelling at Frank, followed by a loud slap, like mean Billy used to hit a pup if it bit someone or something. Suzi continued crying, and Frank yelled until the noise eventually stopped. Meanwhile, Leroy had begun to rub my neck and scratch my back. I don't know if he meant to do it, but it helped me feel calmer.

When it seemed that tv was over, Leroy carried me into the kitchen, put me on the floor, and got something from the fridge (another new word). He cut up whatever and put the pieces on a plate, which he placed on the floor for me, as though offering me kibble. But this was no kibble. I took one piece and it was nothing like anything I had ever tasted. It was wonderful! After I had finished half of it, I looked up at Leroy to see if he was going to yell at me. He just smiled and pushed the plate with his foot, which I understood to mean that it was okay, and that the plate was all mine. I ate as fast as I could before Frank found us and took the meat from me. When I had finished eating but still hoping for more, Leroy took me outside to do my business. When it was done, he took me into his room. There was only one small bed, but Leroy put a big blanket on the floor next to the bed. I thought it was for me, so I curled up on it.

Leroy put a bowl of water and a couple treats like we had gotten at the shelter. He put them on the floor, patted me on the head and turned off the lights. Still nervous, I was so tired that I went to sleep for the entire night.

I was awoken after the sunlight came into our room and I got up to go outside. Same routine everywhere I had been, except for the farm. Leroy was still sleeping but Suzi knocked on the door, entered, and scooped me up while nuzzling my neck and saying quiet words. Her eye seemed darker around the edge. She took me outside and I did my business and more, which she immediately picked up with a metal tool and threw my poop into the trees. Weird, but this was my new lifestyle.

While watching me, Suzi sat on a big table with benches and smoked a cigarette. I hoped that they didn't make her mean like farm Billy and Frank. She let me walk alone into the kitchen, where Frank was standing by the counter drinking another beer as if he had not moved from the night before. Suzi went to a big bag on the floor, put in a cup, and pulled out some kibble, which she put into a bowl before giving it to me. I went to it and looked at the biggest kibble I had ever seen. She watched me struggle to chew the large bites, before saying something angrily to Frank, who reacted by kicking my bowl across the room and slamming the door on his way out. Must have been part of his lifestyle.

Suzi began to cry as she swept-up the mess. Leroy hurried through the door following Frank, and said something to Suzi who looked up uncertain. After she had put the kibble into another bowl, she added water. She waited before putting it back on the floor. I smelled it, but it still had that unpleasant odor like the food from the farm. I bit a chunk, and surprisingly it broke apart in my mouth. I chewed it and most of the other chunks of kibble until they were almost gone.

While I was eating, Suzi had gone back to the couch and the tv. The pictures must have started again because she was staring, unaware of anything else. I was able to jump up on the couch, and she was lying down, inviting me to come to her and what became known as a cuddle. She was stroking my neck, and I saw some water leaking from her eyes. I could sense that she was sad, and I instinctively licked the salty drops of water (tears). She held me tighter and I felt bad for her.

After we rested with safety and comfort, Suzi took me outside, where she let me run anywhere I wanted. I had never done such a thing – no cages, no fences, or no mean people. There were birds that I remembered from the farm, and they were eating something from the ground. I wanted to chase and play with them, so I immediately took off barking. They were all quick and soon sitting in the trees looking down at me in wonder. I don't know why they wouldn't play with me unless they were afraid, like I was of Frank when he yelled.

"Toto, Toto," Suzi grabbed me, but not angry. She was laughing when she took me to sit on the big table with her. Soon she took something from her hand and threw it hard on the ground. I couldn't believe that it hit the ground and went straight up before coming down and rolling down the hill.

"Fetch," said Suzi. I wasn't sure of that word, but she put me on the ground and pointed me to the object (ball), and I followed her. She picked it up and threw it back towards the house. This time I ran after her when she went to get it. I got there first and bit into the ball. It was soft and I was able to pick it up with my mouth. I remember people playing this game at the Humane Society. Now I knew the rules.

"Good dog, Toto," said Suzi as she took it from my mouth. Immediately, she turned and threw it high. When it landed, I raced after it before Suzi had even started. It went far, but I found it quickly and carried it back to her, who took the ball and kept saying, "Good dog, Toto." I recognized the words "good dog," but what was "Toto"?

We played this game every day until I grew too tired to play anymore, but Suzi didn't seem to mind. That was pretty much my life at the cabin: watch tv with Suzi in the morning, eat kibble, play chase the ball, sometimes just walk around the fence-free grounds, all the while Suzi kept saying, "Toto." Whenever I was out of sight, she would yell, "Toto, real loud, and I soon learned that she wanted me. Of course, I learned that it was my one name, like Suzi, Frank, and Leroy. I didn't really care, but what was a Toto?

That was a typical day until Frank and Leroy came home, driving up the long road to the cabin. As soon as they got out of the truck, they went into the house, where Suzi was holding me, after having opened some bottles of beer for them. Immediately I could feel tension and fear from Suzi. The men would often go outside with their beer and sit on the table. Some days, if Suzi did not feel the tension or fear, she would take me out and let me wander alone, while she joined the men on the table. They all seemed nice to each other. Maybe there was a decent life coming after all.

When it was almost dark, Suzi took me inside, and she cooked food for the three of them. Usually, they were pleased. Suzi and Leroy would occasionally give me bites under the table, hiding it from Frank, who never gave me anything, not even kibble. After supper, they would all watch tv. If they had drunk too much beer, Frank became mean to Suzi. He would take her into their bedroom and they would scream at each other, accompanied by slaps. I trembled on the couch, wishing I could help Suzi, but I just had to sit there with Leroy and pretend, like he did, that there was no way to help her.

Some mornings Suzi did not come out of their bedroom until the men had left. When she did, Suzi was usually crying, and she picked me up and hugged me tightly on the couch while mumbling words; the only one that I understood was "Toto." Her eyes were closed shut, like mine had been at the farm. I tried to give her licks, but they did not help. What could I do?

Some days the men did not leave and stayed home all day and drank beer. Suzi and I tried to avoid them, usually playing ball out of their sight, but still there was a constant tension, like we were waiting for Frank to stop our playing and beat Suzi. Instead, a loud sound made us stop. Suzi ran to the front of the cabin with me following. Another blast came as we turned the corner. Frank was there holding a long pipe in his hands. When he saw Suzi, he smiled, but not a nice smile. He shouted something, which made her grab me for comfort, hers and mine.

Leroy took the pipe (rifle, I soon learned) from Frank, held it up to his shoulder and looked down its top as if he could see something special. Then another boom came from the pipe and one of the beer bottles on top of a fence, shattered. Both men laughed and clapped. Then it was Frank's turn, and they seemed to do that all day. Suzi was used to it, but I was afraid of those loud sounds and the game they seemed to be playing.

I just lay by the corner of the house, trying to stay hidden, but ready if Suzi should need me, hoping she didn't, but I was willing to try. Suzi began to make a fire under a metal pan she had brought outside, went into the cabin, and returned with a plateful of meat, like the kind that Leroy and Suzi sometimes sneaked bits to me under the table. It smelled good, and the tension seemed to lessen as the day wore on. I just stayed out of sight and kept an eye on Suzi.

She turned over the meat on the fire and more flames shot up. She put a big piece on a plate and yelled, "Frank," as she put it on the table. He went to his seat at the big outside table and began to put other foods from the bowls that Suzi had also put out. Soon they were all eating while I watched intensely from the side.

Then I saw Leroy's hand drop down with a piece of meat for me. I ran over and ate it very fast; it was much better than kibble. I was able to hide under the table for more meat to come my way. Then a big piece fell on the ground. I immediately picked it up and ran into the yard. I heard a loud, angry voice, and Frank was yelling and chasing me. I dropped the meat but he was still mad. Luckily, I was faster and could evade him without too much difficulty until I felt a big kick in my back leg. It hurt and I rolled in the grass, but he kept coming. Suzi yelled and she stopped Frank enough so that I could keep out of his reach. Despite the pain, I was able to get away down the driveway.

A loud bang came from behind me. It was that rifle that the men had broken bottles with, but Frank had it pointed straight up and no bottles were broken. Still, I had never been so afraid, even when I had been eager to go to Rainbow Bridge. I just ran farther from the house and from Frank, while Suzi followed me and shouted, "Toto, Toto!" I had never been to this part of the woods, even when Suzi and I had just walked around. I ran between some trees until I felt that I was out of his sight. Too tired and scared to run anymore, I just lay down and hoped that I didn't see anyone except for Suzi. I fell asleep.

When I awoke, it was all dark, and I wasn't sure what to do. I heard strange sounds around me and even saw some odd creatures with shining eyes. They felt dangerous to me, but I didn't think they could help me either. I slowly got up, my back leg still hurting. I thought about barking, but what if Frank heard it? I began to walk out of the many trees until it was just grass. I wasn't sure which way to go.

After more time to rest my sore leg, I saw a circle of light coming my way. I didn't know what it was so I tried to stay still as the light got closer. Then I heard, "Toto!" I answered with a bark and the light came closer fast.

"Toto." It was Suzi, who ran to pick me up. After lots of cuddling and neck rubbing, she carried me all the way back to the cabin. Frank and Leroy were in the front room watching tv. Suzi yelled something at Frank, who was still drinking beer and ignored Suzi. She brought me into the kitchen and put down a small plate with meat on it just for me. I wasn't sure if I should touch it and risk another kick from Frank, so I shied away from the plate, but Suzi pushed the plate over to me and said, "Eat." It was a word I knew, so I quickly began to chew all the meat on the plate, temporarily forgetting the pain in my leg.

When I had finished eating, Suzi took me outside to go to the bathroom. She sat on the big table, watching me and noticing my limp. She immediately got up, picked me up, and put me back on the table, where she rubbed my back and scratched my neck. She knew how to make a dog feel better. If only I could help her.

She smoked a cigarette while tending me, her Toto. Suzi stared off into the dark woods, as though deep in thought and hoping to find answers there. She spoke directly to me, "Sorry, Toto," but I didn't understand the rest. She just made me feel safe again after such an awful day.

When we went back inside, Frank was sleeping in his big chair. Leroy was standing by the door to his room and said something to Suzi. Still holding me tight, she passed me to Leroy, who took me in his room and gently placed me on my blanket. Then he patted my head, felt my still sore leg, but he moved it a little and seemed satisfied with his action. He gave me a treat, rubbed my neck a little, and climbed into his bed. Soon I could hear him give his people growl.

The next day Suzi did not talk to Frank, and he seemed angry but did not react. I heard the word "Toto" mentioned several times, but I stayed out of sight. Last time I had been with Frank, I had been scared too much, and he had hurt Suzi.

Days passed without incident, and eventually Frank and Suzi seemed to be back to normal, except that Frank seemed a little more patient with me. He didn't play ball or give me meat or treats or anything fun, but he didn't hurt me, and I was able to live in a world with less fear. I was back to eating big, wet kibble, and it seemed to help Frank be nicer. Leroy and Suzi occasionally sneaked little bites of people food to me under the table. If Frank saw anything, he didn't say a word.

Life seemed better for a while, until one day that the men were drinking and shooting again. I stayed and hid in the cabin, not even going outside with Suzi. Later that day it looked like they were going to start an outside fire on which to cook meat, I was hoping. Soon rain began to fall, big drops and so many of them that they decided not to cook outside. Frank came rushing in, turned on the tv and plopped into his chair.

Suzi seemed upset about something when she came in and watched Frank watching tv. Seemed odd. She sounded angry while she kept pointing at the screen and waited for him to talk to her. He just kept staring at the tv and would yell. Suzi stood in front and continued shouting at him, until Frank lost his mind and backhanded her, knocking her to the floor.

I immediately reacted like I had been ready all day if Suzi had needed any help. Instinctively I jumped and bit the hand that had hit her. The bite didn't last long, but he bled and then started to yell. I was on the floor, too, and Frank kicked me hard in the head. I felt something break and a pain shot through my mouth. When I tried to lick my wound, a piece of tooth fell out, followed by blood.

Suzi was still on the floor trying to shelter me. Frank was about to kick me again when Suzi threw herself on top of me. Frank decided to kick her too. Thankfully, Leroy rushed in, shouted, "No" and pushed Frank away. He, too, fell to the floor, while Suzi tried to get up while shielding me. Leroy helped us while Frank just shouted some more. Suzi took me to her bedroom, locked the door and sat on the bed with me.

She cradled me and cried while trying to look into my mouth. It hurt but I couldn't do anything. She felt bad for both of us, as did I. At least I had tried to help, but I was just too little.

Outside we could see the rain pouring down and one tree was waving and almost falling. I could smell something unusual in the air and grew more afraid at the sound of the wind.

Our cuddle was interrupted when Frank kicked in the door. He was yelling but passed by without hitting either of us. He pulled something that he kept under the bed and began to put his clothes in it. He kept pointing at me and shouting, which made Suzi hold me tighter. He went back to the front room and I felt a little relief, despite my aching tooth.

Suzi had a small bottle and took out a small pill, opened my mouth and put the pill on the back of my tongue; then she closed my mouth, forcing me to swallow. She carried me to the couch and we sat while she rubbed my head and scratched my back. Then something odd happened. Leroy and Frank picked up the big tv and carried it outside. I watched them carefully load it into the truck. The bite I had given Frank was already dry, but I didn't think that he had forgotten about it. That was just Frank's natural way – hold that grudge.

The rain and wind were blowing into their truck and Frank covered the back with a big plastic cloth and tied it tightly. The men made a few more trips for those cases with clothes. They ran, trying to avoid the wind and rain. There was a big crack and a tree fell beside the cabin. It just broke. Why? It had been so big and strong.

Leroy brought bottles of water (odd) and put them in the truck. Suzi and I watched, wondering what would happen next. The falling water became deeper and deeper; the wind brought more water until the whole front yard covered Suzi's feet.

We stood in the kitchen as the water came from the outside into the cabin. Suzi was more scared than I was. She probably knew more than I did. I was being held by my favorite person and although the pain in my tooth lessened, I wished that I were somewhere else, with Suzi.

Then my world shattered even more. Leroy stormed in, took me from Suzi, and gently dropped me to the floor and held me tight. She reacted by shouting, "No! No! No!" over and over. Then Frank ran in and forcefully carried her up and out the door. I barked and tried to help but Leroy held me back. He waited with me as we watched Frank shove Suzi into the truck. She was fighting and crying the whole way.

Leroy slowly carried me to the couch, which had water climbing up the front. Quickly he went to the kitchen and brought back a big bowl of kibble. As if knowing that I wouldn't be able to chew such large, hard chunks with a broken tooth, he poured water over the food. He also had a water bowl, and a handful of treats, which he put at the end of the couch. I didn't know why he had given me so much. I couldn't have eaten that much over several days. Next, he did something really odd. He took a stool he had rested his feet on when he watched tv. The stool was not quite covered with water, yet. Finally, he took the blanket I used as a bed from his room and put it on the couch. Then he talked soft while he scratched my neck and ran out the open front door to the truck.

I watched as he jumped into the truck and they all raced away. Did they forget me? I could see Suzi in the back window pounding her fists and yelling. She needed me, so without thinking I jumped off the couch and onto the watery floor and ran after them, all the while barking. It was hard to run because my feet were under water and my paws were heavier to lift with every effort. I barked and ran but the truck carrying Suzi was going too fast, and they went down the hill and turned away for good.

It was hard to stand with the wind blowing so hard. Down the driveway I could see the creatures that I must have seen when I was running from Frank's shooting. Some were small, like the ones I often saw in the pile of wood next to the cabin and even in the house. There were a couple animals with long ears that were trying to hop over the water, but they never made it very far over the water. Birds could be heard but not seen in the dark skies.

With no idea what to do, I just turned back and began to run back to the house, fighting wind and water as I neared the open doorway. There were no lights, but I could remember where everything in the house was. When I looked back, all I could see were the forest creatures following me. No truck. No Suzi.

I went through the front door and was glad to see that the couch was not yet under water, but half of it was wet. In the cabin it was still hard to run, but at least I could reach the stool and jump to its top and onto the couch. It was almost as if Leroy had put that there for me. He surely did with the kibble, water, treats and blanket. But why did he leave me so alone?

Some creatures put their noses in the door, but left when they realized that the water was everywhere. Sometimes I barked to let them know that I was there, but it seemed to scare them instead, and they all left. Outside was getting nighttime dark, not just storm dark. No tv, no lights, no people. I clawed my bedroom blanket into a pile and lay down in safety like my usual routine, even though I could hear and see the rain and crashing trees. I was scared like never before, even worse than Frank's threats. Why did Suzi and Leroy leave me alone?

Exhausted I fell asleep, despite all the noises and water falling. My eyes opened to the dim daylight and I stretched my legs and walked over to my water bowl and tried to eat something. I couldn't understand why Leroy left me water in a bowl when there was already so much water in the cabin. I really liked the idea of having as many treats as I wanted, but Leroy had forgotten to put water on them, so I had a painful time trying to bite and chew them without using both sides of my mouth. My broken tooth was beginning to hurt more after a full night alone, but I was helpless.

Although the rain and wind seemed to have lessened, they were continuing but causing less damage. Water was still climbing up the couch, and I began to feel it when I hung my paw over the edge. My stool was totally under water, so I didn't dare risk falling off. It looked like a day on the couch, hoping that Suzi would come back for me. I just peed on the couch, hoping that Frank would come back to yell and hit me, and unknowingly save me.

I passed the time staring out the door. No cars, people, or anything. Inside I saw some of the outside animals, but many were now floating on their sides, unable to swim. As the day passed, more and more creatures floated through the door. I never did see the long-eared animals again. Overhead I could hear screaming birds and a loud machine-like noise that passed over the house several times. I barked and hoped that someone might hear me. No response.

The water seemed to be almost done climbing my couch, but it was still high enough for me just to sit still and stare. I imagined that I was on the couch with Suzi watching her shows, including something called "General Hospital," which excited her as she pointed at the screen and talked to me like I understood. Those times had been nice and safe, and I wished that I had it all back again. But thinking about something isn't as good as doing, so the time passed slowly. I pooped once, but it floated away, and I hoped that Frank would step on it.

The outside grew darker again, but this time I think it was only nighttime, not the storm again. Still there were no lights and I was scared, even though I had lived through another day. I thought back to the day at the farm when I was ready to go to Rainbow Bridge.

Maybe that would have been a good day. Was there any life that was good for me or any dog?

Another night and day passed. There was no threatening wind or rain, but the water slowly got higher. The entire couch was now wet up to where I was lying. The stool was completely covered with water, so I wouldn't even dare jump on it. The food and treats that Leroy had left for me were all one wet clump. At times I ate some, but it was even less appealing.

I spent the next day, staring out the door and wishing their white truck would come back to get me. I hoped that Suzi and Leroy were safe, but I really did not care about Frank. Thoughts of that good home I had at that shelter were in my mind, and I wondered if the rest of our group had found better homes than I had. And Bob? Where was he now?

I began to sleep again, reliving that old farm wish to go to Rainbow Bridge, not quite wanting to get there yet, but it was something that ran through my muddled thoughts. Outside was completely black, and I could barely keep my eyes open. No pain, just fear of the unknown.

Still, I kept one eye half-open and listened. My sense of smell was so strong that everything reeked of death. More water was everywhere, and more creatures floated into the cabin, none moving on their own. There was a distant sound, which made me weakly bark. I didn't know what the sound was, but it didn't sound like any creature I knew. It sounded like Frank's truck, but there was no clear sign of it coming up the now missing driveway.

My fur was all wet, and even though it was always hot there. I began to get cold and started to shiver. I shook off the wet, but it only helped a little. Then, I thought I heard a human voice. Again, I barked. My voice was not as loud as I could usually make it, but I tried a few times.

In the distance I could see a light bobbing above the water. A human voice also came from it. I barked more, but some other noise was too loud and nobody answered. The light floated past the door and out of sight, but I gave all I could. Dare I jump into the water and try to chase the light? I didn't know how to swim, but I had seen people on TV do it, and they just kicked their arms and legs. I don't know why they didn't sink, but I didn't really care. Was that my only choice?

The loud noise from outside stopped, so I barked some more. If I jumped, would I still be able to get back to my couch? Suddenly there was a piece of light on my door. I could hear human voices nearer. I barked more and the light got bigger.

Enough thinking. I got onto the edge of the couch and jumped as far as a little wet dog could. When I hit the smelly water, I went straight under. Instinctively I began to kick with all four legs. My body seemed to rise and soon my head was above water. I was so exhausted that I didn't know how much longer I could do that, but I had to try. Finally, my body quit and my legs stopped kicking. My mouth filled with water when I foolishly tried to bark. I kept sinking, looking for a way up and out, but I could see nothing. After my breathing had almost come to an end, I mysteriously rose above the water. A big man held me high with one hand. I felt water come out of my mouth, and it fell on his big bearded face. Instead of slapping me and throwing me like Frank had so often done, I could hear the man say, "Okay, okay," and other words I did not understand.

Slowly he passed me to other people sitting in a boat like the ones I had seen on tv. Several people were in it, and they all seemed eager to touch and hold me. Someone wrapped me in a warm blanket. They dried and hugged me, which made me feel warmer and safer. Each person held me tight before passing me to someone else.

The man in the back of the boat pulled something and that loud noise returned. That caused the boat to go faster, and the woman in the front held a big light, the one I had seen in the doorway. I peeked from under the blanket and saw everything go by fast as we passed. Maybe they could find Bob, too, I thought. We kept finding more people in trouble, and soon the boat was almost full. Even the new people wanted to hold me.

All these nice people confused me. Why were so many people like Billy at the farm and Frank at the cabin, so mean to me, or was it just dogs in general? Other people like Vikki and Pete at the humane society and all these people in the boat seemed kind. I learned that if people were nice to each other and to me, I could be nice, too. The boat grew louder and went faster, then got quieter and slower. The big light was always shining in the front.

Time passed slowly as we found more people and somehow found room for them to sit. When there was no more room, the boat went fast until we finally reached a place where more people were waiting for us. Surprisingly, I was the first one off the boat as I was handed to a man on shore. He held me in one hand, while he helped few other people onto the shore. "Bye," he said as he waved his hand at them and carried me to a car.

It was just us and he gently placed me on a blanket on the front seat of a car. He shut the door and I was worried that I would be left alone, but the man soon appeared on the other side and immediately started, rubbing my neck and talking softly. Then we left. I never learned his name, but he had something hanging from his mirror, like the one Suzi had hanging around her neck. She would often squeeze it and quickly mumble some words when Frank was threatening her. Exhausted I went to sleep, at times seeing patches of bright lights as we drove.

When we finally stopped, I wanted to see where we were. I recognized the place, but how? We went inside and everything seemed familiar. Then I had a wonderful surprise when an excited Vikki came to us and took me from the nice man who had brought me back to her. How had he known to take me here? I didn't ever know, but I was extremely happy. After the water in the cabin, I felt that I would never be safe again.

She put me on a table and looked into my ears and eyes and was shocked when she lifted my lip to check my teeth. She said something, as she nestled my head against her chest. With so much activity from being rescued in the boat and the long drive, I had mostly forgotten my aching tooth. The pain had returned, but I was just happy to be where I belonged.

My old cage was still there for me, but Vikki took me to the big room with all the tables in it and put me on one. Soon I felt a little stick in my neck and I could hardly stand, but not from the pain. What had Vikki given me? And why? I still trusted her and knew that she was a good person.

When I awoke, I still felt weak and Vikki took me outside to pee. I felt better once I had done my business, but I was still puzzled. I lay on the grass just to feel cool and out of harm's way. Vikki waited. Then I noticed something when I went to the water bowl. When I took a drink, some of the water came out of my mouth and fell back into the bowl. I felt with my tongue and my hurting tooth was gone. Nothing hurt any more, but it took a long time before I learned to eat and drink without that tooth. She must have taken it while I was sleeping. I guess Vikki was a good person, after all.

So, I was back where I had started before Suzi had tried to give me a better life. I missed her and never saw Frank or Leroy again, which was good. I often thought about Suzi and our playing with the ball and watching tv, and her overall goodness. I hoped that she was okay and with someone other than Frank, who would take good care of her like she had cared for me.

Life in the humane society was much the same as when I had left, except there were many more dogs now, and there were several that had to share a cage. But we all seemed to get along as if we had all shared the same experiences. Perhaps they all had had to be saved from the water like me. Many of the dogs looked tired and sad, so no canine bothered another dog who looked like it just wanted to be alone. Slowly most of us began to grow closer and often slept touching each other. Vikki checked on us every day. She particularly checked my mouth and ran a finger where my tooth had been. Then she'd say, "Good dog," and scratch my neck. I really had liked Suzi, but maybe Vikki could replace her, maybe even take me home to live with her, too.

During the day many people walked back and forth as they looked at us, like people had before, when Suzi had found me. A few people took some of us, and I still hoped for a good home, though so far, my life had not been good for anyone. Days were all the same – outside, eating, more outside, but not much fun. All the people seemed too busy to stop to play or to watch tv. There's always time to enjoy a dog. I don't know what else they had to do, but they were always moving and talking into phones. Still, when the day was over, we all felt tired. Maybe just tired of waiting, but at least we were safe.

Many days passed without much happening, until one day another big truck parked and began to unload cages and place them in the parking lot. They sat there all day while we watched people put food, water, and a blanket in each cage, like when we had all left the farm. The day was getting darker and it looked like nothing more would happen. I was still outside, lying in the cool grass after eating. Then everything changed.

People came and took us away to the cages. Soon I was being carried away with the rest. Suddenly, Vikki came up and said something to the man carrying me and took me from him. Instead of carrying me in her hand, we cuddled as we walked. She kept holding me tight, while she talked to me constantly in her soothing voice. We stopped and she raised me to her face, still talking but now her eyes had tears. She put my nose on her nose, and I heard the words, "Good bye" again as Vikki put me in a cage and shut the door. Her eyes became wetter with more tears. Before she walked away, she patted my cage, turned, and left.

It was as painful as leaving Suzi. There was nothing I could do except bark, which caused Vikki to turn back and wave her hand. I barked again, but a man came and put his arm around her shoulders and they were gone, for good. First Suzi, then Vikki. What was my problem? Was I a bad dog, like other people had yelled at me? I didn't think so, because so many other nice people called me a "good dog."

My cage began to move and I was carried to another truck with cages stacked on top of each other, but not cramped like the ones from the farm, which had seemed big at the time. Like my last trip to the humane society, the truck was cool and we really couldn't see much into the other cages. I didn't expect Bob to be there, but I barked anyway and waited for an answer. I got several, but not Bob's.

Knowing what to expect, I lay down and shut my tired eyes. It seemed natural that sad dogs were tired dogs. I heard the back door slam shut and we were soon moving. Where would this trip take me? My life just seemed to be a constant worry about if there would be another new life. The farm, Frank, the rising water, the too frequent moving. Nothing much seemed to give me the chance to prove that I was a good dog, except for Suzi and Vikki, and they were gone. Maybe this trip would be better.

I still had no idea of time, except long or short between events. One time on this trip, we stopped and all the dogs got out of their cages to run and go to the bathroom, while the driver and his helper watched us and smoked. Then they put us back into the same cages. They called me "14" and the last dog "28." I don't know what they meant, but I assumed that they were our new names. I guess the name "Toto" was already being used by another dog.

Back to sleep until I felt the truck had stopped again. The back door opened and many new people began to take our cages and bring them into a large room. Once the cages were all inside, the people took us all outside to a large grassy area, where we could all pee and explore. We felt safe but not sure where we were or why. Some of the bigger dogs were led into the building, while we normal dogs were carried inside and put back into cages, like the ones we had just left at the humane society. My cage had all the usual – food, water, blanket, and a big thing for chewing, which I did despite my missing tooth. I enjoyed it because it was something different to do – just chew but not eat.

These new days were like the old days at the last society. New comfortable place, but not a fulfilling life. Sometimes a woman pointed something at us, pushed a button which made a click and caused a flash of light. She did that to all the dogs. Nothing harmful, so I just kept chewing.

Then the day came that Carla, the latest woman to take care of me, put a card on the front of our cages. I could see a picture of myself, like I had when Suzi had used a mirror, on the card. When she did so, she smiled and said, "Hello, Binky." I did not know what that meant, but over time I learned that it was my new name – Binky. I liked Toto, but I guess that Binky was okay, though I had no idea why I had to change names again or what made it special.

Like the last humane society, people would often walk past our cages, and put their fingers through the doors. I never knew what to do when they did. Biting seemed the normal response; why else would they continually do that. Still, I never bit anyone except Frank, who had really hurt me, so now I just sniffed their fingers. The result was usually the same --- they would say, "good- bye" and move on to the next cage

One day some of us were again put into cages, moved into another truck and driven away again. I had no idea where this time. A short time later we stopped, and the truck's back door opened and the cages were quickly taken out and stacked in another big building, but this one had lots of dog things. From my cage I could see big bags of kibble, like Suzi used to get for me. And there were toys and chews, and so many balls. Many people were walking around and picking up things, even bouncing the balls. My cage came to a stop on top of another cage or cages. I couldn't see far, because my fur had grown over my eyes, and I was still confused by the shadows I could see moving.

Overwhelmed by so much new activity outside of the cage, I closed my eyes and waited for what was next. Several people looked at me but nobody ever opened my cage door. I could see other dogs walking around the outside floor, but I could not tell what they were doing. I just waited; my new fur not only hindered my seeing but it also made me hot, not like farm hot, but hotter than the humane society. One man tried to look at my tooth, so I snapped at him and was immediately put back in the cage. I tried to sleep.

Finally, there was someone at my cage door who took a longer look at me. She opened the door and passed me to another woman, who cuddled me, then slowly put something around my neck and put me on the floor. Immediately, I tried to run, but was held back by what she had put around my neck. It had choked me, so I stopped trying to run, and as soon as I did, I could breathe easily. She was holding the other end of what they called a "leash," and I wasn't sure if she was good or bad.

I was standing on the floor, not trying to run any longer, when a man stooped next to me, rubbing my head and talking. He seemed nice for a man. He took the leash and let me walk slowly. I could see the outside and instinctively tried to pull him to the light, but he wouldn't follow me. He started to pick me up in one hand, so I tried to bite him. It was my chance to be totally free. Instinct. He put me down, not angry, and the woman picked me up. I trusted her face and she held me closely.

Then some other woman came to us and started talking. She gave the man a piece of paper while she rubbed my head and kept saying, "Binky, Binky." The man seemed angry at first but the woman barked back at him. Finally, the first woman put me on the floor and we walked around. I could smell wonderful things and treats. The sight of balls took me back to Suzi at the cabin. If this was all for me, I thought that it would be wonderful to live there. I saw the outside again but no longer had a strong desire to escape. I had another nice woman and a safe place to be.

She (Becky) picked me up again and we went back to the man (Larry). Becky and that other woman were looking at him, as if waiting for him to speak. Becky held me tighter, so I licked her again, a trick I had leaned at the humane society. Finally, he said "Okay," which I knew meant yes and Becky smiled big and kissed me on my head, not using her tongue like good dogs did. I just hoped that Larry was going to be more like Leroy than Frank.

Soon another dog from our group was brought over and we sniffed each other. He had an unpleasant odor, like a sickness, which I hadn't smelled in the truck. After some time, the woman took away my companion and put him back in his cage. Larry and Becky seemed upset for some undetectable reason. I never saw any of my humane society friends again, but it turned out good, because I left the big place with all the food and toys and treats to go to another home. For better or worse?

Instead of riding in a cage, I sat on Becky's lap in a car. Rarely I used to sit on Suzi's lap when Frank drove his truck, but this was nicer. I was sitting high enough to see all the new wonders outside. Becky opened the window, and I could stick my head outside while she held me by the neck and back end, even though I had no plan to jump to freedom. The fresh air felt cool and renewing. Today had been a good day, and, if possible, may get even better.

The sights were too much for my experiences. There were so many cars, buses, and trucks all moving at once. An occasional honk would sometimes startle me, but I felt safe in the car with my two new people. So many smells – some unpleasant and some wonderful, depending on where we were. The noises were constant, like when I had first gone to the humane society, only these seemed louder and more annoying, night or day. And everything moved too fast.

Finally, we pulled into another big building, not as big as the society, but a large door magically opened for us, and Larry drove the car into a room big enough for two cars. Where were we? Do I stay or try to escape? Where would I go? I still wasn't big enough to get away from a person's grip and I did not want to bite Becky. I let her carry me out of the car, through some more people doors, and we were outside again. She put me on the ground and I began to run as fast as I could.

Everywhere I went there was a fence or growing things to block my progress. It was a big outdoor place full of good smells and soft grass. Still, I kept looking for escape spots, if not for now, maybe for the future if everything stopped being good. After being born at the farm and living with Frank and escaping the flood, I had learned to always seek someplace better and safer. That was how my whole life had been. It was a tough lesson, but it was part of me now.

Soon I was tired and saw Becky and Larry watching me and smiling. Larry bent down and I instinctively ran to him. He carried me up some stairs to another big door and took me into the kitchen, which was much bigger and cleaner than the one at the cabin. He put me on the floor next to a water bowl full of cold water and I drank as much as I could. No one stopped me.

Once I was done and drooling all over the floor, Larry started to scratch my back, and it felt so good. We walked through several rooms and they had so much new stuff, including a huge tv, much bigger than the one at the cabin. The place was full of new scents and I was afraid that my nose might stop working from so much activity. I wondered if Becky and I would watch shows every morning. Okay by me. Was this how they lived? Was I going to live here too? Where were all the other people? Was there someone special to take care of me if I needed anything? Was that bowl of water only for me? Maybe I shouldn't have drunk so much, but memories of the farm always haunted me.

Larry and Becky sat on the couch, and as I watched, still unsure of what to do, Becky patted the space next to her. I instinctively jumped up next to her. Suzi had often done that unless Frank was sitting next to her, but Larry did not seem to mind. As soon as I was on the couch, they both began to talk quietly while they petted me. Then Larry surprised me by reaching into his pocket and giving me a treat. I snapped it out of his hand and immediately jumped down and ran to a hiding place (desk) and began to dig into the floor to try to hide this new treasure. Frank had often taken treats and toys from me if he had been drinking. Larry had acted like he wanted me to have it for myself, but I still didn't trust him.

Suddenly I was being carried away by Becky as she kept shouting, "No, no, no!" Not sure what I had done wrong exactly, but she was mad about something. I was sure that Larry had meant to give me that treat, and I ran through the open back door and hid outside. Later that night I went back to the hiding place and the treat was still there. Slowly I ate it in front of them. Oddly, I was rewarded with a scratching and a "Good dog." It was going to be a while for this dog to understand and adjust.

Just when I thought that it was dark enough outside to go to sleep, Larry and Becky went out on their upstairs deck and turned-on lights that flooded the whole yard, complete with a small area where water flowed over some big stones, nothing to fear. They sat and looked over the yard while they drank beer, and I hoped that it did not affect them the way it had Frank. They had put an old shirt on the deck for me to lie on. I looked at it and Larry threw a treat on it. My immediate instinct was to grab it, run down the stairs and hide it. Instead, maybe it was an invitation to sit with them and have a treat. It was such a different reaction from the first treat they had given me. I sniffed it, then lay on the shirt and ate it.

"Happy hour," Becky told me, whatever that meant. It was something we all did almost every night, and it was good but that first night I just wanted to have one more search of my new yard. Mostly dark, but those lights showed me parts to check closer. Then I heard Larry yell," Binky! Binky!" I wasn't sure what that meant either, but it sounded familiar. I was smelling something unusual under a bush, but I ignored it for now. Hopefully we would do this again tomorrow.

Then I heard Becky call me by the name that they used at the last society, and I thought that maybe she had forgiven me for the last time that she had yelled, "No!" and scared me enough to make me run and hide. Growing trust, this time I went to her immediately.

They were both standing in the doorway, laughing about something, and I went between them into the kitchen, both giving me pats on my back. They ate at a table, but I didn't know if I would have anything special, so I just went to my kibble and began to crunch. It was still kibble, but this tasted a little different.

After eating we went to the front room and Becky sat on the couch, while Larry brought some big cushion and put it on the floor. It didn't look as good as Leroy's old blanket, but it would be fine. Then he patted it like he wanted to me to lie on it. When I didn't respond, Becky carried me to the cushion and placed me in it. Soft, I was reminded of the bed I had sometimes shared with Suzi without Frank. It was the perfect size, and I could rest my head on the edge, almost like someone had made it for me. I could have slept there except that I would miss scratches and petting. Instead, I decided to sit by Becky, where my wishes came true.

Larry put another pillow in my "bed," so I jumped down and cuddled in the warmth and tried to sleep in my new surroundings. So much had happened since I woke-up that morning that I could hardly move. I went to sleep and when I stirred, I noticed that both

Becky and Larry were gone. Lights were on but there were no people. Time to find them, hoping that they hadn't left for good, like so many others had deserted me. It was my first night there. How was I supposed to know the routine?

Luckily, the first room searched, I found them sleeping. I learned how to jump high from the nights that Leroy left room for me to join him on his bed. So, I leapt and landed right between them, where I tried to snuggle into the warmth of their legs. I thought I heard them whisper something as I went to a deep sleep.

I got up when Becky shook me and I followed her outside, running down the outside stairs. I realized how bad I had to poop, and it made me feel much better. Then Larry came out and called, "Ernie, Ernie," but I only gave him a blank stare. Then Becky called "Ernie" and having done this routine many times before, l suspected that I was again getting a new name. I raced up the stairs to her. Surprisingly, she gave me a treat. I began to wonder about this woman's mind.

If that wasn't enough to comprehend, Larry went down the stairs, looked up at me and called "Ernie" again. Not sure if I was getting a new name or what was happening, I ran down to him. He gave me a treat. What kind of people were these? I learned that my new name was Ernie, and that Binky was no more. Treats can train a dog to do almost anything.

Except to climb trees. There were too many happenings in my new yard that I was rarely bored. I recognized little furry creatures like the ones I had seen at Suzi's especially during all the water. I would chase them but I didn't want to hurt them. I remembered so many of them floating lifelessly at the cabin. They were so small, and one time in this new yard, I did swipe one playfully who rolled over, but I never hurt him. The biggest challenge was the squirrels that could climb trees and walk across wires between houses. And, of course, birds. Life wasn't fair. Birds could not run faster than me, but they flew straight up to the safety of the trees. Still, they provided good sport.

The next day we all went to a new place, where they left me in the hands of someone named "Lori." I didn't know what was happening, if they were just getting rid of me or what. I couldn't have been that bad of a dog in only one day. Lori seemed nice, so I let her put me in a big tub like they had used at the humane society.

Then she sprayed me with water. Still not fond of too much water, but this spray was warm and didn't smell bad, like the flood. My feet were on solid ground, so I wasn't afraid. Lori rubbed some flowery smelling stuff into my fur and massaged me, even my butt. After a few minutes of just standing still, she rubbed me again while she sprayed all the good-smelling stuff off me. I really didn't know what she was doing, but it sure felt wonderful, even better than Vikki's washing. Lori even spent extra time on my head and ears and was careful by my eyes, which were finally normal again.

Just when I thought it couldn't get any better, the water went somewhere and Lori picked up my soaking wet body in a warm towel. I began to tremble, not because of the cold, but memories of being wrapped in a towel was too much like the flood and the woman in the boat who had also tried to warm me in a towel, wondering then if I was going to die. Instead, Lori put me on a table and put a rope around my neck to force me to stand and to keep up my head. A loud noise started and hot air blew all over me. She went back and forth over my body, and soon I was no longer wet but enjoying the warmth. What kind of place was this? They took two elements I had learned to hate from my past lives, water, and heat, and turned them into pleasurable experiences.

Next Lori helped me feel even better. At first, I was afraid of the unknown sound, as Lori ran something up and down my sides, I felt like pieces of me were falling off. Was it okay if I didn't feel any pain? I thought that people would probably worry if their sides started to fall off. My body felt much lighter without my fur. I still couldn't move my head, but I trusted Lori; so far, she had only done things that felt good. She even cut fur away from my eyes, and I was shocked at how clear everything looked. Then she cut my nails, but I didn't mind. I would still be able to run, and I doubted that I would ever be able to climb trees. Lucky squirrels. Wondered if Lori ever cut the squirrels' nails.

I was put into a cage alone, and I saw many other dogs in cages. They all looked clean and happy. Like so many other times, they vanished quickly, before I even got to know them. Finally, it was my turn and Lori took me from the cage, put a collar around me and led me to the front. Larry and Becky were waiting, looking like they didn't even know me. I immediately ran to them and covered them with kisses and whimpers. I had been afraid that I would never see them again. They both had small tears in their eyes. I couldn't have been that ugly.

Lori came over one more time to pat my head. I would see her many more times over the years, and I always got excited when we went to visit her. I wondered if people ever did this to each other – warm water with good smelling stuff, hot air, and shortened hair. Why wouldn't they?

We all went home and I was eager to see if we returned to the big house and yard or if I was being moved again. As soon as Larry opened the car and back doors, I ran like a crazy dog, just to get rid of all that energy I had built-up while I had that noose around my neck. With so much fur gone, the air felt even cooler and my vision was clearer. I ran so fast that I think I could have run up a tree and gotten one of those squirrels, but, lucky for them, Lori had taken all my nails.

Time passed as I settled into my new home, now feeling like my "forever home," a term I had often heard. In dog time it was probably only a month, give or take. We all went to a new place resembling other places I had been, but I could not exactly remember. Once inside Larry had me sit on a scale and then he put me on a table in a small room. Seems like I spent a long time sitting on similar tables that were all the same and I grew anxious. A man (Keith) came in and extended his hand for me to sniff. He smelled like lots of other dogs, but seemed friendly and even gave me a small treat. Larry and Becky were in the room with me, so I felt safe.

Keith reminded me of Vikki from the humane society as he shined a light in my eyes and ears. He even checked my teeth and put his finger where my missing tooth had been. He put something on my chest and checked my legs, nails, and everything a normal dog has. I assumed that Keith in his white coat was nice like Vikki, and he ruffled my head when he left. And I got another treat, but I really didn't like his treats and I wondered if I saved it for Larry, if he would eat it. Still, like Lori's, I wouldn't mind coming back here.

Every day Larry and Becky took me for a walk around the neighborhood. I think they had done this before, maybe a lot! They greeted everyone and sometimes stopped to talk while I tried to patiently wait to get onto the next smells. When another person was also walking a dog on a leash, we stopped and I would extend my nose to his dog's nose, but when I got too close, I would hear a growl, so I immediately went into protective mode and barked and lunged at him. I wasn't going to bite him unless he had continued his attack. I just wanted to acknowledge him like a possible friend and to protect Larry. How else could I communicate? Big dog or small dog, no one seemed to let me sniff their snouts without growling and reacting the same way. I guess no dogs in the neighborhood had been raised around other dogs the way that I had. Larry seemed puzzled by my behavior.

One night Larry took me to another unusual place. Unlike most trips to stores, this time I did not have to wait in the car. Still leashed I followed him into the store and was immediately frightened. It was exactly like the place where Larry and Becky had found me and took me home. Were they not happy with me and bringing me back? Not again. Why couldn't I find a forever home? I liked them and had been a good dog, I thought.

Larry led me around the store, and just like the last time, I could smell kibble, rawhides, toys and treats. We finally went to a smaller area where several other dogs and masters were waiting. Were we all going home with a different master? Was one of these dogs going home with Larry to his big house and yard, and was I going home with another person? I was scared but still wanted to smell and play with the other dogs. Maybe somehow, they could communicate about their owners before we all left. Then . . .

Another man (Jon) was in the center of our circle and talking to all of us. He made an irritating clicking noise with something in his hand, and he passed a noisemaker to each owner. I did not like Jon, especially when he kept saying things to Larry, which caused tension that I could detect. After a while we all walked around the store. No time for nose or butt sniffs. One time the noisemaking leader held my leash while Larry walked away down the aisle. Soon he stopped and bent over for me to come to him. I felt the leash loosen and I raced down the aisle to Larry who gave me a little treat. Why? I would have come to him anyway. No treat needed.

We did some more inane acts in the store, while the man kept making that clicking noise. I'd met a lot of people in my life, but this one, though not cruel, was one of the first on my list to maim. The guy didn't even give edible treats.

Next week Becky took me to see that same clicker guy. I had a feeling that Becky did not like Jon either. She probably wouldn't have gotten into trouble if she had bit that nasty noisemaker; people did not usually bite other people who had deserved it. By the time Becky and I had finished doing those same activities from last week with Larry, I could also sense tension in her, and she never got stressed. In fact, she told Larry that she would never go back. Maybe if Jon had given us all better treats. . .

Larry and I went to see Jon a few more times and it was never fun. No playing or treats, just clicking. What purpose did these trips have? On our last week we all got papers, which made Larry laugh, ruffle my head, and took us home, never to return. That night we were all sitting on the couch and Larry was cradling my head, looking me in the eyes and he said something which made both Larry and Becky laugh. I didn't understand, but I felt relieved because I belonged with those two and hopefully nothing would ever part us.

One morning a new worry arrived, floating down from the sky. I didn't think that it came off the roof or trees or birds, maybe the clouds, but I just stared, trying to understand if it was good or bad. Larry and Becky were both there, and, other than some unpleasant words said to nobody, they showed no outward fear. Cautiously I stepped off the downstairs porch and onto the white stuff hiding the lawn.

Larry walked into the middle of the yard and called me. If he could stand there, it must be safe. After slowly walking out to him, taking high steps in case the white ground caved-in, I was still puzzled. Some landed on my nose, and I tried to lick them off, but I couldn't reach them. I really didn't need to because in seconds they were gone. Then Larry rubbed my head with the white stuff (snow), and I shook it off. What was I supposed to do? All the neighbors seemed to have it in their yards.

Larry patted his legs, then started to run after me. Couldn't catch me; he was too slow. I began to race around the yard in a circle, like I had the first day. Surprisingly, my paws slipped from under me and I rolled in the snow. It didn't hurt but I was surprised and immediately got up and continued my escape from Larry. Then Becky joined in and threw balls of snow at both of us. I remember playing catch with Suzi and a ball, only these balls did not bounce but broke in my mouth when I jumped to catch them. Then Larry started to throw snowballs at Becky, and I wished that I could do so, too. They both decided to chase me and I fell many times but I was always was ready to play. I had come a long way from the farm.

Finally, Larry realized that he could never catch me and quit, so we all went inside. I was so thirsty that I almost emptied my water bowl. Then I went to my bed and slept, to rest up for our next outside playing. I hadn't worked that hard since Suzi's cabin had all that water, and I had been forced to survive alone.

When I recovered after a long sleep, snow became a big part of my life. The snow was piled so high that Larry had to clear enough space in the back yard for me to use as my private bathroom. I was still a little guy, compared to the big dogs of most neighbors. Some days I could catch and eat the snow. Larry and Becky had a machine that shot snow far and kept sidewalks clean so that we could still take a walk every day. I would have been fine with skipping the walk on some days, but I wanted to please Larry, so we put on our coats. Mine had my name on it so that we didn't get them mixed-up.

I felt the air grow colder and unpleasant, but they rarely let me get too cold. I was thankful that I had a good home. When I did get too cold, I would involuntarily shake. Of course, they would wrap me in a warm blanket and rub my body until I fell asleep on their laps.

It was during this cold season that people brought trees into their houses and put lights and ornaments on them and in their yards. Odd custom I thought, but everything looked nicer. Then a new person came into my life. Odd, his name was also Larry and he lived there, too. Why did it take so long to meet him if he lived there? Was he my brother, like Bob had been? Though big, he seemed a nice man, and some nights I even slept with him in his bed downstairs, where they kept him. He would even let me cuddle on the couch. Some days he would walk me even in the cold. It was strange walking down the sidewalks and not being able to see the houses because of the high snow. At times there was so much snow that big Larry and I walked down the middle of the street in the huge tracks that ran through the neighborhood.

One night Larry let me out for a final pee, and I was happy to go because the three of them were intently involved watching some play-off game, and they would often yell, stand, and clap, which always made me nervous, even though they were eating popcorn. Lots of shouting, either anger or cheerfulness. And why did they have to stand and clap so much? I was ready to escape to the cold outside. Maybe they'd be normal when they let me in again.

I walked around a little, just in the area that Larry had made my bathroom. But now there was a new clear path leading to the gate. I hadn't seen anything outside of our backyard for a long time, since the snow had decided to cover our grass. I cautiously walked to the gate, and there was a small opening that I could fit through. I decided to explore this; it looked different from the normal grassland of the warm seasons. The driveway was clear, so I was easily able to get to the sidewalk. I could see as far as possible either way. The only problem was that I could not see over the high walls made by the snow. Which way to go?

I kept moving, but I really could not see much, just look at the endless tunnels of white surrounding me. Soon there was another clear driveway, so I turned down it and was on the big street. Everything was so much wider, making it easier to see more things --- houses, half-buried fire extinguishers which I had watered many times, and parked cars, but I had walked far enough that I did not clearly recognize anything. I wished that I could see our gate again and that I hadn't left the yard. I kept walking, wanting for someone to recognize me, but there was no one out this late and in the chill. I began to feel the same helplessness that I had suffered when I had been waiting to be rescued from the flood, only now I wasn't wet but close to frozen.

As time passed my eyes were beginning to freeze shut, like they had stuck together at the farm. I had never felt such penetrating cold. I kept moving, if only I knew which way to go. Sometimes I just stopped and barked, hoping that someone would recognize the sound of a distressed dog. The problem was that when I stopped, my pads were almost stuck to the freezing street. They felt better if I kept moving.

Finally, I saw some bright lights that vaguely looked familiar. I tried to run towards them, but not only was I cold, I was tired and scared. I didn't know how long I had been outside. Still the lights drew me closer to come inside. I got to the big door and waited for it to open. I had often seen Larry and Becky stand before a door, wait for it to open, and they walked through. I was ready to enter, but I had to wait for someone to come out; no one did. I had been there before with Larry but never inside. Barking seemed to help in most places, but not this time.

Finally, a man ran up and opened the door but he put his foot out to stop me from following him inside. Not roughly, but enough to deny me entry. I barked anyway. I waited for the man to come back out. He did, but he left by the far door. 'Help! I'm really freezing!' I barked again and the door opened. Another man came out and held the door partly open, as though inviting me inside. Suddenly I found my racing legs and went inside, where the warmth immediately devoured me. I was shaking uncontrollably. He picked me up and talked to my face like I knew what he was saying. My vocabulary had grown over the years, but I was too cold to understand. I wanted to say "thank you," so I did the only thing I knew – a smack on his hairy face. He giggled and placed me on the floor.

Then he disappeared, but I was just happy to be out of the cold. I could see all kinds of food, but I wasn't really hungry, just glad to be in the safe warmth. When he (Tom) came back, he was carrying a bowl of water, which he put behind the counter. The last time I had been this afraid it was because of the rising water at the cabin. Now I felt relieved to have some water in a bowl. He watched me drink, while taking a box off the shelf. He ripped it open, reached inside, and brought out a treat. I could not believe it. When I had finished eating that one, he gave me another. I hadn't been hungry until this man had begun feeding me treats. This place couldn't be Rainbow Bridge, but it was like I had imagined part of it many times. I stopped eating, plopped on my side, and went to sleep. I was able to sleep anywhere, having had a wide background and experience of killing time.

I was awoken by a woman who took me from Tom's hands and put me into a warm car. There was a cage in the back, but she (Karen) put me in the front seat with her, and rubbed my head the whole time. I had stopped shivering by then, but welcomed the warmth and concern I found in Karen and her car. I wasn't even worried about where we were going, but I was hoping to Larry and Becky's house. I wondered if they even knew that I had been gone. We drove to some other not far place and Karen carried me inside. She put me on the floor and I simply followed her into another room, where she put me on her desk and said something to a man, who was dressed exactly like her. He got something from his desk and pointed it at my neck, then told Karen something that she wrote down. Then he called someone on his phone. Soon I heard him say "Larry Ehrhorn" and I realized that he was probably talking to my Larry Ehrhorn. I barked once, but Karen said "No," so I stopped because I trusted her. After a short time when the man unsuccessfully tried to play ball with me, Karen took me back to the same warm car and we drove away again. Why? Odd, but if he had called Larry, why wouldn't Larry just come to get me? We drove for a long while in the night, and I almost got cold just looking out the window.

We stopped at another building and she carried me in. It, too, was warm, so I wasn't worried about being released to the cold. Did all these people I had met just help dogs? If so, bless them. I saw a sign on the wall and recognized two words that I had learned long ago – "Humane Society." Did that mean that I was going to be held until someone new wanted me? Was my life with Larry and Becky all over just because I went through that gate? I'm sure the humane society would give me food and water, a blanket, and take care of me, but I would miss something I could not name. It was a feeling that came from people and spread to me and to other people. I'm sure it had a name, but I did not know what it was called, just that it was important and pulled me through some rough times. I had really liked my last life, or was it still my current life, and I didn't want to leave it.

The woman behind the desk took me to another room with a table on it. Again! Is there no end to tables for dogs? Karen had ruffled the top of my head and even kissed my head before she left. The new woman (Jodi) checked me like so many others had – eyes, ears, legs, heart, teeth, pads, etc. Apparently, everything was good, and she brought me to a large cage. She put me inside and shut the door. I could see a few other dogs that had watched my arrival. This cage was just like all the others I had been in – water bowl, kibble, blanket, and a rawhide chew. Not much else to do after such an active night, and I was just glad to be able to sleep in a warm place.

I slept soundly and was awoken by the same woman. Jodi carried me to a door, and I gave my society inmates a last look, hoping our lives would turn out well for all of us.

Good start. She took me through another door and there were Larry, Becky, and big Larry waiting for me. I ran so fast that I slipped on the tile floor. Even Becky let me give her dog kisses. They slipped a leash around my neck and off we went. We had almost reached the outside when Larry went back to the counter to talk to Jodi; she had some papers to give him. When he returned, he was furious, but I didn't think it was at me. Becky drove home and he let me sit on his lap while he constantly scratched my head.

When we got home, Larry immediately went to his chair and I was quick to join him. He wasn't angry with me yet, and gradually we both fell asleep. Almost sleeping but I could hear Larry talking about something. I heard my name and the word "dog," but not "good dog." More like "worst dog."

The snow was gone after a few warm days, but it left behind wet, muddy yards. Still, I was able to explore some more area, but I never checked the gate again. The worst part was that whenever my feet got muddy, which was almost every time I went out to the back yard, someone always lifted me into a large tub of water and washed my paws, like Lori had so often done. The next part of my life moved the same – snow came and went, rain poured, which made me anxious, hot season for relaxing outdoors, but I never went hungry or thirsty again. I had experienced plenty in a dog's life, but this home had been the best part of it. I wondered and hoped that Bob was living a good life, too.

One day during a warm season Larry took me on our usual neighborhood walk. I saw one of those chipmunks hiding in some bushes. As we passed him, I thought I'd at least scare him and barked while I pushed my head between the bushes. Larry pulled me back fast, but something had cut my eye. I had experienced pain, but this was different. My eye watered and a burning sensation spread. I couldn't help it, but I yelped and cried to let Larry know that I really hurt and wasn't playing.

He carried me home but it didn't stop the pain. Larry brought me to the sink where they bathed me and he called for Becky, who came running to help. She put a cold, wet cloth on my eyes, which momentarily eased the pain, but only as long as she left it there. They kept checking my eye, but all I could do was try to keep it shut and whine. I never cried anymore, but I just couldn't control anything. In the past if it had itched, except at the farm when it was stuck shut, I could usually scratch it to help, but not for this.

Soon we were all in the car, and Larry drove fast to the vet's office. Keith looked at my eye with a bright light. Then Larry tried to *hold up my head as the vet put some drops in my eye. I tried to get loose, but Larry held me tight. Despite my days at the farm and my life during the flood when I thought that Rainbow Bridge might be calling me, I wasn't ready for the agony those eye drops gave me. They hurt me like the drops that Vicki had given me at the first humane society.*

Why would they do something like that to me? I had thought that they all liked me and would take good care of me. Perhaps that is what they were doing, but I understand how. To make matters worse, Keith wrapped a heavy plastic cone around my neck so that I could hardly move. They put me on the floor, where I could move a little without seeing much. I guess that it took my mind off the burning a little, but what was I supposed to do? Were they going to take that big thing off me or was I supposed to adapt to another change?

Larry carried me to the car while I hung my head, hoping the cone would fall off. I was still in pain but glad to be out of the vet's office. I sat on Larry's lap the entire way home, where he carried me up the stairs and put me on the floor. I went right for my water bowl but this thing held me back from reaching the water. Becky immediately filled a different bowl and helped me guide the cone over the bowl and I just drank and drank. Then Larry put down a different bowl of kibble, but I couldn't reach it or eat; I really was not hungry, anyway. My eye was still itching but not burning as much. I just made my way to my bed and fell onto my side into the bed, like the cone gave me any other choice. Even when Becky cooked me fresh meat, I didn't want it.

After a difficult sleep and a few tedious and wearisome days later, we all went back to the vet, who listened to them about our last few days. It paid off, because he took off my collar. It felt good to move my head again, but my eye still itched, and I immediately wanted to scratch it. The vet stopped my paw and said, "No, Ernie!" Keith had never raised his voice to me.

We went home and Becky held me, grabbing my paw when I tried to scratch. The first days were agonizing and the constant itch would not stop, except when I was finally able to sleep. They both yelled, "No!" when I tried to scratch, but I couldn't help but try.

I lost my appetite and really did not eat much, even leftovers on Sunday steak night. Kibble was substituted with some soft food, but it did not taste good either. After so many trials in my life, when I thought that I had finally found my forever home, I just wasn't happy. Then it got worse when Larry had to carry me up and down stairs because my legs were just too weak. I was ceasing to be a dog.

One day we went back to the vet, who checked me over, but did not try to put drops in my eye. He stroked my back while he talked to Larry and Becky, who almost seemed to be crying. We all returned home and Larry tried to put a leash on me for a walk. I was just too tired, like I had been at the farm when I had hoped to see Rainbow Bridge. They took turns paying special attention to me that night — petting, scratching, talking softly -- but I just wanted to sleep.

Days later we again returned to the vet's office. Larry held me on his lap, and I could feel his sadness while his eyes dropped tears on me. We were sitting in our usual examination room when Keith came in with a somber look. He said a few words and Larry put me on the table, not the floor. The doctor had a towel, which he put under me. He also had a tray with some needles like others I had felt. Really no pain.

Becky stood by me at the table and rubbed my neck, while Keith gave me a shot, just like before. I could see Larry staring at me, and I think I knew why he was sad. I was sad, too, and I really wanted to let him know that I was okay, but I could only stare at him. Then I felt another shot, but it was deeper and harder in my leg, and I couldn't help but cry out. Becky picked me up in the towel and set me on Larry's lap. He petted me and said something about, "best, worst dog," which I remembered as everything went dark and pain and fatigue left me forever.

After what felt like a long, relaxing rest, dim light began to seep into my eyes. Slowly I opened them and knew that I had finally made it to Rainbow Bridge. After so much suffering as a pup and young dog, I had finally achieved my desire — a life without pain, hunger, thirst, loneliness, or fear, a flawless life for a dog, and slowly I remembered the last, best part of my life and the remarkable years.

Suzi, Vicki, Larry and Becky, and so many decent people were kind and had helped me, so that my life had not been entirely unpleasant or wasted. Amazingly, as I looked around me, I felt that I already knew many of these dogs and people. I knew simply everyone's name like they had been old friends. They had lived in Larry's heart and mind, where he always thought of them and unconsciously shared them with me. In the spirit of a good universal world, all of those connected to him were also linked to me and to each other.

Larry's childhood first pets, Ginger and Susie, were the first that instilled a love of dogs and animals in general. They both barked, "Hi, Ernie," to me. As a teen, Pepper and ZsaZsa drew Larry closer to all of us in heart. Running across the grass on his short, stumpy legs and long ears flying awkwardly came the show dog basset hound Dexter. Larry's adult phase introduced him to Macbeth, who had suffered a sad puppyhood, having lost sisters Lucy and Ruby, and he had eventually been parted from the rest of his littermates. Larry had picked Macbeth out of a shop window and they had shared many good years. I could feel their losses as they were all reunited and found each other again. Macduff followed Macbeth, and though he only lived a short five years, he bonded with Larry and appreciated what he had done for a sick border collie. Dickens was patiently waiting in a single-file line, while other dogs took turns jumping onto the back of a cow. No matter each dog's size, there was no problem jumping high enough. I thought that I had never stood on a cow either. I'd have to join the line sometime. Even Teddy, who was so small and had done so much good, came running through the endless field to greet me. I barked back.

Standing on Rainbow Bridge were a few people I was able to relate to my flowing memories. Nana and Bud, who were attached to Teddy for his care when they had grown old. I was surprised to see Suzi, who was smiling and waving and calling "Toto! Toto!" She was without Frank or Leroy, indicating that only she had died and the other two were still alive, or that they had been forced to take different path.

I had often heard people refer to heaven. I never knew what it meant, but everyone I met seemed to like the idea. Now that we were at Rainbow Bridge, I remembered another word I had often heard but was unsure of its meaning. It was an emotion that made people feel closer in their hearts. It was called "love." Now, every day was going to be a glorious day.

Who wouldn't want me?

You'd better run!

Epilogue

"The best things in life are . . . rescued."
Anonymous

Hi! My name is Jack, and if you hadn't guessed by now, I am next in line after Macbeth, Macduff, Dickens, Teddy and Ernie. When I go to Rainbow Bridge, I will officially be the "best worst dog" that Larry ever had.

For now, I am going to enjoy myself while waiting for my summons. In keeping with tradition, Larry named me for Jack London or a current cultural literary figure name Jack Reacher. Personally, I think I was named after his favorite, Jack Daniels

My reason for writing this page, besides a promised treat, was to emphasize my origin. I was found walking the streets of Houston, Texas. I don't recall anything before being picked-up by a kind stranger who took me home one night. The next day he called a place called "Lola's Lucky Day," a canine rescue service. I was like so many dogs that often are abandoned or lost and are always in search of a forever home. In fact, on this day (12/12/2021) according to two reliable sources (American Society for the Prevention of Cruelty to Animals and the Humane Society of America) 3.1 million dogs (surrendered, stray, homeless) enter one of the nation's 3,500 shelters. Of that number, 390,000 lost dogs are euthanized, mainly because of a lack of space and/or adopters. Those numbers are even higher for cats. Best recommendation is to say 'No!" to unreliable pet stores and to ignore "pets-for-sale" advertisements, unless it is someone you know and trust.

The people at Lola's Lucky Day rescue took me in, cared for me, fostered me to other nice people, and posted a brief description and a picture of me (I was called "Scrappy" then.) As you can see, I was and still am, extremely cute, and Larry found my picture on the internet. It had been only four months after Ernie had made his final journey, and Larry felt, as did Becky, that something important was missing in their lives. Even his wife said that he was happiest with a dog. Most people are.

Being one of those discarded dogs, Larry thought that I would be more experienced to ask all of you to adopt a dog in search of its forever home. Almost every breed has its own website (I'm a border terrier) but there's nothing wrong with a good old mutt, like Macbeth and Teddy had been. Please avoid puppy mills/farms and support legislation to close and ban all such places. Beware of pet shops and dishonest breeders, who are only trying to make a profit.

Lola's Lucky Day works with a companion office in Wisconsin. You can virtually find a suitable dog anywhere, and it will somehow find you. After a long 26-hour trip (truck broke down), I was again fostered, until one day when Larry and Becky stepped out of an elevator at my current foster home in an apartment on Atwood Avenue in Madison, Wisconsin. He knelt and I ran to him as fast as I could. I sensed that he would give me a good life, except for Wisconsin winters. After two years, I'm not ready to go anywhere, except up that pictured tree to chase squirrels and birds.

Please take the time to research before getting a dog and bringing it home. Certain dogs may be good with children, or not. Some do not do well in confined areas, whether caged while owners are gone to work or a lack of space to exercise.

Make a dog and yourself/family complete and happy. Now can I have my promised treat?

About the Author

Larry Ehrhorn was born in 1947 (post-Revolutionary War) and raised in Chicago and its suburbs, steadily moving west. Attended Northern Illinois University and graduated with a Bachelor of Art in Speech/Theatre with an English minor in 1970. Job market pushed toward high school English teacher, where he spent the next thirty-three years in three small, rural Wisconsin towns. Quite the contrast from a megalopolis of ten million to towns of six hundred. Finally moved to Madison, where he still enjoys his life with his wife Becky of forty-two years. Accompanying them was always a dog to help create a gratifying life.

He is also the author of "Four Months in Brighton Park, which relates his last four months at Wheaton Community High School in 1965 with some altered details Larry is currently retired and still living in Madison with his wife Becky and simple access (two hours) to his son Larry, daughter-in-law Nikki and three grandkids, Madison Allie, and Mason. And, of course, his dog Jack, a border terrier rescued from Houston, Texas.